Monte Carlo Simulation and Resampling Methods for Social Science

We dedicate this book to our wives, Dawn and Melissa.

Monte Carlo Simulation and Resampling Methods for Social Science

Thomas M. Carsey
University of North Carolina at Chapel Hill

Jeffrey J. Harden
University of Colorado Boulder

Los Angeles | London | New Delhi
Singapore | Washington DC

Los Angeles | London | New Delhi
Singapore | Washington DC

FOR INFORMATION:

SAGE Publications, Inc.
2455 Teller Road
Thousand Oaks, California 91320
E-mail: order@sagepub.com

SAGE Publications Ltd.
1 Oliver's Yard
55 City Road
London EC1Y 1SP
United Kingdom

SAGE Publications India Pvt. Ltd.
B 1/I 1 Mohan Cooperative Industrial Area
Mathura Road, New Delhi 110 044
India

SAGE Publications Asia-Pacific Pte. Ltd.
3 Church Street
#10-04 Samsung Hub
Singapore 049483

Acquisitions Editor: Helen Salmon
Editorial Assistant: Jessica Miller
Production Editor: Olivia Weber-Stenis
Copy Editor: QuADS Prepress (P) Ltd.
Typesetter: C&M Digitals (P) Ltd.
Proofreader: Susan Schon
Indexer: Molly Hall
Cover Designer: Anupama Krishnan
Marketing Manager: Nicole Elliott

Copyright © 2014 by SAGE Publications, Inc.

All rights reserved. No part of this book may be reproduced or utilized in any form or by any means, electronic or mechanical, including photocopying, recording, or by any information storage and retrieval system, without permission in writing from the publisher.

Library of Congress Cataloging-in-Publication Data

Carsey, Thomas M., 1966

Monte Carlo simulation and resampling : methods for social science / Thomas M. Carsey, University of North Carolina at Chapel Hill, Jeffrey J. Harden, University of Colorado Boulder.

pages cm
ISBN 978-1-4522-8890-1 (alk. paper)

1. Social sciences—Statistical methods. 2. Monte Carlo method. 3. Social sciences—Methodology. 4. Social sciences—Research—Computer simulation. I. Harden, Jeffrey J. II. Title.

HA29.C33 2014
300.1′518282—dc23   2013007917

This book is printed on acid-free paper.

13 14 15 16 17 10 9 8 7 6 5 4 3 2 1

CONTENTS

ACKNOWLEDGMENTS

The seed for this book was planted by a conversation Carsey had with two colleagues at the University of North Carolina at Chapel Hill (UNC–Chapel Hill), Jim Stimson and Mike MacKuen. The conversation centered on teaching graduate-level quantitative methods classes, and Jim said something like, "If you really want students to understand the properties of a model or the model's underlying assumptions, make them simulate a sample of data that has those properties." The idea is really very simple—statistical tools are useful, but only to the degree that we understand how the assumptions of the method comport with the data-generating process we are studying.

Our collaboration began as professor and student in 2007. Since then, it has included stints as professor and teaching assistant, as dissertation chair and PhD student, and as coauthors. During this time, we also taught a week-long intensive ICPSR (Inter University Consortium for Political and Social Research) course on these methods in the summer of 2011 at the Odum Institute for Research in Social Science at UNC–Chapel Hill. Preparing and teaching that course convinced us of the need for this book.

Since that first comment from Jim, we have benefited greatly from a number of others in putting together this book. First and foremost, we are grateful to the students at UNC–Chapel Hill and the University of Colorado Boulder who have taken courses, labs, and workshops from us that featured various portions of this material. Their positive feedback and constructive critiques have significantly shaped the content and style of this book.

As we began to formulate a plan for the book, we benefited from several informal conversations with colleagues at UNC–Chapel Hill. Those with whom we talked the most include Kevin Banda, Skyler Cranmer, Justin Gross, and Justin Kirkland. As we prepared the manuscript, a number of colleagues around the country read all or parts of the book and provided very helpful feedback. These folks include Jake Bowers, Bruce Desmarais, Mike Hanmer, Dan Hopkins, Chris Mooney, and Jenny Wolak. We are also grateful for feedback from SAGE reviewers Wendy K. Tam Cho, Laron K. Williams, and Paul Johnson. Each person provided extremely helpful responses and comments that made the book better.

We would also like to acknowledge the support provided by the Odum Institute at UNC–Chapel Hill (http://www.odum.unc.edu/), where Carsey has been Director since 2011. The Odum Institute provided logistical and organizational support for the summer class we taught, and also supported numerous R short courses taught by Harden. Paul Mihas in particular helped with these efforts. The Odum Institute is a world-class organization with excellent staff who make working there a real joy.

Finally, we want to thank our families. They have had to listen to us talk about this for quite some time and provided nothing but encouragement and support. This is especially the case for our wives, to whom we dedicate this book.

All of the R code used in this book for all of the simulations we present, as well as the R code we used to construct the figures in the book, is available on the website for the book, located at www.sagepub.com/carsey.

1

Introduction

Social scientists study questions that affect all of our lives: What causes (or prevents) war? What policies promote economic growth? How are cultural values transmitted across generations? What best promotes learning among children? These and a myriad of others are important questions, which makes getting good answers to them important as well.

In many cases, scholars seeking answers to their research questions turn to quantitative methods and the analysis of data in the hope that doing so will shed light on which theoretical explanations for these processes hold the most promise. In doing so, scholars want more than just a description of the data they have; they want to be able to make inferences about the larger population from which their data was drawn. This book introduces scholars to a set of methods we believe will assist in this effort—Monte Carlo simulation and resampling methods. Learning about these methods will help scholars ask better questions, generate more complete answers, and provide deeper assessments of both quantitative methods and substantive theory. Readers will not be experts in these methods when they finish this book, but they should have a deeper understanding and a solid foundation on which to build.

This book is for any student or researcher looking for another set of tools that they can use in their research. This is not a statistics textbook, but we spend a lot of time discussing how these tools can be used to better understand, implement, and evaluate statistical methods. This book is not purely theoretical either, though developing tools to help scholars evaluate theories provides the fundamental motivation for the book. Rather, the book is about using computer-based simulation methods to better evaluate statistical methods and substantive theories.

We think this book will be especially useful to scholars who have some training in quantitative methods, but who feel there is a gap between their training and many of the methods they see used. In particular, we suspect that there are many scholars who have read articles or books that employ simulations that they are able to follow at some level, but would be hard-pressed to replicate. This book will show researchers how to use these methods in their own work.

Based on our own experiences in the classroom, we also believe that simulation and resampling methods provide an excellent means for learning more deeply about commonly used statistical methods as well as new cutting-edge techniques, even for those with somewhat limited mathematical backgrounds. Many students who cannot always follow all of the math are left with "pointing and clicking" their way through statistical software when doing their research without developing a clear intuition about what is happening "under the hood" to their data. Simulation provides a means of addressing this shortcoming.

Finally, we believe that even sophisticated users of quantitative methods can improve their understanding of both the methods they use and the theories that guide their substantive research through the creative application of simulations. Simulation and resampling methods permit scholars to evaluate the performance of cutting-edge methods across a range of contexts that might describe real data. These methods also permit researchers to explore new theoretical and methodological innovations in the controlled environment of their computer.

In short, we hope the book is helpful to a broad audience and that it helps them meet a variety of goals. We think Monte Carlo simulation and resampling methods bring together some of the best aspects of quantitative analysis of observational data, experimental analysis, and the value of making clear formal statements about the underlying data-generating process (DGP) that produces the sample data we have. The book can be read alone, or it can provide a good complement to traditional textbooks on quantitative methods.

1.1 CAN YOU REPEAT THAT PLEASE?

Monte Carlo simulation and resampling methods have a lot to do with the phrase "in repeated samples." This phrase comes up in nearly every quantitative methods course, well, repeatedly. For example, when evaluating a sample of survey data, we want to understand how the data would change if we gave the same survey questions to another sample of respondents, then another one after that, and another one after that. The concept of "in repeated samples" is important because researchers are generally interested in inference—that is, we do not simply want to describe what is going on in the one sample of data we have in our hands. Rather, we want to be able to generalize the patterns we find in our sample of data to all of the observations that *could have been* in the sample. In other words, we want to infer conclusions about the larger population from which our sample was taken based on our analysis of that sample. Concepts taught in quantitative methods courses—such as inference, bias, efficiency, and measures of uncertainty—are typically learned based on the logic of repeated samples. In short, understanding the concept of "in repeated samples" is extremely important for all social scientists doing quantitative analysis.

However, class discussions about the concept of "in repeated samples" are often just theoretical or hypothetical. With limited resources, we cannot administer the same survey many times to different samples. In fact, if sufficient funding to field surveys to multiple samples was available, most researchers would either just increase their sample size initially or avoid repetition and use different questions. In other cases, collecting another sample may be impossible; for instance, we cannot create a new set of countries from which to collect economic indicators since 1945. The end result is that students may come away with a vague notion of what "in repeated samples" means in the abstract because it is generally only encountered as an assumption—students rarely see it in action.

Monte Carlo simulation solves this problem. Simulation allows analysts to easily create many samples of data in a computing environment, then assess patterns that appear across those repeated samples. Monte Carlo simulation is a valuable tool for everyone from students just beginning to learn statistical methods to applied researchers looking to test the consequences of estimator assumption violations to advanced researchers developing and evaluating new statistical techniques or directly testing substantive theories. In this book, we demonstrate the utility of Monte Carlo simulation in three different areas: (1) as a means of learning and understanding fundamental principles of statistical methods, (2) as a powerful tool for assessing new methods and comparing competing methods, and (3) as a method of evaluating substantive theories about social processes. The wide range of applicability enjoyed by these tools reflects the increasing prominence of simulation-based methods in empirical quantitative research.[1]

This book is applied in nature and includes numerous examples. We emphasize the development of a deeper understanding of key concepts such as DGPs, populations, sampling, and statistical estimators. Our goal is to help readers use these tools to make connections between substantive theory, empirical evidence, and the quantitative methods they use in that process. We examine both numerical and graphical methods of evaluating simulation results hoping that this combination fosters a more complete understanding of simulation and resampling methods.

We illustrate every concept and construct every example using the statistical programming environment R, which is freely available. More information about R can be found online at `http://cran.r-project.org/`, the website for the Comprehensive R Archive Network (CRAN). Additionally, all of the R code presented in this book, along with the code we used to produce all of the figures in the book, can be downloaded at the book's website, located at `www.sagepub .com/carsey`. Before you continue reading, you should download R and install it on your computer. You should also read the accompanying manual "An Introduction to R." You can find a link to the manual under the "Help" menu

---

[1]This is particularly evident in the social sciences, where simulation has been used to evaluate and compare statistical models (e.g., Bollen, Ray, Zavisca, & Harden, 2012; Cameron & Trivedi, 2005; Desmarais & Harden, 2012; Feng, McLerran, & Grizzle, 1996; Green & Vavreck, 2008; Harden & Desmarais, 2011), evaluate substantive theory (e.g., Adler, 2000; Adler & Lapinski, 1997), assess the uncertainty of estimates after they have been computed (e.g., Gelman & Hill, 2007; King, Tomz, & Wittenberg, 2000), and solve for model parameters that are otherwise intractable via Markov Chain Monte Carlo (MCMC) methods.

within R and on the CRAN website. In Chapter 3, we provide a basic introduction focused on using R to perform simulations and resampling analyses. Thus, reviewing the general manual first will prove extremely helpful to R newcomers. There are also a series of packages in R that provide extensions to the functions that are part of the base system for R. We describe several packages in greater detail as we encounter them throughout the book. A complete list of the R packages we use is provided at the end of this chapter—you might want to go ahead and install them all now.

1.2 SIMULATION AND RESAMPLING METHODS

Social scientists increasingly use statistical simulation techniques to help them understand the social processes they study and the statistical methods used to study them. This book examines two types of computer simulation techniques that are quickly becoming essential tools for empirical social scientists: (1) Monte Carlo simulation and (2) resampling methods.

While the rest of this book elaborates on what these methods involve, we begin with basic definitions here. We define a Monte Carlo simulation as any computational algorithm that randomly generates multiple samples of data from a defined population based on an assumed DGP. The DGP is the mechanism that characterizes the population from which simulated samples of data are drawn. Then, the researcher explores patterns that emerge across those simulated samples (Mooney, 1997). Most important, the researcher controls all aspects of the population DGP, which allows for precise comparison of competing theoretical models and/or statistical estimators.

Resampling techniques are similar in that they also draw multiple simulated samples of data. However, rather than making draws from a theoretical population DGP defined by the researcher, resampling techniques draw multiple simulated samples from the researcher's actual sample of data. Both techniques are used to evaluate how well a given statistical model characterizes the underlying population DGP. In that sense, both can be useful to evaluate either the assumptions of statistical estimators or substantive theory. However, in Monte Carlo simulation, the true population DGP is known because the researcher constructs it. With resampling techniques, the true population DGP remains unknown.

1.2.1 Simulations as Experiments

We find it helpful to think of Monte Carlo simulation as a way to use your computer as an experimental laboratory. Like in a lab, the analyst conducting the study has control over the environment. The study then generally consists of manipulating various conditions of the laboratory environment and observing the consequences. In a traditional laboratory experiment, a scientist might divide two groups of patients, survey respondents, or fruit flies into equivalent groups (often by using random assignment). Then, each group within a study is treated in exactly the same way except for one factor: (1) one set of patients gets the new drug and the other gets a placebo, (2) one group of survey respondents gets a question about a policy proposal that focuses on the costs of the program while another group gets a version of the question that focuses on the benefits of the program, and (3) one set of fruit flies is exposed to air containing a potential pollutant while the other group is exposed to air that does not contain that element. Then, the researcher observes the consequence of changing that one factor. The idea is that if everything else about the groups is equivalent (e.g., "all else is equal"), then any differences between the groups that appear within a study can be attributed to the one difference in how they were treated. This is often called the treatment effect.

Computer simulations follow the same basic logic. The researcher uses a computer to simulate some process or environment that describes or characterizes some phenomenon that the researcher wants to study. A simulation study typically involves allowing the process being simulated to unfold or evolve over many iterations or across many observations. The patterns that emerge describe the process under study. These patterns can be compared with what was expected based on some substantive or statistical theory. Frequently, the researcher then manipulates one facet of the simulation and then reruns it. The patterns that emerge from this second run through the simulation are then compared with the patterns that emerged from the first run, and any differences are attributed to the change that was made. Again, this can be thought of as the treatment effect.

In this way, the power of simulation is similar to the power of experimental design. Researchers can achieve a high degree of leverage on causality because of the control they have over the experimental setting and the manipulation of the treatment. Of course, determining that a treatment caused some difference to emerge does not necessarily provide an explanation for why the treatment had an impact. Did the drug work because it stimulates the immune system or because it killed the virus? Was the effect direct or because it interacted with other chemicals in the human body? Similar challenges with explanation can emerge in complex simulations, though many of the simulations shown in this text are simple enough that we should be able to see why the treatment has the effect that it does.

Of course, the limitation of experimental work regarding generalizability outside of the laboratory setting also confronts those doing simulations. Labs and simulations create a controlled environment that are typically dramatic simplifications of the real world. Thus, how treatments work outside of the lab, or outside of the simulation, is always subject to some uncertainty, though we can frequently access that uncertainty in simulation studies. Still, experiments and simulations can provide insights to researchers that help them substantially improve their ability to describe and explain the world outside the lab.

1.2.2 Simulations Help Develop Intuition

In presenting the material that follows, we do not wish to suggest that simulation is always a replacement for analytics (though sometimes it can be a replacement when analytics are too complex). The precision and rigor of statistical formulas and mathematical proofs are a critical part of systematic empirical analysis. The point we aim to make is that simulation can serve as a *complement* to analytic expressions. In particular, simulation can help with the development of intuition to better understand and visualize analytic results. For instance, while it can be demonstrated formally that measurement error in an independent variable leads to bias in the estimate of an ordinary least squares (OLS) regression coefficient, illustrating this bias through simulation can make the consequences of measurement error much more accessible to many students.

Simulation can also complement analytics by showing the magnitude of effects. Continuing with the measurement error example, simulation can help us assess how changes in the amount of measurement error influence bias. Does an increase in measurement error lead to an increase in the amount of bias? If so, is this increase linear, or does it follow some other pattern? What happens when there is also measurement error in a second independent variable? What if those two variables are correlated? Again, simulation provides a method of answering questions like these through illustration and visualization that should help foster intuition and understanding. Furthermore, analysts can tailor their simulation to reflect features of their own sample. This facilitates learning about real data in the controlled environment of a simulation.

Of course, simulations can be extremely useful in situations where there is no analytic solution available or the statistical properties of an estimator are not known. An obvious case is when employing a maximum likelihood (ML) estimator with a relatively small sample.[2]

1.2.3 An Overview of Simulation

As defined above, the typical Monte Carlo simulation involves drawing multiple random samples of data from an assumed DGP that describes the unobserved process in the larger population of how a phenomenon of interest is produced. It is the true or real DGP that scholars are ultimately interested in evaluating. Of course, we rarely know what the true DGP is in the real world—we just see the sample data it produces. Most of our research is about trying to uncover the underlying DGP or test predictions that emerge from different theories about what the DGP looks like. Most DGPs are assumed to be a mixture of some systematic, structural, or deterministic component and some random or stochastic component. A Monte Carlo simulation requires the researcher to specify what DGP he or she plans to evaluate. In other words, the researcher must present a mathematical expression of how the data of interest are produced. That theoretical DGP must include both the systematic and stochastic components of the process. Once a theoretical DGP is defined, researchers use a computer to randomly generate a large number of samples of data. Those samples can be treated as samples drawn from a population described by the theoretical DGP specified by the researcher.

Once a large number of these simulated samples are generated, the researcher can summarize patterns across those samples. That summary can then be compared

---

[2]See Long (1997) for a useful discussion of what constitutes a "small" sample for ML.

with the true DGP. This might be the final goal of the simulation, but just as common is a project that involves making a change to the theoretical DGP and rerunning the entire simulation to see if the change in the DGP results in a different pattern emerging among the new simulated samples of data.

This discussion highlights the important distinction between the population and a sample taken from a population. Statistical inference is about using a sample of data to draw conclusions about the population that produced that sample of data. Whether our inference is directed at description or causality, inference is about the population. In Monte Carlo simulations, the researcher has knowledge of the true population DGP because the researcher specifies it as part of the experiment. That is not the case in typical empirical research, either observational or experimental.[3] Because we know the true DGP in a simulation, we are able to use simulations to draw correct inferences under a range of circumstances.

1.2.4 Resampling Methods as Simulation

Before closing this chapter with a couple of simulation examples, we want to briefly introduce resampling methods and how they relate to simulation. Resampling methods include a wide array of techniques that are useful for social scientists, and several books have been written about them.[4] We include resampling methods in this book because of their clear connection to Monte Carlo simulation methods. As mentioned above, resampling techniques also draw multiple samples in an iterative process, but from the observed data rather than a researcher-defined theoretical DGP. The true population DGP remains unknown in resampling methods, but if the observations in our one sample of data represent a random sample from a larger population, drawing multiple samples from those data in some form (which we will describe in Chapter 8) can be assumed to approximate the distribution in the population.

The specific resampling methods we will discuss in this book are permutation/randomization testing, jackknifing, and bootstrapping. Permutation tests are conducted by randomly reshuffling observations (or groups) to break the observed relationships between cases. Next, you compare the observed data to the reshuffled data to see how likely a random reshuffling process would produce a data set like the one you actually have. In jackknifing, new samples are created by iteratively removing one observation or group of observations at a time from the data. As such, each new "sample" of data is really just a subset of the total sample of data with which the researcher started. Bootstrapping involves repeatedly creating new data sets by drawing observations (or groups of observations) from the observed data at random *with replacement*. These three methods are all primarily means of assessing variability in statistical estimates and/or testing hypotheses. We will discuss their relative strengths and weaknesses in more detail as we present them.

---

[3]In fact, if we had knowledge of the true population DGP in the real world, we would not need statistical analysis to make inferences about it.

[4]See, for example, Efron and Tibshirani (1993), Good (2005), Mooney and Duval (1993), or Chernick and LaBudde (2011).

1.3 OLS AS A MOTIVATING EXAMPLE

OLS regression is a workhorse model in the social sciences. It is also a special case of a large class of generalized linear models (GLM) that are very widely used.[5] Because of its importance, we illustrate the basics of a simulation here by conducting one for OLS.

The standard OLS regression model assumes that some dependent variable (often labeled Y) is a linear function of some set of independent variables (often labeled as Xs), where that relationship is described by a set of parameters (often labeled as βs), and some random stochastic component (often labeled as ε). This random component (also called the residual, the disturbance term, or the error term of the regression model) is a random variable with defined/assumed probabilistic properties. That random component represents the sum of all unmodeled factors that might affect Y as well as any part of Y that is fundamentally stochastic. So a statistical model like the one shown below in Equation 1.4 illustrates that the dependent variable of interest has two fundamental components: (1) a systematic (or deterministic) component represented by everything on the right-hand side of the equals sign *except* ε_i and (2) a random (or stochastic) component that is represented by ε_i.

Another way to think about this is that we are developing a probability model for a random variable Y. In OLS regression, we are developing a conditional probability model for the dependent variable given the independent variables and a stochastic term.

$$E(Y|X_i) = f(X_i) \tag{1.1}$$

We read this as "the expected value of Y given X as being equal to some function of X." OLS is designed specifically to model the expected mean of Y conditional on some function of a set of independent variables. Because Y is a random variable, we assume that it is not fully determined by some function of the independent variables. Rather, we expect some portion of Y to remain stochastic, or random. Thus, the individual values of Y that we observe in our data are the conditional expected value of Y given X plus the random component.

$$Y_i = E(Y|X_i) + \varepsilon_i \tag{1.2}$$

In OLS regression, the conditional mean of Y is expressed as a linear function of X. In other words,

$$f(X_i) = \beta_0 + \beta_1 X_{1i} + \beta_2 X_{2i} + \cdots + \varepsilon_i \tag{1.3}$$

---

[5]In fact, we devote Chapter 5 entirely to OLS and Chapter 6 to GLMs.

Thus,

$$Y_i = \beta_0 + \beta_1 X_{1i} + \beta_2 X_{2i} + \cdots + \varepsilon_i \qquad (1.4)$$

The various β terms in Equation 1.4 are called the parameters or coefficients of the regression model. OLS produces estimates of these parameters using a sample of data. In many statistics texts, you will see the β parameters reported as shown in Equation 1.4 when they are meant to represent the unknown parameters that describe an underlying population DGP, but they will be reported with "hats," such as $\widehat{\beta_0}$ and $\widehat{\beta_1}$ when referring to estimated values of those parameters based on a sample of data.

The variables X and Y are subscripted with an "i" to indicate that they represent variables with values that change for each ith observation in the data set. The residual, ε, is also subscripted because every observation has one. Notice that the β parameters are *not* subscripted by i. That is because we only estimate one value for each parameter—they do not change from observation to observation in the data set.

When we plan to run an OLS regression to analyze data we have in our hands, the data contain observed values for X_i and Y_i. We use those values to mathematically calculate estimates of the parameters. Those estimates of the βs could then be combined with the observed values of X_i to produce fitted values (also called expected values) of Y_i, often denoted as $\widehat{Y_i}$ and pronounced as "Y hat." Thus, $\widehat{Y_i}$ would equal the intercept.

From this logic, we can see that ε_i captures the difference between the actual value of Y_i and the fitted value $\widehat{Y_i}$. In other words,

$$\varepsilon_i = Y_i - \widehat{Y_i} \qquad (1.5)$$

which we could read as *residual = actual value – fitted value*. All of the elements we have described thus far are represented in Figure 1.1, which is based on a simple regression model that includes one independent variable and five data points.

In Figure 1.1, $\widehat{\beta_0}$ shows what the value of $\widehat{Y_i}$ would be when X_i is zero. This is the point where the estimated line crosses the y-axis. Again, $\widehat{\beta_0}$ is an estimate of the intercept (sometimes also called the constant). Figure 1.1 shows that $\widehat{\beta_1}$ represents how much $\widehat{Y_i}$ changes for a one-unit increase in X. In other words, $\widehat{\beta_1}$ represents the estimated marginal effect of X on Y. When we increased X by one unit moving to the right on the x-axis, to get back up to the line, we had to increase by $\widehat{\beta_1}$ on the y-axis. The gap between the fourth data point in our data set and the estimated line is labeled ε_4. That gap is the residual, or the error in $\widehat{Y_i}$ compared with the actual value of Y_i, for the fourth observation. Finally, the entire regression line in Figure 1.1 is defined by the full regression equation for $\widehat{Y}$. In case you are interested, the R code we used to produce Figure 1.1 is reproduced below. Graphics code for the entire book can be found in the appendix.

| Figure 1.1 | Component Parts of a Simple Regression |

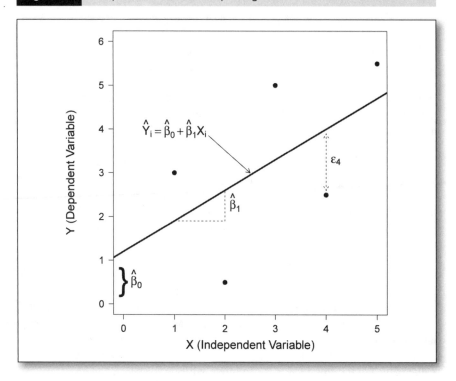

```
# OLS Example
eq <- expression(hat(Y)[i] == hat(beta)[0] + hat(beta)[1]*X[i])
slope <- expression(hat(beta)[1])
intercept <- expression(hat(beta)[0])
error4 <- expression(epsilon[4])
brace <- expression("}")
x <- c(1, 2, 3, 4, 5)
y <- c(3, .5, 5, 2.5, 5.5)
m <- lm(y ~ x)
m
yhat <- predict(m)

par(mar = c(5, 5.25, .5, .5))
plot(x, y, xlim = c(0, 5), ylim = c(0, 6), pch = 19, cex = 1.2, xlab = "",
  ylab = "", axes = FALSE)
abline(m, lwd = 3)
text(1, 4, eq, cex = 1.5)
arrows(1.675, 3.85, 2.5, 3, length = .1)
arrows(4, y[x = 4] + .1, 4, yhat[x = 4] -.1, code = 3, length =.1 ,
  lty = 2)
segments(1, yhat[x == 1], 2, yhat[x == 1], lty = 2)
segments(2, yhat[x == 1], 2, yhat[x == 2], lty = 2)
```

```
text(2, (yhat[x == 1] + yhat[x == 2])/2, slope, pos = 4,
 cex = 1.5)
text(4, (y[x == 4] + yhat[x == 4])/2, error4, pos = 4, cex = 1.5)
text(0, .5, brace, cex = 4)
text(.05, .5, intercept, pos = 4, cex = 1.5)
axis(1, cex.axis = 1.25)
axis(2, cex.axis = 1.25, las = 2)
title(xlab = expression("X (Independent Variable)"), cex.lab = 1.5)
title(ylab = expression("Y (Dependent Variable)"), line = 3.75,
  cex.lab = 1.5)
box()
```

OLS regression rests on a number of assumptions about the DGP, including the independent variables are fixed in repeated samples, the residuals of the model are independently and identically distributed (iid), and the residuals are distributed normally. OLS also assumes that the independent variables are not perfectly collinear. A weaker version of this condition notes that a high level of collinearity among independent variables has consequences for OLS.

The assumption about independent variables being fixed in repeated samples includes assuming that the X variables do not contain stochastic components and also that the X variables will be uncorrelated with the residuals of the model. The strongest form of the assumption—that the values of the X variables are strictly fixed—stems from early work in experimental analysis. The typical example given is to imagine a farmer who divides her land into multiple plots and then applies a fixed amount of fertilizer to each plot that varies across plots. As numerous textbooks point out, however, the notion that the typical social science researcher truly has data that includes fixed values for the Xs is not plausible. Most social science work analyzes observational data, such that the observed values of the independent variables are random at the very least due to random sampling. As Fox (2008) explains, "Under these circumstances, we assume that the explanatory variable is measured without error and that the explanatory variable and the error [term of the regression model] are independent in the population from which the sample is drawn" (p. 102).[6]

The iid assumption states that there is no serial or spatial correlation among the residuals and that the variance of the residuals is constant. The normality

---

[6]Gujarati and Porter (2008) explain that the strong assumption of the Xs being fixed in repeated samples simplifies the discussion of the classical OLS regression model. Also, they note that "even if the X variables are stochastic, the statistical results of linear regression based on the case of fixed regressors are also valid when the Xs are random, provided that...the regressor X and the error term [of the OLS regression model] are independent" (pp. 62–66). Greene (2011) presents this using slightly different language. He notes that if the Xs are assumed to be random vectors rather than fixed, then the basic assumptions about OLS become assumptions about the joint distribution of Y and the Xs. However, Greene states that, whether fixed or random, it is most important that the independent variables are generated by a mechanism unrelated to the residuals. Of course, this is also a very challenging assumption in applied statistical work because there are not obvious ways to make use of the sample data to evaluate this assumption.

assumption means that the residuals are assumed to be drawn from a normal probability distribution (rather than some other probability distribution, of which there are many that we will explore in this book). The normality assumption is particularly relevant for inference and hypothesis testing.

OLS regression on existing data makes use of that sample of data to compute estimates of the model's parameters, which you can then use to draw inferences about the population DGP that might have produced the sample data. The ability of OLS to allow you to do this successfully depends on whether the assumptions about the DGP described above, however, are met. This presents a challenge because we don't know the DGP—if we did, there would be no need to derive estimates of it using sample data. There are a lot of tests and other diagnostics we can perform to try to determine whether it is plausible to believe that all of the OLS assumptions are met, but we can never know for sure.

What happens if we violate an assumption of OLS, but we proceed anyway? Well, that depends on the particular assumption in question and the severity of the violation. In general, violations of OLS assumptions lead to consequences in terms of producing estimates that are biased and/or inefficient. Bias refers to getting estimated parameters that are systematically off target compared with the true population parameters for the DGP. Inefficiency refers to getting less precise estimates of those parameters. For methods like OLS that are so common and widely used, the consequences for most violations can be derived analytically. However, simulations can help illustrate the consequences of violating OLS assumptions in different ways and to different degrees.

The typical empirical study that employs OLS does so to use a sample of data to make inferences about an unknown population DGP. In contrast, the typical simulation study focused on OLS starts with the researcher specifying a DGP for a hypothetical population, using that DGP to generate simulated data, and then determining whether OLS is doing a good job of producing estimates from the simulated data that match the researcher-defined DGP. This is sometimes described as exploring whether the statistical estimator in question—OLS in this case—successfully recovers the parameters that characterize the DGP. In the next section, we work through an example showing relevant code in R, but we are not going to discuss the code much at this point. We want to focus on the example for now and getting a feel for how simulations are constructed. We will start delving into the details of doing them in the later chapters.

1.4 TWO BRIEF EXAMPLES

To preview the remainder of the book, we close this chapter with two brief examples: (1) a statistical simulation and (2) a simulation about substantive theory. These examples illustrate how the process of generating repeated samples from a DGP can be used to evaluate a statistical estimator and understand a social process, respectively. At this point, readers should focus on beginning to see the logic behind simulations rather than the specific details of these particular simulations and the code used to run them. The rest of the book is devoted to unpacking such details.

1.4.1 Example 1: A Statistical Simulation

In this first simulation, we demonstrate that OLS is an unbiased estimator when all of its assumptions hold. We create a true DGP by setting the values of the model's parameters. Then, we create many data sets from this DGP, adding random error to each one. Next, we estimate the parameters with OLS on each of those data sets. We conclude by examining all of those parameter estimates. Formally, the model we simulate is given in Equation 1.6:

$$Y_i = \beta_0 + \beta_1 X_{1i} + \varepsilon_i \qquad (1.6)$$

The necessary R code to simulate this model is below. First, we set the seed of the random number generator, which allows us to reproduce the exact same random numbers each time. Next, we set the number of simulations (500), the true values of the parameters ($\beta_0 = 0.20$, $\beta_1 = 0.50$), and the sample size (1,000). We create an independent variable X. Then, inside a `for` loop (code that repeats for a specified number of times), we create the dependent variable Y as a function of the parameters (the "systematic" component of the DGP) and a normally distributed error term (the "stochastic" component of the DGP). Notice that in this setup, all of the assumptions of OLS hold (i.e., no measurement error in the independent variable, error term is normal with a mean of zero and constant variance).

After creating that dependent variable, we estimate an OLS regression model and save the parameter estimates. We repeat this process in the `for` loop until we have 500 saved estimates of β_0 and 500 saved estimates of β_1. Each set of estimates comes from a data set created from the same DGP. The only differences between the data sets are those that emerge due to the random error. This means that the only differences in our parameter estimates from one data set to the next also stem from that same stochastic component of the model. Repeating the process 500 times using the same DGP in this way (the set parameters plus random error), we mimic the concept of repeated samples.

```
# Statistical Simulation
set.seed(123456) # Set the seed for reproducible results
reps <- 500 # Set the number of repetitions at the top of the script
par.est <- matrix(NA, nrow = reps, ncol = 2) # Empty matrix to store the
                                             # estimates
b0 <- .2 # True value for the intercept
b1 <- .5 # True value for the slope
n <- 1000 # Sample size
X <- runif(n, -1, 1) # Create a sample of n observations on the
                     # independent variable X

for(i in 1:reps){ # Start the loop
Y <- b0 + b1*X + rnorm(n, 0, 1) # The true DGP, with N(0, 1) error
model <- lm(Y ~ X) # Estimate OLS model
par.est[i, 1] <- model$coef[1] # Put the estimate for the intercept
```

```
                                        # in the first column
        par.est[i, 2] <- model$coef[2] # Put the estimate for the coefficient on
                                        # X in the second column
            } # End the loop
```

After completing the simulation, we can then evaluate the results. One way to do so is to plot the distributions of the parameter estimates. Figure 1.2 gives histograms of β_0 (Panel a) and β_1 (Panel b). Notice that in each case the estimates are centered very near the true value (the mean of the β_0 estimates is 0.1996 and the mean of the β_1 estimates is 0.4950) and symmetrically distributed. No individual sample produced estimated values for β_0 and β_1 that were exactly the same as the true values, but Figure 1.2 shows that there is no systematic pattern to the "misses." In each graph, about half of the estimates miss on the low side of the true parameter and half miss above it. This simulation shows us that OLS does in fact produce unbiased estimates of model parameters when the assumptions of OLS are met.

This example illustrates one of the basic ideas behind simulation that we will highlight throughout the book. By creating a DGP, then using an estimator to recover that DGP, we can better understand the estimator and evaluate its performance. Consider what might happen to the distribution of the estimates if we

Figure 1.2 Histograms of 500 Simulated β_0 and β_1 Estimates

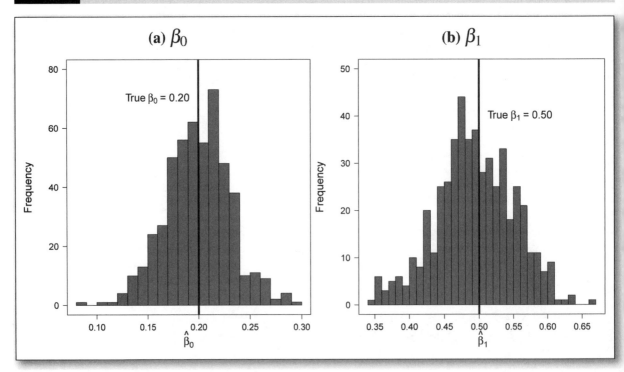

changed the code above to give the error term a nonzero mean or nonconstant variance. Similarly, what would happen if we added a second independent variable that was correlated with the first one? We address these and other questions in the chapters that follow.

1.4.2 Example 2: A Substantive Theory Simulation

In Chapter 7, we present a detailed discussion of three examples where simulation can be used to directly evaluate a substantive theory. One of those examples explores something called Zipf's law. George Kingsley Zipf, a linguistics professor, first published his result that has become known as "Zipf's law" in 1932 (Zipf, 1932). Zipf discovered that how frequently individual words appear in long passages of text tends to follow a power law. Specifically, if you sort all the words in a long document in order of how often they are used, the frequency with which a word appears tends to be proportional to the inverse of that word's rank. In other words, Zipf's law proposes that word frequencies in a large document follow what is called a power law relative to their rank order of frequency with an exponent equal to −1.

We will talk more about what that means in Chapter 7, but for now, we illustrate what Zipf's law looks like with Mary Shelley's classic book *Frankenstein*. Figure 1.3 plots the expected relationship between a word's frequency and its rank if Zipf's law were correct along with the actual relationship between the frequencies and ranks of the top 40 words that appear in *Frankenstein*. Figure 1.3 suggests that Zipf's law provides a good description of this particular text. Furthermore, it is important to note that this finding is not unique to *Frankenstein*. As Zipf (1932) and others show, it exists in many different text documents.

This leads to the question of why this pattern emerges so regularly. A number of scholars have offered plausible explanations based on signal theory, efficiency in communication, and satisficing behavior, to name a few. However, Li (1992, p. 1) and others note that few scholars actually gave serious attention to a comment made by Miller (1965) suggesting that randomness might be a plausible explanation. Mitchell (2009) describes Miller's alternative explanation as imagining what would happen if monkeys typed randomly on a keyboard with "words" being separated from each other every time the monkey happened to hit the space bar. We share the view articulated by Li (1992) that Miller's comment really suggests a plausible null hypothesis. Without spoiling the surprise, what we show in Chapter 7 is how to construct a simulation that captures the process of random word generation and evaluates the result of such a DGP against Zipf's law.

1.5 LOOKING AHEAD

In closing this introduction, we give a brief preview of what this book does and does not cover.

| Figure 1.3 | The Rank and Frequency of the 40 Most Frequently Used Words in *Frankenstein* |

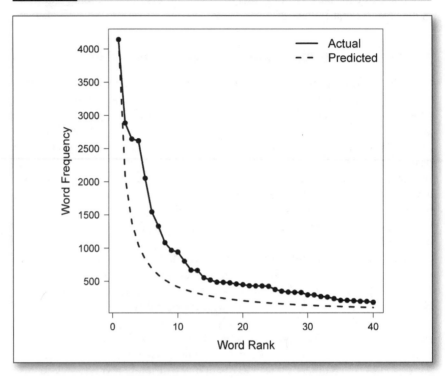

1.5.1 Assumed Knowledge

This book is not a textbook in the traditional sense, and it is not meant to be a first course in statistics or R. While a key goal is to provide an accessible look at the material, we assume readers have some basic knowledge of probability (which we review briefly) and have had some exposure to statistics, including multiple regression models, hypothesis testing, concepts such as bias and efficiency, and potentially maximum likelihood estimation. Readers need not have perfect understanding of these concepts, but coming to the book with some knowledge is important. By the end of the book, it is our hope that these readers will have a much deeper understanding of these tools and concepts by seeing them illustrated through simulation.

1.5.2 A Preview of the Book

Chapter 2 gives a brief summary of key concepts from probability theory. Chapter 3 provides a basic introduction to R. Note that Chapter 3 is not meant to be a comprehensive introduction to R, but rather an introduction to what you need to know to do simulations. Readers familiar with probability and R can skip to Chapter 4, which begins the main content of the book with some basics about random number generation and its role in simulation methods. Chapter 5 details DGP creation, basic properties of statistical estimators, and how to evaluate simulation results in the context of the linear model. Chapter 6 extends the material from Chapter 5 to simulations of GLMs. We also discuss practical issues that arise in implementing simulation in Chapter 6.

In Chapter 7, we shift from statistical simulation to the use of simulation to evaluate substantive theory. Chapter 8 discusses resampling methods as a simulation-based means of evaluating uncertainty. Finally, in Chapter 9, we demonstrate other useful simulation-based methods. These methods include simulation as a means of generating quantities of interest from statistical models and cross-validation (an out-of-sample prediction method for evaluating model fit). We draw conclusions about the role of simulation in empirical social science research in Chapter 10.

In the end, we will not provide enough coverage of any one topic to make the reader an expert. However, we hope that we cover enough methods in enough detail to provide researchers with a basic understanding of these methods and a solid foundation for using them in their own research.

1.6 R PACKAGES

As we mentioned above, one of the main strengths of R is its large library of user-written packages. Below is a complete list of the packages we use and/or discuss in this book.

- arm (Gelman et al., 2012)
- boot (Canty & Ripley, 2011)
- bootstrap (Tibshirani & Leisch, 2012)
- combinat (Chasalow, 2010)
- DAAG (Maindonald & Braun, 2012)
- doSNOW (Revolution Analytics, 2011a)
- foreach (Revolution Analytics, 2011b)
- foreign (DebRoy & Bivand, 2011)
- lda (Chang, 2011)
- lme4 (Bates, Maechler, & Bolker, 2011)
- MASS (Venables & Ripley, 2002)
- moments (Komsta & Novomestky, 2012)
- mvtnorm (Genz et al., 2011)
- normalp (Mineo & Ruggieri, 2005)
- pcse (Bailey & Katz, 2011)
- pscl (Jackman, 2011; Zeileis, Kleiber, & Jackman, 2008)
- quantreg (Koenker, 2011)
- rms (Harrell, 2012)
- RTextTools (Jurka, Collingwood, Boydstun, Grossman, & van Atteveldt, 2011)

- `sandwich` (Zeileis, 2006)
- `snow` (Tierney, Rossini, Li, & Sevcikova, 2011)
- `survival` (Therneau, 2012)
- `tm` (Feinerer, Hornik, & Meyer, 2008)
- `topicmodels` (Grün & Hornik, 2011)
- `twang` (Ridgeway, McCaffrey, Morral, Griffin, & Burgette, 2012)
- `twitteR` (Gentry, 2012)
- `VGAM` (Yee, 2010)
- `Zelig` (Imai, King, & Lau, 2012)
- `zipfR` (Evert & Baroni, 2008)

Probability

2.1 INTRODUCTION

The concept of probability plays a major role in Monte Carlo simulations and resampling methods. Both methods produce a series of samples of data that display variance precisely because the process of generating them included a probabilistic component. Of course, all statistical inference is also probabilistic, so quantitative researchers should be comfortable with working in a probabilistic world.

A probability is a number between 0 and 1 that describes how likely something is to occur. In the simplest example, if we toss a fair coin into the air, the probability that it will land on Heads is 0.50. That is, there are two possible outcomes—Heads or Tails—and each one is equally likely to occur. We know that it will come out to be either Heads or Tails for sure. So the probability of getting one *or* the other equals 1 because 1 is the maximum value any probability can take on. If we divide that evenly between the two possible outcomes, then $1 \div 2 = 0.50$, meaning that there is a 0.50 probability of the coin coming up Heads. Again, the basic intuition behind probability rests on how likely an event is to occur.

Another way to think about probability is, if you repeated a process lots of times, what proportion of them would you expect to result in a given outcome? If we flipped a coin a thousand times, you would expect that about 500 times, or 50% of the observations (0.50 in terms of a proportion) would be Heads. This makes good sense for what we will define below as discrete events, but we will have to adapt that intuition a bit for continuous events. Note also that the idea of an "expected outcome" plays a major role in hypothesis testing.

Thus, we can define probability in terms of the *relative frequency* with which an event will occur if we repeated our "experiment" a great many times.[1] This is a classic "frequentist" interpretation of probability that lies at the heart of traditional or "classical" statistics.[2] From this perspective, the probability of an event,

---

[1] We told you that this "in repeated samples" concept would come up again and again.

[2] The alternative view of probability is the Bayesian view, which is beyond the scope of this book (see Gill, 2007).

A, occurring is defined in what is called the limit. This means that as the number of trials of our experiment increases toward infinity, the relative frequency of the event occurring will converge toward the true probability of it occurring in any given trial.

We can also define a probability in terms of a logical consequence of some assumptions. We did that when we defined the probability of a single coin toss coming up "Heads" as equal to 0.50. We did not have to flip the coin many times to reach this conclusion. Rather, we assumed that there were only two possible outcomes that were each equally likely to occur. In frequentist statistics, inference about the population DGP based on sample data generally rests on some form of hypothesis testing. Hypothesis testing involves making probabilistic statements about whether the sample we have in our hands looks like what we would have expected it to look like given some assumption about the population DGP.

Now that we have defined some basic terms, we can turn our attention to the role of probability and probability distributions in statistical inference. This section will cover basic rules regarding probabilities. It will then cover discrete and continuous random variables in more detail. We conclude with some discussion of common discrete and continuous probability distributions. Note that we will only hit the basics in this chapter. A full treatment of probability and probability theory is beyond the scope of this book.[3]

2.2 SOME BASIC RULES OF PROBABILITY

Probability theory involves the study of uncertainty. We have intuition about probability already because we encounter it in our daily lives. What is the chance it will rain today? Will our favorite player get a base hit this time at bat? Will our first child be a boy or a girl? Who will win the election? What are the chances that a dispute between countries will escalate into war? In a bit of mathematical irony, there is actually a great deal of precision in the study of probability. There are a number of formal rules and basic features of probability that we must review. Before we can get a handle on these rules, we need to consider some basic ideas from set theory.

2.2.1 Introduction to Set Theory

A set is merely a collection of objects. Those objects are usually called the elements of the set. When talking about sets, the whole set is usually represented by a capital letter and its elements by subscripted lowercase letters. So a set called *A* would be represented as

$$A = \{a_1, a_2, \ldots, a_n\} \tag{2.1}$$

[3]For additional references, see Durrett (2010), Greene (2011), Gujarati and Porter (2008), Rao and Swift (2005), Stroock (2011), or Varadhan (2001).

where the above expression says that the Set A is made up of n elements that run from a_1 through a_n.

There are several types of sets. The set that contains all possible outcomes is often called the universal set. This is sometimes denoted as a capital S. A set that contains no elements at all is called the empty set, or the null set, and is often denoted as $\varnothing$. Sets also consist of subsets. A set is a subset of itself, but any partial collection of elements from a set is a subset of that set. The null set is also a subset of a set. To illustrate all of this further, let's return to the coin flipping example. A coin can either land on Heads or Tails. So we might define the universal set for tossing a single coin like this:

$$S = \{h, t\} \tag{2.2}$$

where the universal set, S consists of elements h for "Heads" and t for "Tails." The set of all of the possible subsets of S is

$$\mathbb{P} = \{\varnothing, \{h\}, \{t\}, S\} \tag{2.3}$$

where the symbol $\mathbb{P}$ represents the set of all possible subsets. This is sometimes called the power set. It can be shown that the power set of any set with n elements will have 2^n subsets. If we want to say that A is a subset of B, we can write that as $A \subset B$. This means that all of the elements of A are in the Set B.

Another important property of sets is the union. The union of two sets, A and B, is a set whose elements belong either to A, or to B, or to both. The union of A and B is symbolized like this: $A \cup B$. Elements that are in both A and B would only be counted once in the union of A and B. Thus, if the set of classes you are taking this semester is Statistics, Biology, U.S. History, and American Government and the set of classes your friend is taking is Statistics, Chemistry, Creative Writing, and American Government, then the union of those two sets is Statistics, Biology, U.S. History, American Government, Chemistry, and Creative Writing.

In contrast to the union, the intersection of two sets, A and B, is that set of only those elements that appear in both A and B. This is written symbolically as $A \cap B$. The elements would only be counted once. Returning to our classes example, the intersection between your set of classes and your friend's set of classes would be Statistics and American Government.

The key difference between the union and the intersection is whether we are talking about the elements that are in A *or* B or the elements that are in both A *and* B. The word "or" indicates the union of two sets, while the word "and" indicates the intersection of two sets. It is sometimes helpful to note that the union symbol $\cup$ looks sort of like the letter "u," which is the first letter in union. Also, the intersection symbol sort of looks like the letter "n," which you can hear in the words "intersection" and "and."

Three other useful notions in set theory are the complement of a set, the difference between sets, and the sum of sets. The complement of a Set A are all those elements of the universal set that are *not* in A. Thus, the complement of your set of classes would be all of the classes that were available this term that you did not take. The difference between two sets consists of all the elements in A that are not in B. Thus, the difference between A and B is the elements in A minus the intersection of A and B. The difference between your set of classes and your friend's set of classes would be Biology and U.S. History. Finally, the sum of two sets is a set that contains all the elements of both. Unlike the union, common elements are counted twice in the sum of two sets.

2.2.2 Properties of Probability

Now that we have a basic (frequentist) understanding of probability and some key elements from set theory under our belts, we can begin to define the properties of probability more clearly. All probabilities fall between 0 and 1, inclusive. In other words, the probability of an event happening cannot by definition be negative, nor can it be greater than 1. The probability of some event, E, happening, often written as $P(E)$, is defined as $0 \leq P(E) \leq 1$. If you consider all of the elements of the universal set, S, for an event as all the possible outcomes of that event, then the sum of the probabilities of all of those outcomes must equal 1.[4] So the probability of getting Heads on the toss of a fair coin is $\frac{1}{2}$ and the probability of getting Tails is also $\frac{1}{2}$. Thus, $\frac{1}{2} + \frac{1}{2} = 1$. The probability of getting a 1 on the roll of a standard six-sided die is $\frac{1}{6}$, and of a 2 is $\frac{1}{6}$, and so on, leading to $\frac{1}{6} + \frac{1}{6} + \frac{1}{6} + \frac{1}{6} + \frac{1}{6} + \frac{1}{6} = 1$. If E is a set of possible outcomes for an event, then $P(E)$ will equal the sum of the probabilities of all of the events included in Set E. Finally, for any set of outcomes E, $P(E) + P(\text{not } E) = 1$. This is to say that the probability of E plus the probability of the complement of E equals 1.

2.2.3 Conditional Probability

So far we have been examining the probability of occurrences of events that are independent of each other. When we toss a coin a second time, the fact that it came up Heads or Tails the first time is irrelevant to the probability of it coming up Heads or Tails the second time—the probabilities remain at 0.50 for each. If the probability of an event occurring is not independent of other events, the probability is defined as conditional. Conditional probability refers to the probability that one event might happen given that another event has already happened that could affect it. For example, the probability that a citizen might turn out to vote could depend on whether the person voted in the last election (if voting is habit forming), or it could depend on whether that person lives in a place where the

---

[4]To be precise, the possible outcomes or elements of the universal set cannot themselves be divided into smaller subsets.

campaign is close and hotly contested. In the first case, the probability of voting depends on a previous act of voting, which suggests that the act of voting or not is *not* the same as flipping a coin repeatedly. In the second example, the probability of voting is conditional on some other factors, which in many statistical models would be described as covariates or predictors of voting.[5]

Regardless, the conditional probability of Event E happening given that Event F has happened, is generally written like this: $P(E|F)$. This conditional probability can be computed as follows:

$$P(E|F) = \frac{P(E \cap F)}{P(F)} \qquad (2.4)$$

From this definition of conditional probability, we can now state a formal definition of independence of events. First, we can say that events E and F are independent if

$$P(E|F) = P(E) \qquad (2.5)$$

which also implies that $P(F|E) = P(F)$. In both expressions, the probability of one event by itself is the same as the probability of that event given another event. In other words, the probability of E occurring is unaffected by whether F has occurred or not, and vice versa. Another way to think about independence is that two events E and F are independent if

$$P(E \cap F) = P(E)P(F) \qquad (2.6)$$

This second expression captures what is called the "multiplicative" rule regarding conditional probabilities.

2.2.4 Simple Math With Probabilities

How we combine the probabilities associated with different events depends on whether we are interested in their intersection or union, and whether they are independent or not. When two events are independent and we want to know the probability of E or F, we can just add them together. If we are drawing a single card from a standard deck of playing cards, and we want to know the probability that it is a Club or a Heart, we can compute it as

$$P(\text{Club} \cup \text{Heart}) = P(\text{Club}) + P(\text{Heart}) = \frac{1}{4} + \frac{1}{4} = \frac{1}{2} \qquad (2.7)$$

We have to alter our calculation, however, if our events are not independent. Suppose I draw a single card from the deck again, and this time I want to know the probability that it is a Club or a face card (e.g., a Jack, Queen, or King). There

---

[5]We will discuss covariates a great deal throughout this book.

are 13 Clubs in a standard deck, and there are 12 face cards. However, three of the face cards are also Clubs. To keep from double-counting these cards when adding the two probabilities together, we must also subtract the common elements. Thus, the probability of drawing a Club or a face card can be computed like this:

$$P(\text{Club} \cup \text{Face Card}) = P(\text{Club}) + P(\text{Face Card}) - P(\text{Club} \cap \text{Face Card}) \quad (2.8)$$

which in this case would be $\frac{13}{52} + \frac{12}{52} - \frac{3}{52} = \frac{22}{52} \approx 0.423$. Notice in both of the previous examples that we were interested in the probability that a card drawn from a deck had one attribute or another. We wrote that "or" in our equations as the *union* between the set of outcomes that could satisfy the first condition and the set of outcomes that could satisfy the second condition. The operation we did to compute the probability was addition, with the subtraction of the intersection of the two sets if they were not independent.

When you are interested in the probability that an observation falls into both Set *E and* Set *F*, then you are interested in the probability of the intersection of *E* and *F*. We compute the probability of an intersection between two sets using multiplication. Returning to our deck of cards, suppose we want to know the probability of drawing a single card that is a face card *and* is Red. We could compute this as follows:

$$P(\text{Face Card} \cap \text{Red}) = P(\text{Face Card})P(\text{Red}) \quad (2.9)$$

which would equal $\frac{12}{52} \times \frac{26}{52} = \frac{312}{2704} = \frac{6}{52} \approx 0.115$. Of course, this example is pretty simple because we could have just counted the number of red face cards in a deck of 52 cards and got to $\frac{6}{52}$ directly. However, not all probability problems are this simple, nor are they always governed by simple assumptions like those we can apply to the toss of a fair coin or a draw from a single standard deck of cards. However, the basic operations we covered here apply to more complicated problems.

2.3 RANDOM VARIABLES AND PROBABILITY DISTRIBUTIONS

A probability distribution describes the range of values that a random variable can take on and the probability of each value occurring. For a continuous variable, the *probability density function* (PDF) describes the relative likelihood that a realization from the distribution will take on a particular value. Note that this is *not* a probability; because the range of possible values in a continuous variable is infinite, the probability that any one exact value will occur is zero. Probability with continuous variables is conceptualized in ranges, as in the probability of a realization falling between two values. This is computed from the PDF by finding the area under the curve in that range. For a discrete variable, the PDF is defined as its *probability distribution function* or alternatively its *probability mass function*

(PMF). In this context, the function can be directly interpreted as probabilities because the discrete values represent the only possible values taken on by realizations from the distribution.

The CDF stands for the cumulative distribution/density function. The CDF captures the probability that a random variable takes on a value less than or equal to a given value. Graphically, a PDF is a curve that rises and falls as the probability of different values for the random variables changes. The total area under the PDF curve sums to 1 because the entire probability space for a random variable must sum to 1. The CDF generally starts at or near zero and then rises until it reaches or approaches 1. While a PDF might rise and fall, the CDF steadily rises from left to right.

Figure 2.1 illustrates this using the normal distribution. Panel (a) plots a standard normal PDF for a random variable X. In this particular example, X has a mean (μ) of 0 and a standard deviation (σ) of 1. The height of the PDF at different values of X represent how likely it is to observe that X takes on values at or near this level in relation to other values.[6] Thus, values down around -3 appear to be rather unlikely, values near the mean of X are much more likely, and values up near $+3$ are rather unlikely again.

Panel (b) of Figure 2.1 shows the CDF for the same random normal variable X. The curve plotted in that graph represents the total area under the PDF curve in Panel (a) that falls below a given value for X. So while the PDF rises and falls (in the familiar "bell-shaped" curve that represents the normal distribution), the CDF continuously rises. In this case, the CDF rises slowly at first because of the skinny tail of the PDF at low values of X, then much faster because of the large mass of the PDF near the mean of X, then more slowly again because of the skinny tail at high values of X.

That the PDF in Figure 2.1, Panel (a) is highest at the mean of the random variable is worth emphasizing. The expected value of a random variable is the mean of that variable. This is true for any random variable regardless of the probability distribution it follows.[7] This does not mean that if we make a single draw from a given probability distribution that the value of that single draw is most likely to be the mean.[8] What it means is that, in repeated samples, the average of the values we draw from our samples will approach the mean of the underlying population as we draw more and more samples.

---

[6]The normal distribution is a continuous distribution over the real number line. Thus, as mentioned above, the probability of taking on any *exact* value down to what decimal place the computer allows is zero. We'll learn that it is better to consider a slice of the PDF between two values of X and treat the area under the curve in that slice as the probability of observing a value of X in that range.

[7]An odd exception is that the Cauchy distribution does not have a defined mean (it also has an infinite variance). Of course you can compute a mean from any sample of observations drawn from a Cauchy distribution, but at the population level, the mean is not defined.

[8]In fact, if the single draw is an independent draw, the most likely value to draw would be the mode, not the mean.

Figure 2.1 PDF and CDF of a Normal Random Variable, X, With $\mu = 0$ and $\sigma = 1$

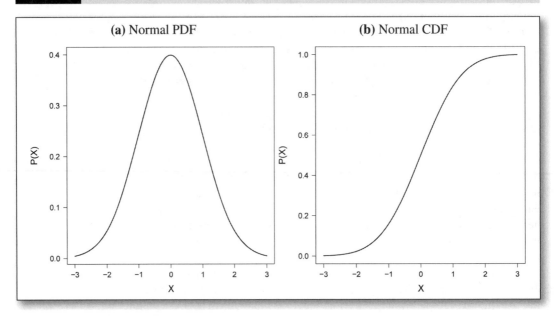

This is a powerful result. There is a class of statistical models focused on modeling the expected value of a dependent variable as a linear function of one or more independent variables. OLS regression is one such model. Researchers use these models to explain values of a dependent variable that might come from any of a number of probability distributions, some of which we will describe later. Nearly all of these models express the expected value of the dependent variable conditional on one or more independent variables. More specifically, they estimate the probability that the dependent variable takes on some value conditional on the values of the independent variables. When these conditional probability models are predicting the expected value of the dependent variable, they are most often predicting the mean.

There are a multitude of common probability distributions already built into R. We will discuss several of them in the sections below and in later chapters. Each distribution has a name (which is often abbreviated in R). You can access these distributions in four different ways by typing one of four letters in front of the name of the distribution. For example, one of the common continuous probability distributions is the normal distribution. It is abbreviated in R as norm. If you want to access the PDF of the normal distribution, you precede it with a d, like this: dnorm(). If you want to access the CDF of the normal distribution, you would type pnorm(). Preceding a distribution name with a q returns the quantiles of the distribution. Starting the distribution with an r allows you to draw random samples from the named distribution.

If events are associated with probabilities, then a function that assigns real values to the events that occur also assigns probabilities to those real values. Such functions are called *random variables*. It is the assignment of real values to events that leads to a random variable. The real values of the random variable inherit the probabilities of their corresponding events. The links between the values of a random variable and the probabilities assigned to those values result in probability densities and probability distributions for the random variable. Thus, a random variable is a mapping of events to the real number line. The values that a random variable can take on fall on the real number line between $-\infty$ and $+\infty$. A random variable can be thought of as a random number drawn from a larger population that is described by a range of possible values and the PDF that describes the relative likelihood of all of those possible values.

"Random" does not mean "haphazard" or otherwise unpredictable in the long run. A random variable is random in that any given observation or trial might be uncertain. However, the underlying distribution of probabilities associated with each possible outcome produces a predictable structure to the pattern of events that occur over the long run. It is hard to predict the outcome of a single flip of a coin—it will be either Heads or Tails, with an equal chance of either outcome. However, if we flip the coin many times, the distribution of Heads and Tails will settle down to a stable predictable frequency distribution. This can be seen in Figure 2.2. In this figure, we simulate tossing a fair coin 200 times. We plot the proportion of flips, called trials, that are scored as a "success," which in this case means coming up Heads. The figure also plots a horizontal line at 0.50 on the y-axis that represents the expected probability of getting Heads on a single toss.

Figure 2.2   Cumulative Frequency of the Proportion of Coin Flips That Produce Heads

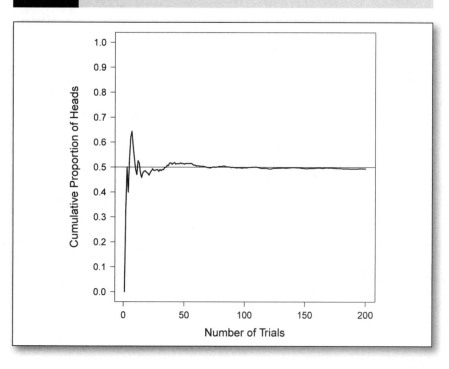

Looking at Figure 2.2 you can see that the proportion of tosses that produce a Heads bounces around above and below the 0.50 line early on. However, as the number of tosses increases, the proportion that are Heads begins to fluctuate less and starts to settle down near the 0.50 level. Figure 2.2 demonstrates that just because one observation or a small number of observations might be hard to predict, a large number of trials reveals something systematic about the underlying probability distribution. This demonstrates an important probability theorem: The law of large numbers, which holds that the average of results from a large number of trials will converge to the expected value. Thus, order emerges from a series of independent random events. You can perform this experiment yourself with the following R code.

```
# Coin Flips
set.seed(23212) # Set the seed for reproducible results
n <- seq(1, 200, length = 200) # Number of trials
heads <- numeric(length(n)) # Empty vector for heads in one set of trials
c.heads <- numeric(length(n)) # Empty vector for cumulative
                              # proportion of heads

k <- c("0 Heads", "1 Head") # Two sides of the coin
p <- c(.5, .5) # Probabilities of heads  and tails

for(i in 1:length(n)){ # Start a for loop over the n trials
# Count the number of heads from n[i] trials
heads[i] <- sum(sample(k, size = n[i], prob = p, replace = TRUE) == "1 Head")
# Compute the cumulative proportion of heads
c.heads[i] <- sum(heads[1:i])/sum(n[1:i])
}
```

Types of Random Variables

There are two basic types of random variables: (1) discrete and (2) continuous. A discrete random variable maps events to values of a countable set (e.g., the integers), with each value in the range having probability greater than zero. A continuous random variable maps events to values of an uncountable set (e.g., the full set of real numbers), providing any interval of values (from its range) a positive probability. However, the probability of any specific value for a continuous random variable is zero. Below we examine discrete and continuous random variables in more detail.

Before proceeding, we present a final piece of notation here. The mean of a random variable, which is the expected value of the random variable (defined by assumption or by the frequentist appeal to repeated samples) is generally symbolized by the Greek letter μ, while the sample mean is represented with a "bar" over the variable name, as in $\bar{x}$. The variance of a random variable is generally symbolized by σ^2, which is the square of the Greek letter "sigma," while the sample variance is represented by s^2.

2.4 DISCRETE RANDOM VARIABLES

We have seen several times the distinction between categorical and continuous variables. Categorical variables take on values that fall into specific categories, while continuous variables can take on any value within a given range, including fractions. In probability theory, the underlying probability distributions and probability densities for categorical variables are called discrete distributions/densities. For continuous variables, they are called continuous distributions/densities.

As noted above, discrete random variables map values from the real number line to integers or categories that describe the probability of a discrete outcome occurring. If X is a discrete random variable, then the range of X is the set of all k where $P(X = k) > 0$. The probability distribution of X is the specification of these probabilities for all k values of X. Note that our rules governing probabilities also ensure that $\sum P(X = k) = 1$.

For example, suppose we toss a coin three times, each time recording whether it comes up Heads or Tails. Let's abbreviate Heads as H and Tails as T. One possible sequence of how three tosses might come out is *(H, T, T)*. The set of all possible outcomes, then, is the set *(H, H, H), (H, H, T), (H, T, H), (H, T, T), (T, H, H), (T, H, T), (T, T, H), (T, T, T)*. If X is the number of Heads, it can be either 0, 1, 2, or 3. If the coin we are tossing is fair, then each of the eight possible outcomes are equally likely. Thus, $P(X = 0) = \frac{1}{8}$, $P(X = 1) = \frac{3}{8}$, $P(X = 2) = \frac{3}{8}$, and $P(X = 3) = \frac{1}{8}$. This describes the discrete PDF of X. Note that the individual probabilities of all of the possible events sum to 1. The cumulative PDF would be represented like this: $P(X \leq 0) = \frac{1}{8}$, $P(X \leq 1) = \frac{4}{8}$, $P(X \leq 2) = \frac{7}{8}$, and $P(X \leq 3) = \frac{8}{8}$.

You can use the `sample()` function in R to generate observations of a discrete random variable. Suppose the Vector k contains the values you are sampling, and the Vector p contains the associated probabilities of each value being selected. Together, these two vectors describe the PDF for some discrete random variable. To draw a sample of n observations from this PDF, we could enter the following code into R:

```
a.sample <- sample(k, size = n, prob = p, replace = TRUE)
```

As we will learn in Chapter 3, the `sample()` function in this case requires several inputs, or arguments, such as the vector of possible outcomes (k) and the size of the sample you want to draw (n, which can be set to any number). If you do not specify `prob`, R will assume that you want to assign equal probabilities of selecting any of the elements in Vector k. R also assumes by default that once you draw an observation, it cannot be selected again. This is called sampling *without* replacement. That would be appropriate if you were trying to simulate a sampling process where the probability of an outcome occurring was dependent on the outcomes that had occurred already. When the outcomes are independent of each other, then the appropriate sampling technique is to sample *with* replacement. In this case, if we happen to get 3 Heads in our first trial, that has no impact on the chances of getting 3 Heads on the second, or third, or 483rd trial. Thus, even though we drew a 3 the first time, we want R to have the same probability of drawing a 3 in each of the subsequent trials.

Returning to the example of tossing a coin, we could use the following code in R to draw a sample of 800 trials of tossing a coin three times and counting how many Heads were produced each time:

```
set.seed(47586) # Set the seed for reproducible results
n <- 800 # Sample size I want to draw
k <- c("0 Heads", "1 Head", "2 Heads", "3 Heads") # Possible
# outcomes
p <- c(1, 3, 3, 1)/8 # Probability of getting 0, 1, 2, or 3 Heads
a.sample <- sample(k, size = n, prob = p, replace = TRUE)

table(a.sample)
0 Heads 1 Head 2 Heads 3 Heads
    96     293    312      99
```

The final part of our R code summarizes the results of the experiment in a frequency table. In 800 trials, we would expect to get 100 occurrences each of 0 Heads and 3 Heads and 300 occurrences each of 1 Head or 2 Heads. This is based on the relative frequency notion of probability from multiple trials compared with our expected frequency given the assumption that the coin we are tossing is fair. You can see from the example above that we got close to the outcomes we expected, but we did not get exactly the expected distribution. That tells us something about probabilities: They have formal and strict rules, but they remain somewhat uncertain in terms of resulting observed outcomes. This uncertainty would be eliminated if we did the experiment an infinite number of times, but we generally want answers sooner than that, which means that we do our real work in the context of finite sample sizes. Before moving on, we note that the comparison of expected outcomes to observed outcomes lies at the heart of hypothesis testing and statistical inference, which is what makes this discussion of probability theory so important for quantitatively oriented social scientists.

2.4.1 Some Common Discrete Distributions

Recall that the PDF of a random variable describes the PDF associated with the probability that a given random variable will take on one of its possible values. In contrast, the CDF of a random variable describes the CDF, which corresponds to the probability that a given random variable will take on a value equal to or less than a given value. There are a number of common probability distributions for discrete random variables. It is beyond the scope of this book to provide a great deal of mathematical detail about them, but we do want to provide a brief description of a few that are most common. This will prove useful when we shift to simulating these types of variables in later chapters.

Discrete probability distributions (PDFs and CDFs) can be represented as a smooth curve like the normal shown in Figure 2.1. However, this is somewhat misleading because discrete variables can only take on a set of fixed integer values. Thus, we present discrete PDFs and CDFs using what is called a "spike" plot. Such a plot presents a single line, or spike, for each discrete value of the random variable with the height of the spike indicating the expected probability of observing that value. Recall that the PDF for discrete random variables can be directly interpreted as a probability that the variable takes on a particular value exactly.

Bernoulli

A random variable that follows a Bernoulli distribution is one that can take on only two values: 0 or 1. The distribution of a random variable, X, distributed as a Bernoulli is described by $p = P(X = 1)$. Often, the term *success* is given to outcomes when $X = 1$ and *failure* to outcomes when $X = 0$. A coin toss, the example we have seen several times in this chapter where $X = 1$ if the coin comes up Heads, is a Bernoulli random variable where $P(X = 1) = 0.50$. A sequence of coin tosses that are independent of each other can be described as a series of Bernoulli random variables or Bernoulli trials. A Bernoulli random variable has a mean $\mu = p$ and a variance $\sigma^2 = p(1 - p)$. The `sample()` function in R can be used to generate a draw or a sequence of independent draws from a Bernoulli distribution.

Binomial

A binomial random variable is a variable that counts the number of successes from a series of n Bernoulli trials. There are two key components to define a binomial random variable: (1) the number of trials (n) and (2) the probability of success on any given trial (p). The possible range of a binomial random variable, X, is then from 0 all the way up to n. The probability distribution for a binomial random variable, X, is written as

$$P(X = k) = \left(\frac{n!}{(n-k)!k!} \right) p^k (1 - p)^{n-k} \tag{2.10}$$

In this equation, k is the number of successes from n Bernoulli trials that we want to evaluate. The symbol $n!$ is read as "n factorial" or "the factorial of n." The factorial operation in mathematics means to multiply $n \times (n - 1) \times (n - 2) \times \cdots \times 2 \times 1$. By convention, $0! = 1$. The mean of a binomial variable is $\mu = np$ and the variance is $\sigma^2 = np(1 - p)$. In R, the name for the binomial distribution is abbreviated as `binom`.

Figure 2.3 shows the PDF (Panel a) and CDF (Panel b) for a binomial random variable, X, with 10 trials and a probability of success on any given trial equal to

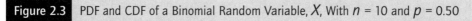

Figure 2.3 PDF and CDF of a Binomial Random Variable, X, With n = 10 and p = 0.50

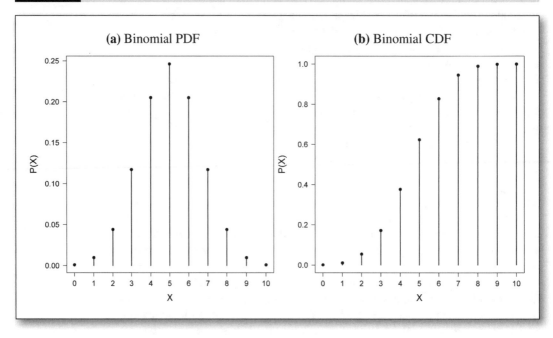

0.50. As noted above, these are spike plots rather than smooth curves because the random variable we are describing is discrete.

Panel (a) of Figure 2.3 shows that the highest probability is associated with observing 5 successes out of 10 trials, when p = 0.50. That probability is about 0.25, which can be computed in R as follows (see Chapter 4 for more on this code).

```
dbinom(5, size = 10, prob = .5)
[1] 0.2460938
```

This is not surprising because the mean of a binomial random variable, μ equals *np*. In this case, $\mu = np = 10 \times 0.50 = 5$. The mean is relatively more likely than other values. Observing 0 successes or 10 successes is very unlikely. Figure 2.3, Panel (b) shows how the cumulative probability of observing 0 successes, 1 or fewer successes, 2 or fewer successes, 3 or fewer successes, all the way up to 10 or fewer successes steadily grows from 0 to 1. These cumulative probabilities can be computed using the pbinom() function in R. Suppose we want to know the probability of observing 5 or fewer successes in 10 trials where p = 0.50 for any one trial. We could type

```
pbinom(5, size = 10, prob = .5)
[1] 0.6230469
```

From this we get a probability of about 0.62 of observing 5 or fewer successes in 10 trials with the probability of success for any one trial equal to 0.50.

While the binomial distribution is for discrete variables based on the number of successes from n Bernoulli trials, it can be shown that as n increases, the binomial distribution can be approximated by the normal distribution. Alternatively, if np is held constant while n increases, the binomial distribution approximates the Poisson distribution, which we discuss below. The multinomial distribution is a generalization of the binomial distribution. While the binomial distribution is based on the successes of a Bernoulli trial, which can have only two outcomes— success or failure—the multinomial distribution can accommodate a process that has m outcomes possible on each trial where m can be greater than two.

Poisson

A Poisson random variable is a variable that counts the number of events or the number of occurrences of an event, usually for a given time period, area, or some other unit. Examples might include the number of presidential vetoes in a given year, the number of students who graduate with a perfect GPA (grade point average), or the number of terrorist attacks that occur in a given year.

The Poisson distribution has a single parameter, often denoted as the Greek letter "lambda" (λ). This distribution assumes that the events being recorded are generally rare given a particular interval. In other words, this distribution best approximates variables where the typical count of the number of events is pretty low. The probability distribution for a Poisson random variable, X, is written as

$$P(X = m) = \left(\frac{\lambda^m}{m!} \right) e^{-\lambda} \qquad (2.11)$$

Figure 2.4 shows the PDF (Panel a) and CDF (Panel b), respectively, of a Poisson random variable with $\lambda = 5$. Panel (a) demonstrates that the most likely count to observe from a Poisson random variable with $\lambda = 5$ is 5. That is not surprising, as λ is the mean of a Poisson random variable.

One feature of the Poisson that makes it both attractive but sometimes limiting is that both the expected mean and the expected variance of a Poisson random variable are equal to λ. This can be problematic when using the Poisson distribution as part of a statistical model because many times count variables evidence "overdispersion." That occurs when the observed variance of the random variable is larger than its observed mean. When estimating models for a dependent variable that is a count, scholars frequently turn to the negative binomial distribution, which is a generalization of the Poisson distribution that allows for overdispersion.

2.5 CONTINUOUS RANDOM VARIABLES

Continuous random variables map the underlying probability to observed values, or realizations, of a variable just like discrete random variables. The difference is

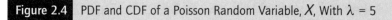

Figure 2.4 PDF and CDF of a Poisson Random Variable, X, With $\lambda = 5$

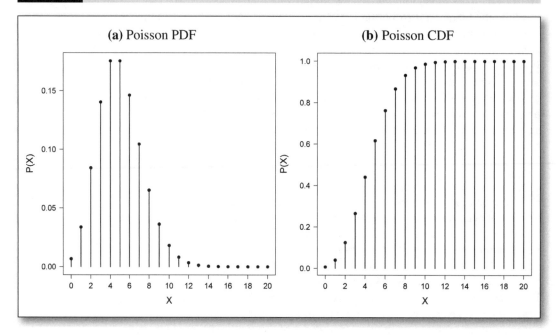

that the observed values of continuous random variables are not limited to discrete integers. Rather, they can (theoretically) take on any value on the real number line. Continuous PDFs and CDFs are, thus, represented by smooth curves rather than spike plots.

This can be a bit misleading at first. Look again at the normal distribution in Figure 2.1, Panel (a). The figure suggests that the probability of observing a value of -1 is about 0.24 because that is how high the PDF curve is when $X = -1$ in this particular example. However, the probability of observing a value of X that is *exactly* -1, which is to say *exactly* -1.000000000 out to as many decimal places as your computer can handle, is actually zero. The PDF of a continuous variable represents the relative probability of observing values near a given value of X compared with values near other values of X. More precisely, continuous PDFs are generally used to describe the probability of observing a value less than or equal to some given value of X, greater than or equal to some value of X, between two values of X, or not between two values of X. This is shown in Figure 2.5 using the normal distribution.

There are four graphs in Figure 2.5. All four present the same normal distribution. In each of the graphs, an area under the normal distribution is shaded. That shaded area corresponds to the probability of observing a value for a random normal variable, X, drawn from this distribution that falls in the shaded range. Thus, the top left graph in Figure 2.5 shades the area corresponding to values of

Figure 2.5	Areas Under a Normal Distribution

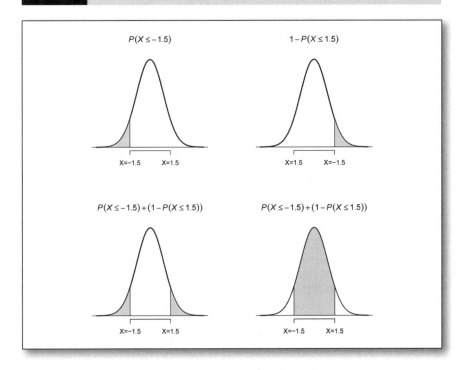

X that are equal to or lower than -1.5. This is often read as shading some portion of the "lower tail" of the distribution. This graph is labeled $P(X \leq -1.5)$. The top right graph shades the area for values that fall at or above $+1.5$. This is called shading some portion of the "upper tail" of the distribution. For convenience, we label this graph as $1 - P(X \leq 1.5)$. This reminds us that the total area under the PDF must sum to 1. It is also common to refer to the probability space to the left of some dividing line, using 1 minus that probability to refer to the area above that dividing line.

The lower left graph shades both tails of the distribution. It is labeled $P(X \leq -1.5) + (1 - P[X \leq 1.5])$. The two probabilities are added together to denote the probability that X lies in either the lower shaded region or the upper shaded region. The lower right graph shades the area between the lower and upper cut points. In other words, it shades the area not in the tails, where the starting points of the tails in this example are set at -1.5 and $+1.5$. The lower right graph could be labeled as 1 minus the sum of the two-tail probabilities. However, we have labeled it as $P(X \leq 1.5) - P(X \leq -1.5)$ to again follow the convention of referring to the space to the left of a specific value. This expression says take the entire area at or below $+1.5$ and subtract from that the area that is at or below -1.5—that lower tail.

To summarize, continuous random variables are variables that map noninterval values to the underlying PDF in a slightly different manner than with discrete random variables. By short hand, we still describe the probability of a continuous random variable taking on a given value using a PDF, but remember that the PDF in this context is a relative measure of the likelihood of observing some small range of values.

2.5.1 Two Common Continuous Distributions

There are a number of continuous probability distributions widely used in statistical analysis. While there are many probability distributions that are not discussed below, those that are discussed constitute some of the main distributions used in applied statistical analysis. Again, we do not spend a great deal of time on the mathematical properties of these distributions. However, we will point out how many of them are related to each other and, by extension, related to the normal distribution.

Uniform

The simplest continuous distribution to understand is the uniform distribution. The uniform distribution is defined by an upper and lower bound, with the probability space allocated evenly, or uniformly, between the two bounds. Values outside the bounds do not occur, or could be said to occur with zero probability. If the lower and upper bounds are defined as a and b, respectively, then the PDF of the uniformly distributed random variable, X, can be written like this:

$$P(X \mid a,b) = \begin{cases} \dfrac{1}{(b-a)} \\ 0 & \text{otherwise.} \end{cases}$$

This expression illustrates that the probability of observing a random variable X given the lower and upper bounds a and b is just 1 divided by the upper bound minus the lower bound if X falls within those bounds and zero if it does not fall within those bounds. The expression $\dfrac{1}{(b-a)}$ defines the probability as evenly distributed throughout the range between a and b. Figure 2.6 shows the PDF and CDF of a uniform random variable, X, with the lower bound, a, set at -2 and the upper bound, b, set at $+2$.

Panel (a) shows that the probability distribution is at zero below values of -2. It rises straight up at -2 and then is flat until reaching the upper bound of $+2$, where it drops immediately down to zero again. The flat but raised curve between -2 and $+2$ constitutes the probability space of the uniform distribution, which is spread out evenly. Like all PDFs, the total area under that curve in Figure 2.6 sums to 1. Panel (b) of Figure 2.6 shows the CDF of the uniform random variable X. Again, it stays at zero for values below -2. It then rises linearly from 0 to 1 as we move from -2 to $+2$ on X.

Figure 2.6 PDF and CDF of a Uniform Random Variable, X, Bounded by -2 and +2

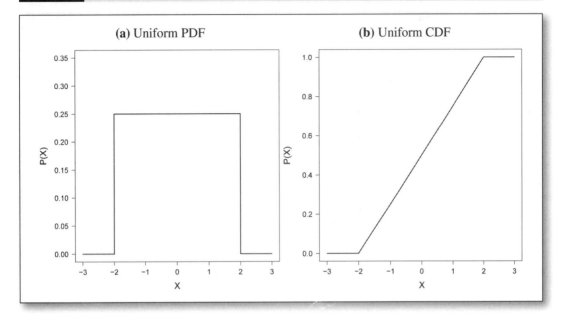

Like all probability distributions, the expected value of the uniform distribution is its mean. In this case, the mean of a uniform random variable is simply $\mu = \frac{a+b}{2}$. Given that the variable is distributed uniformly, the center location between the lower and upper bound is the mean. The variance of a uniform random variable is $\sigma^2 = \frac{(b-a)^2}{12}$.

The uniform distribution is very useful in simulation. Most computer functions that generate random variables from other distributions do so by first creating a random uniform variable and then feeding that variable into the equation that defines a given probability distribution. R and other statistical computing programs have many of these operations already built in. However, if you need a probability distribution that is not already available, as long as you know the formula that describes it, you can often generate a sample of observations that follows that distribution by feeding a random uniform variable through the equation. We demonstrate an example of this in Chapter 4.

Normal

We have already introduced the normal distribution by using it as an example so we will only briefly review it here. The importance of the normal distribution in statistical analysis, however, cannot be understated. Many other common distributions are either related to the normal or begin to approximate it under a variety of circumstances. More important, the central limit theorem (CLT) states that the distribution of the means of repeated samples drawn from *any* distribution will follow a normal distribution as long as the samples from which the means were computed are large enough, the samples are randomly and independently drawn, and the observations within each sample are randomly and independently drawn.[9] Thus, the CLT provides the foundation for hypothesis testing in classical frequentist statistics.

The PDF of the normal distribution presented in Panel (a) of Figure 2.1 displays its signature "bell-shaped" curve. Most of the mass of the PDF is concentrated around the mean of the distribution, with much smaller amounts out in what are called the distribution's "tails." The corresponding CDF, presented in Figure 2.1, Panel (b), displays what is also a classic inverted "S-shaped" curve. The normal distribution has two parameters that define it: (1) its mean, μ, and (2) its variance, σ^2. Note that we could just as easily use the standard deviation, σ, instead of the variance since the standard deviation is just the square root of the variance. The formulas are as follows:

$$\mu = \frac{\sum x_i}{n} \tag{2.12}$$

$$\sigma^2 = \frac{\sum_{i=1}^{n}(x_i - \bar{x})^2}{n} \tag{2.13}$$

Note the use of n rather than $n - 1$ in the equation for the variance. That is because we are defining the population variance, σ^2 and not the sample variance s^2. Of course, when n gets large, the difference between the two becomes negligible. In practice, however, we use $n - 1$ in our calculations from a sample to account for the degree of freedom lost in estimating the mean, which itself is part of the formula for the variance (see below for more on degrees of freedom).

The PDF for the normal distribution is more complicated than we have seen before. For a random variable, Y, the function is

$$P(Y = y \mid \mu, \sigma) = \frac{1}{\sigma\sqrt{2\pi}} \exp\left[-\frac{1}{2}\left(\frac{y - \mu}{\sigma}\right)^2\right] \tag{2.14}$$

It is worth noting the special case when $\mu = 0$ and $\sigma^2 = 1$ (which also means that $\sigma = 1$). When this is the case for a random variable, it is said to follow a *standard normal distribution*. This is important because of how the standard normal distribution relates to other distributions described in this chapter. This is also related in spirit to the construction of so-called standardized variables. Standardizing a variable transforms the variable from its original values into a variable that has a mean of zero and a variance (and, thus, standard deviation) of 1.

---

[9]There is no formal definition of "large enough" for the CLT, but the common rule of thumb is sample sizes of 30 are generally large enough for the CLT to kick in.

Importantly, standardizing a variable will *not* change its distribution. It will only change its scale of measurement.

2.5.2 Other Continuous Distributions

We now return to the discussion of several more probability densities for continuous variables. The remaining three distributions covered are "sampling" distributions. Sampling distributions describe characteristics of samples drawn from a larger population. We most often make use of sampling distributions as they relate to statistics we compute from data rather than regarding the distribution of individual variables.

Recall that statistics are things we calculate or compute from the data we have in our hands. We also noted that when we conduct inference, we typically use statistics calculated from our data as estimates of some parameter that describes the entire population. All of these statistics are computed from the variables we have in our sample of data. If those variables are random variables—which they would be if the sample was randomly selected—then the statistics we compute are based on random variables. Because statistics are functions of random variables, they are themselves also random variables. As a result, all statistics have an associated probability distribution—specifically, a sampling distribution.

Thus, the next three distributions presented below can be thought of as just three more continuous probability distributions and that would be correct. However, researchers are interested in these distributions because of their central role in classic hypothesis testing. Hypothesis testing generally involves computing a statistic of some sort with a known distribution and then comparing that statistic to the expected value of the distribution to determine how likely we were to get the result we obtained due to chance.

The sampling distributions considered below also have another attribute—their shapes are all influenced by how many degrees of freedom (*df*s) they have. Degrees of freedom describe how many values in the final calculation of a statistic are allowed to vary. This is a way of describing how much information is available to compute a statistic. All else equal, the greater the *df*, the greater the amount of independent information you have in your data with which to compute a statistic. From a practical standpoint, the fact that the shapes of these sampling distributions change based on the *df* available is a way of saying that these distributions adjust to how much information you have in your sample. Remember, probability distributions are about describing uncertainty. If we are computing a statistic based on a sample, our uncertainty about that statistic should depend on how much information we have.

Chi-Square

The chi-square distribution, often written as χ^2, is a probability distribution that only takes on positive values. It is a continuous distribution, so it can take on any positive value on the real number line. If you have a random standard normal variable—meaning a random normal variable with $\mu = 0$ and $\sigma = 1$, then the squared values of that variable will follow a χ^2 distribution with 1 df. If n observations from a standard normal variable are squared and then summed, the resulting sum has a χ^2 distribution with $df = n$. Formally, the PDF of the χ^2 given $df = n$ is

$$P(x \mid n) = \frac{1}{2^{\frac{n}{2}} \Gamma\left(\frac{n}{2}\right)} x^{\frac{n}{2}-1} \exp\left(-\frac{x}{2}\right) \tag{2.15}$$

The symbol Γ stands for the Gamma distribution. The expected value, or mean, of the χ^2 distribution is n. Its expected variance is $2n$. Figure 2.7 plots several χ^2 distributions with different degrees of freedom. The graph shows that at 1 df the χ^2 distribution is a downward sloping curve. As the df s increase, the distribution first goes up and then goes down. The mass under the curve is also being pulled to the right. As df increase, the χ^2 distribution begins to approximate a normal distribution.

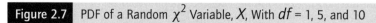

Figure 2.7   PDF of a Random χ^2 Variable, X, With df = 1, 5, and 10

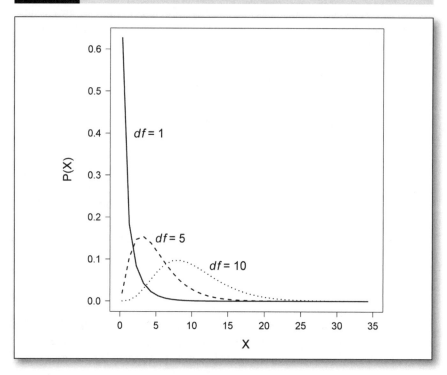

Student's t

The Student's t distribution gets its name from the person, Student, who discovered it. The density is defined such that, if Z is a standard normal random variable and U is a random χ^2 variable with df equal to n, and if Z and U are independent of each other, then $\dfrac{Z}{\sqrt{U/n}}$ follows a Student's t distribution with n df. Formally, the t PDF with $df = n$ is defined as

$$P(t \mid n) = \frac{\Gamma\left(\dfrac{n+1}{2}\right)}{\sqrt{n\pi}\,\Gamma\left(\dfrac{n}{2}\right)}\left(1+\frac{t^2}{n}\right)^{-\frac{n+1}{2}} \tag{2.16}$$

The Student's t, often just called the t distribution, is bell shaped like the normal, but it has a shorter peak and somewhat fatter tails than does the normal. Figure 2.8 shows just how similar the Student's t and the normal distributions can be. When $df = \infty$, the t is equivalent to the standard normal.

Figure 2.8 Comparison of the Student's t and Normal Distribution PDFs

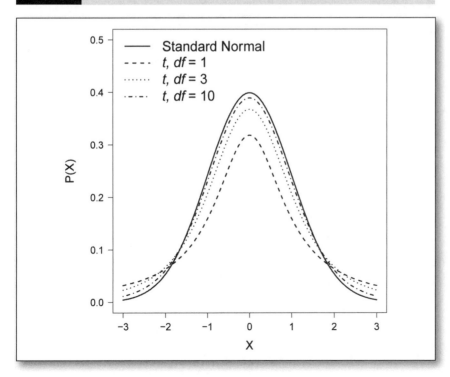

The solid line in Figure 2.8 reproduces a standard normal PDF ($\mu = 0$, $\sigma = 1$). The dashed line represents a t distribution with 1 df. The dotted line represents a t distribution with $df = 3$ and the dot-dash line is a t with $df = 10$. Note that the three t distributions show the lower peak and the fatter tails compared with the normal distribution. Figure 2.8 also shows that as the dfs increase, the t distribution starts to approximate the normal distribution.

F distribution

The last distribution we want to consider is the F distribution. Like the χ^2, the F distribution is bounded at zero but can reach any positive real number. This distribution is defined such that, if A_1 and A_2 are independent random variables that each follow χ^2 distributions, with degrees of freedom of df_1 and df_2, respectively, then the following expression holds:

$$F_{df_1 df_2} = \frac{A_1/df_1}{A_2/df_2} \tag{2.17}$$

What this means is that the ratio of two independently drawn random χ^2 variables follows an F distribution. The two df parameters (for the numerator and denominator,

Figure 2.9   Comparison of F Distribution PDFs

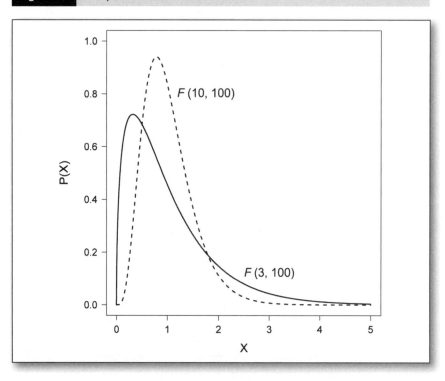

respectively) combine to control the distribution's shape. The PDF of the F distribution is defined as follows.[10]

$$P(x \mid df_1, df_2) = \frac{\sqrt{\dfrac{(df_1 x)^{df_1} df_2^{df_2}}{(df_1 x + df_2)^{df_1 + df_2}}}}{xB\left(\dfrac{df_1}{2}, \dfrac{df_2}{2}\right)} \ . \tag{2.18}$$

Figure 2.9 shows that the F distribution appears similar in shape to the χ^2 distribution. This is not surprising given that the F consists of a ratio of two χ^2 distributions. Figure 2.9 also suggests that as the df increase, the F distribution gets stretched out like the χ^2 and itself also begins to approach an approximately normal distribution.

2.6 CONCLUSIONS

This chapter presented an overview of probability theory and probability distributions. Probability theory provides the foundation for statistical inference, and much of that inference relies on the common probability distributions discussed in this chapter. We only scratched the surface of these very important topics, but our modest goal was simply to provide some basic rules about probability, a working understanding of what a probability distribution is, and sense that all of these various distributions, definitions, and operations have a great deal in common. In particular, you should come away from this chapter with a sense that the normal distribution is at the heart of classical inferential statistics. In the chapters that follow, we will use the normal and other distributions in creating the DGPs that we wish to simulate.

---

[10]The symbol B denotes the beta function (see Press, Teukolsky, Vetterling, & Flannery, 2007).

3

Introduction to R

In this chapter, we provide a brief review of the statistical environment R, which we use in all of the examples throughout the book. R holds several advantages both for general use and for the specific purpose of conducting simulations. Among these advantages include the fact that it is open-source and free, it utilizes a flexible programming style, it has a very large library of user-written packages that allow users to extend its functionality, and there is a lot of help with R available online.

What follows is not a comprehensive look at R and all that it has to offer. R is quite large and complex, and so a full treatment of its capabilities is beyond the scope of this book. We cover some very basic information about R along with some additional features relevant to conducting simulations that are critical for understanding the material in the rest of the book. There are several useful full-length introductions to R, listed below, which we recommend for readers who wish to learn more. For a general overview of R, we suggest Matloff (2011). For applied statistics texts that use R, we recommend Cohen and Cohen (2008) and Fox and Weisberg (2010). Those looking for more advanced treatments of statistical programming in R should consider Chambers (2008), Rizzo (2008), and Jones, Maillardet, and Robinson (2009).

3.2 WHAT IS R?

R is a platform for the statistical programming language S. R is widely used in statistics and has become quite popular in social science. R can be used as either a programming language or as a tool used to perform standard statistical analyses similar to Stata, SAS, or SPSS.

R has an extensive number of operations built into it that you might think of as commands, or what R calls functions. Every function has a name followed immediately by a set of parentheses. Within the parentheses, you provide arguments that control what the function does. Most functions have default operations they will perform, so much so that some functions do not actually need any arguments included within the parentheses to generate results. However, the default settings of a function can be changed in many ways. Users can also write their own functions in R, and R also carries an extensive library of user-written packages that can be used to conduct a wide variety of statistical analyses, graphical presentations, and other functions.

3.2.1 Resources

Again, the review here is not meant to be comprehensive. As questions emerge about R, here are a few resources you may want to consider:

- Within R, there is "Introduction to R," which is located in the "Help" pull-down menu under "Manuals" as well as the ? and `help()` commands.
- As mentioned above, there are many good books on R, including Braun and Murdoch (2007), Rizzo (2008), Cohen and Cohen (2008), Jones et al. (2009), Fox and Weisberg (2010), Horton and Kleinman (2011), Matloff (2011), and Chernick and LaBudde (2011).
- Springer's Use R! series covers a broad range of specific topics in R. (`http://www.springer.com/series/6991`).
- To do a web-based search, use `http://www.rseek.org/` (powered by Google).
- The Nabble-R help forum is useful for asking questions: `http://r.789695.n4.nabble.com/`.
- Quick-R is a great resource for SAS/SPSS/Stata users looking for how to execute an operation in R that they already know how to do with one of those other programs: `http://www.statmethods.net/`.

3.3 USING R WITH A TEXT EDITOR

R is an actual programming language. That means you type code and submit it rather than use the "point-and-click" approach or pull-down menus found in many software packages. Code is usually saved in what most users call "script" files, which are text files that contain R code. Script files are saved with the ".r" or ".R" file extension. We strongly recommend using a text editor to manage script files. A text editor is a program used to open, edit, and save text files. There are many text editors available, and a great majority are free to use. See this website for several examples: `http://www.sciviews.org/_rgui/projects/Editors.html`. Some, such as Tinn-R (Windows), Aquamacs (Mac), and RStudio (Windows/Mac/Linux) have several functions designed to make working with R easier. These features include buttons and/or commands to send code directly to R and color schemes for the text that make it easier to visualize and understand your R code.

Using a text editor makes submitting commands to R quicker and organizing your code easier. Additionally, using a text editor that is separate from R protects you from losing code if there is a problem with your R session. While there is a basic text editor within R, we do not recommend using it. If you submit a command that causes R to freeze or crash before saving your code, the unsaved code will be lost. If you manage code in a separate text editor, it will not be affected by problems in R.

3.4 FIRST STEPS

To obtain R for Windows, Mac, or Linux, go to The Comprehensive R Archive Network (CRAN) at `http://cran.r-project.org/` and download the executable file. CRAN also has instructions for installation. After installing, open R. All of the commands you will use will be entered at a command prompt:

```
>
```

3.4.1 Creating Objects

Simulation and resampling methods produce a considerable amount of data (i.e., many simulated or resampled data sets, statistical estimates from those data sets, and summaries of those estimates). One of the key strengths of R is that it makes organization of this information relatively easy through the creation of objects. In its simplest form, this means that you can store anything you do in R with a name, then look at that object, run another command on it later, overwrite it, or delete it as you see fit.

Here is a basic example. We want to create an object called x that is the value 2. We use R's assignment operator, which is the "less-than sign" and a hyphen, (<–) to do this:

```
x <- 2
x
[1] 2
```

The first line of code creates an object named x and assigns to it the value of 2. The second line of code just types the name of that object. The third line is not code, but rather output produced by the second line. Specifically, when we typed the name of the object x, R printed the value of that object, which is 2, to the screen. The [1] is just an index counting the number of elements that are being printed on the screen.

We can now use this object x later in the code. Objects can be just about anything in R, including single numbers, vectors, matrices, lists, data frames, output from statistical models, letters, and text. All of these types of objects are created in the same way as the example above by using the assignment operator. In writing R code, you will likely create many different objects, which makes organization important. Below are some tips on naming objects to keep in mind.

- Expressions and functions in R are case-sensitive.
- Anything following the pound character (#) R ignores as a comment.
- An object name must start with an alphabetical character, but may contain numeric characters thereafter. A period may also form part of the name of an object. For example, x1 is a valid name for an object in R. However, names of objects in R cannot have spaces.
- You can use the arrow keys on the keyboard to scroll back to previous commands.
- To list the objects you have created in a session, type the following functions as shown here: objects() or ls() (both do the same thing).
- To remove all the objects you have created from the active R session, use the following function and arguments rm(list = ls(all = TRUE)).
- You can save the objects you have created during your R session in what R calls a workspace file—which gets saved with the extension .RData—in two different ways:
    1. Select the "Save Workspace ..." option under the "File" menu in the R terminal. Then, choose a location on your computer for the file.
    2. Use the save.image() command with the desired file name as its argument, as in save.image(''example.RData'').[1]
- There are also two options for loading an existing .RData file into R:
    1. Select the "Load Workspace ... " option under the "File" menu in the R terminal. Then, find the file location on your computer.
    2. Use the load() command in the same way as save.image().

3.5 BASIC MANIPULATION OF OBJECTS

R has many functions that create, change, or summarize objects. Below are a few basic functions you should be familiar with for later topics in the book. Remember that after creating an object, you can display that object on the screen simply by typing its name.

3.5.1 Vectors and Sequences

To create a vector of numbers or text, use the c() function. As we will see, this very simple command is used in several different applications. Also notice that by typing the object's name we can print that object on the screen.

```
my.vector <- c(1, 2, 3, 4, 5)
my.vector
[1] 1 2 3 4 5
```

To create a sequence of numbers, use the colon : or the seq() function. To repeat a pattern, use the rep() function.

---

[1] You can also specify the desired file path inside the save.image() command.

```
# This makes a sequence from 0 to 10, increasing by 1 each time
my.sequence <- 0:10
# This makes a sequence from 0 to 10, increasing by 2 each time
my.sequence2 <- seq(0, 10, by = 2)
my.sequence
[1] 0 1 2 3 4 5 6 7 8 9 10
my.sequence2
[1] 0 2 4 6 8 10
# This uses c() to repeat the pattern "1, 2, 3" 8 times
my.repetition <- rep(c(1, 2, 3), times = 8)
my.repetition
[1] 1 2 3 1 2 3 1 2 3 1 2 3 1 2 3 1 2 3 1 2 3 1 2 3
```

As you can see, an object may contain many individual elements. R keeps track of all of those elements by indexing them. To reference specific elements from a vector, use the square brackets [] with the proper index number included within those brackets.

```
# This displays the 4th element in my.sequence
element.4 <- my.sequence[4]
element.4
[1] 3
# This uses c() to reference multiple elements
element.4.and.6 <- my.sequence[c(4, 6)]
element.4.and.6
[1] 3 5

# This makes a sequence with all of the elements of my.sequence
# except the 3rd element
no.3rd.element <- my.sequence[-3]
no.3rd.element
 [1] 0 1 3 4 5 6 7 8 9 10
```

To draw a sample from your vector, use the sample() function:

```
# Sampling with and without replacement
with.replace <- sample(my.sequence, replace = TRUE)
no.replace <- sample(my.sequence, replace = FALSE)
with.replace
 [1] 9 4 0 5 0 1 6 5 9 7 6
no.replace
 [1] 4 10 7 3 5 1 9 8 6 2 0
```

3.5.2 Matrices

To create a matrix, use the matrix() function. There are several arguments available for this function. To learn about them, type ?matrix.

```
# This makes a 3 x 3 matrix with the numbers 1 through 9,
# entering by columns. Notice the use of the colon :
my.matrix <- matrix(1:9, nrow = 3, ncol = 3)
my.matrix
      [,1] [,2] [,3]
[1,]    1    4    7
[2,]    2    5    8
[3,]    3    6    9

# Still use square brackets to reference elements
# This references the element in row 2, column 2
row2.col2 <- my.matrix[2, 2]
row2.col2
[1] 5

# This references the entire third row
row.3 <- my.matrix[3, ]
row.3
[1] 3 6 9

# This references the entire second column
col.2 <- my.matrix[ , 2]
col.2
[1] 4 5 6
```

3.6 FUNCTIONS

R is built on lots of different functions. As noted above, the basic structure of a function is the name of the function, followed by parentheses. Arguments to the function are listed inside the parentheses, separated by commas. Here are a few more examples of functions that compute basic summary statistics.

```
# Calculate the minimum, maximum, mean, median,
# and 25th and 75th percentiles of my.sequence
min(my.sequence)
[1] 0
max(my.sequence)
[1] 10
mean(my.sequence)
[1] 5
median(my.sequence)
[1] 5
quantile(my.sequence, .25)
25%
2.5
quantile(my.sequence, .75)
75%
```

```
7.5
# Or we could just use the summary() function
summary(my.sequence)
   Min. 1st Qu. Median  Mean 3rd Qu.  Max.
    0.0     2.5    5.0   5.0     7.5  10.0
# Two more: variance and standard deviation
var(my.sequence)
[1] 11
sd(my.sequence)
[1] 3.316625
```

3.6.1 Matrix Algebra Functions

R can also perform several useful matrix calculations and perform linear algebra.

- `det()` computes the determinant of the matrix.
- `diag()` references main diagonal of the matrix.
- `t()` finds the transpose of the matrix.
- `solve()` finds the inverse of the matrix.
- `eigen()` returns eigenvalues and eigenvectors of the matrix.
- Matrix multiplication is done by putting the `%` sign on either side of the `*`. For example, to multiply Matrix A by Matrix B, you would type A `%*%` B.

Another function that is useful when working with matrices is `apply()`. This function applies another function to either all of the rows or all of the columns of a matrix. The first argument is the name of the matrix, the second argument is a number—either 1 (for rows) or 2 (for columns), and the third argument is the name of the function you want to execute for every row or column. For example, to compute the mean of all of the columns in `my.matrix`, we type

```
col.means <- apply(my.matrix, 2, mean)
col.means
[1] 2 5 8
```

3.6.2 Creating New Functions

You can also make your own function with the `function()` command. Using this tool to create your own function requires the following three things: (1) a list of the arguments the new function will take, (2) definitions of the calculations the function will perform, and (3) instructions for what to return when it is done. For example, let's make a function called `average()` that will calculate the mean of a vector. Of course, there already is a function called `mean()` to do this task, but this will allow us to check that our own function is correct.

To begin, we assign the name `average` to our function and in the parentheses list the argument the function will take. In this case, the function requires a vector, which we name `the.vector`. The name of the arguments could be anything. The key is to make sure that the name in the first line matches the name used in later lines. After writing the argument(s), the next step is to use the open curly bracket ({). It is also a good idea to type the close curly bracket a few lines down (}) right away so you do not forget to do so later. Any code inside the {} will operate in the function.

Inside the function, we create three objects. `S` is created by adding all of the elements in `the.vector` using the `sum()` function. `L` is the number of elements in `the.vector`, created with the `length()` function. Finally, `A` is created as `S` divided by `L`. By dividing the sum of all the elements in `the.vector` by the number of elements, we obtain the average. Finally, the line `return(A)` tells the function to produce only the object `A` as output; the objects `S` and `L` do not exist outside of the function.[2]

```
# This function requires one argument, a vector, called "the.vector" here
average <- function(the.vector){ # Start the function
S <- sum(the.vector) # Step one: Take the sum of all elements in the.vector
L <- length(the.vector) # Step two: Find no. of elements in the.vector
A <- S/L # Divide to get the average
return(A) # Only return the final result
} # Close the function

# Check to make sure it works
mean(my.sequence)
[1] 5
average(my.sequence)
[1] 5
```

3.7 WORKING WITH DATA

Loading data into R is an important task for researchers. We demonstrate some basics here, but there is a great deal on data management we do not cover. In particular, in the examples below we use a data set that has already been "cleaned." For more on the data preparation capabilities of R, see `http://www.stat methods.net/management/index.html` and Spector (2008).

3.7.1 Loading Data

R can read data from several formats, such as CSV files, Excel worksheets, or files from several different software packages. We will demonstrate this last approach here by importing a Stata file into R. To do so, the `foreign` package is required. To install a package for the first time, use the `install.packages()`

---

[2]Note that instead of creating these three objects we could also accomplish this task in one line of code: `return(sum(the.vector)/length(the.vector))`.

function. To load a particular package into the current R session, use the
`library()` function.[3]

```
install.packages("foreign") # This is not necessary after the first time
library(foreign)
```

In this example, we use Ehrlich's (1973) data on crime in the American states,
which are publicly available at `http://www.statsci.org/data/gen
eral/uscrime.html` and included in the replication materials associated
with this book.[4]

To follow along, locate the file "crime.dta" and load it into R using the `read
.dta()` function. You can point R to the proper directory on your computer by
including the full file extension inside the parentheses or by using the `setwd()`
function, which stands for "set working directory."[5] Keep in mind that R requires
forward slashes in file path names.

```
# Option 1
crime <- read.dta("<your file path here>/crime.dta")
# Option 2
setwd("<your file path here>")
crime <- read.dta("crime.dta")
```

This creates a single object in R called `crime` that includes all of the data that
was in the original Stata file named `crime.dta`.

3.7.2 Exploring the Data

Once loaded, you can inspect the data. To look at the variable names, use the
`names()` function.

```
names(crime)
 [1] "pctmale1424"        "south"               "education"
 [4] "police1960"         "police1959"          "lfrate"
 [7] "malesper100females" "population1960"      "nonwhite"
[10] "unemployment1424"   "unemployment3539"    "wealth"
[13] "inequality"         "imprisonment"        "avgtimeserved"
[16] "crime1960"
```

---

[3]Veteran users will note that this is not strictly necessary for the foreign package
because it gets loaded automatically when R starts. We thank John Fox for bringing this to
our attention.

[4]Note that we have changed variable names in the examples so that they are more informative, but we have not changed the data. This data set can also be accessed through the MASS
package in R by typing `data(UScrime)`.

[5]The related function `getwd()` ("get working directory") will display the current working
directory.

We see that the object named `crime` has 16 other named objects or elements within it. In this case, each of those objects corresponds to the name of a variable in the original data set. When R reads a data set, it becomes what R calls a data frame. To reference specific named objects within another object, you use the dollar sign ($). Thus, to reference a specific variable in the `crime` data frame, we would type the name of the data frame, the dollar sign, and then the name of the variable inside that data frame (with no separating spaces). For example, to use the `summary()` function to summarize the variable `pctmale1424`, type

```
summary(crime$pctmale1424)
   Min. 1st Qu. Median  Mean 3rd Qu.  Max.
  11.90   13.00  13.60 13.86   14.60 17.70
```

3.7.3 Statistical Models

R can estimate several types of statistical models either in the default packages that are loaded when you start an R session or in user-written packages. We illustrate this by estimating a basic OLS model using the `lm()` function. We model `crime1960`, the state crime rate in 1960 (number of offenses per 100,000 people), as a function of several independent variables. The dependent variable is listed first, then the ~ sign. All independent variables are entered after that and must be separated with the + sign. You also need to specify the data frame that R should use when it estimates the model. Finally, it is a good idea to assign the results of this model to an object, like `ols.1`, so you can make use of it later. Here, we include five independent variables: (1) `imprisonment`, (2) `education`, (3) `wealth`, (4) `inequality`, and (5) `population1960`.

```
ols.1 <- lm(crime1960 ~ imprisonment + education + wealth +
inequality + population1960, data = crime)
```

Analyzing Results

If you just typed the name of the object `ols.1`, R would report out the individual coefficient estimates of the regression model we just performed, but nothing else. To see a more complete set of results from the OLS regression we just performed, you can use the `summary()` function.

```
summary(ols.1)

Call:
lm(formula = crime1960 ~ imprisonment + education + wealth +
    inequality + population1960, data = crime)

Residuals:
    Min      1Q Median     3Q    Max
-525.23 -178.94 -25.09 145.62 771.65
```

```
Coefficients:
                 Estimate   Std. Error   t value   Pr(>|t|)
(Intercept)    -4213.3894    1241.3856    -3.394   0.001538 **
imprisonment   -3537.8468    2379.4467    -1.487   0.144709
education        113.6824      65.2770     1.742   0.089088 .
wealth             0.3938       0.1151     3.422   0.001420 **
inequality       101.9513      25.9314     3.932   0.000318 ***
population1960     1.0250       1.3726     0.747   0.459458
---
Signif. codes: 0 *** 0.001 ** 0.01 * 0.05 . 0.1   1

Residual standard error: 297 on 41 degrees of freedom
Multiple R-squared: 0.4744,       Adjusted R-squared: 0.4103
F-statistic:    7.4 on 5 and 41 DF,  p-value: 5.054e-05
```

If you wanted to include all of the other variables in the data frame as independent variables, you could use a period in place of the variable names after the ~ symbol, like this:

```
ols.2 <- lm(crime1960 ~ ., data = crime)
summary(ols.2)


Call:
lm(formula = crime1960 ~ ., data = crime)

Residuals:
    Min      1Q   Median      3Q      Max
-395.74  -98.09    -6.69  112.99   512.67

Coefficients:
                     Estimate   Std. Error   t value   Pr(>|t|)
(Intercept)        -5984.28873  1628.31880    -3.675   0.000893 ***
pctmale1424           87.83016    41.71387     2.106   0.043443 *
south                 -3.80341   148.75514    -0.026   0.979766
education            188.32435    62.08838     3.033   0.004861 **
police1960           192.80425   106.10969     1.817   0.078892 .
police1959          -109.42185   117.47754    -0.931   0.358830
lfrate              -663.82786  1469.72926    -0.452   0.654653
malesper100females    17.40688    20.35385     0.855   0.398995
population1960        -0.73301     1.28956    -0.568   0.573846
nonwhite               4.20446     6.48089     0.649   0.521279
unemployment1424   -5827.10553  4210.28973    -1.384   0.176238
unemployment3539     167.79967    82.33595     2.038   0.050161.
wealth                 0.09617     0.10367     0.928   0.360754
inequality            70.67210    22.71652     3.111   0.003983 **
imprisonment       -4855.26506  2272.37476    -2.137   0.040627 *
avgtimeserved         -3.47901     7.16528    -0.486   0.630709
---
Signif. codes: 0 *** 0.001 ** 0.01 * 0.05 . 0.1    1
```

```
Residual standard error: 209.1 on 31 degrees of freedom
Multiple R-squared: 0.8031,     Adjusted R-squared: 0.7078
F-statistic: 8.429 on 15 and 31 DF,  p-value: 0.0000003539
```

As you can see, the `lm()` function produces a lot of results that are stored within the object to which those results are assigned—in our second example, the object `ols.2`. Several of those results are stored as objects with specific names that can be referenced from the objects `ols.2` or `summary(ols.2)` for further analysis. For example, you can place the coefficients, residuals, and Adjusted R^2 into objects. This is done with the dollar sign notation introduced above.

```
ols.2.coef <- ols.2$coef # Coefficients
ols.2.res <- ols.2$residuals # Residuals
ols.2.adjr2 <- summary(ols.2)$adj.r.squared # Adjusted R^2
```

To get the covariance matrix of the parameter estimates, use the `vcov()` function. To get the standard errors—which are calculated as the square root of the diagonal of the covariance matrix—you can use the `sqrt()` and `diag()` functions together with the `vcov()` function, like this:

```
ols.2.vcv <- vcov(ols.2)
ols.2.se <- sqrt(diag(ols.2.vcv))
ols.2.se
     (Intercept)    pctmale1424              south            education
    1628.3188012     41.7138658        148.7551439           62.0883782
      police1960      police1959             lfrate   malesper100females
     106.1096855     117.4775442       1469.7292602           20.3538506
  population1960        nonwhite   unemployment1424     unemployment3539
       1.2895554       6.4808929       4210.2897270           82.3359549
          wealth      inequality        imprisonment         avgtimeserved
       0.1036661      22.7165189       2272.3747553            7.1652755
```

As we work through examples of simulations, you will see that being able to extract specific elements from the results of a statistical analysis and place them into another object will be extremely helpful.

Interaction Terms

Sometimes your statistical analysis might call for the inclusion of multiplicative interaction terms. R can process multiplicative interaction terms on the fly. Let's say we want to consider a variant of the `ols.1` model where `wealth` is interacted with `inequality`. This can be done by adding `wealth*inequality` as an independent variable in the model. Note that we name this model to a new object called `ols.3`.

```
ols.3 <- lm(crime1960 ~ imprisonment + education + wealth +
inequality + population1960 + wealth*inequality, data = crime)
summary(ols.3)

Call:
lm(formula = crime1960 ~ imprisonment + education + wealth +
    inequality + population1960 + wealth * inequality, data = crime)

Residuals:
    Min      1Q   Median      3Q     Max
-508.58  -181.31  -31.79   149.36  722.56

Coefficients:
                      Estimate    Std. Error   t value   Pr(>|t|)
(Intercept)        -5219.728170  2007.751404    -2.600    0.0130 *
imprisonment       -3771.366086  2424.301941    -1.556    0.1277
education            125.279960    68.198088     1.837    0.0736 .
wealth                 0.558991     0.282755     1.977    0.0550 .
inequality           146.289040    73.973716     1.978    0.0549 .
population1960         0.932072     1.390148     0.670    0.5064
wealth:inequality     -0.008418     0.013141    -0.641    0.5254
---
Signif. codes: 0 *** 0.001 ** 0.01 * 0.05 . 0.1 1

Residual standard error: 299.2 on 40 degrees of freedom
Multiple R-squared: 0.4797,    Adjusted R-squared: 0.4017
F-statistic: 6.147 on 6 and 40 DF, p-value: 0.0001245
```

We do not have the space to devote extensive attention to the interpretation of regression results, especially when interaction terms are included. The point we want to make here is that estimating OLS regression models using the lm() function in R is relatively straight forward, as is the inclusion of multiplicative interaction terms in such models.

3.7.4 Generalized Linear Models

Generalized linear models (GLM) can be estimated in a similar way to the OLS examples we have presented. Here we will do a brief example using logistic regression on the determinants of voter turnout. These data come from the Current Population Survey (CPS) in 2000 as part of the Zelig package (Imai et al., 2012). The dependent variable is whether a respondent reported having voted or not in the 2000 general election (vote). Independent variables include each respondent's income, education, age, and whether or not they were female.

We start by opening the data. Instead of using the `foreign` package like we did above, this time we use the `data` function to call a specific data set named `voteincome` that is already located within the `Zelig` package. We call the package first, then the data set.[6] To see what data sets are available in a given package (such as `Zelig`), type `data(package = ''Zelig'')`.

```
library(Zelig)
data(voteincome)  # Use 2000 CPS data
```

The syntax to estimate a logit model is similar to that of OLS. In this case, we use the `glm()` function. In addition to the formula for the model and the data, we need to specify the logit model through the `family` argument. In this case, because the dependent variable has two categories (voted or did not vote), we want the binomial distribution. We then specify a logistic link function with `(link = logit)`. Then, we can name it to an object and use `summary()` function as before to see the results.

```
logit.1 <- glm(vote ~ income + education + age + female,
     family = binomial (link = logit), data = voteincome)

summary(logit.1)

Call:
glm(formula = vote ~ income + education + age + female,
 family = binomial(link = logit), data = voteincome)

Deviance Residuals:
  Min     1Q Median     3Q    Max
-2.42470.3936 0.4869 0.5913 1.0284

Coefficients:
            Estimate Std. Error z value  Pr(>|z|)
(Intercept)-0.877591  0.375796  -2.335  0.019529 *
income       0.094331  0.021666   4.354 0.0000134 ***
education    0.224927  0.090063   2.497  0.012510 *
age          0.016464  0.004328   3.804  0.000142 ***
female       0.309880  0.151031   2.052  0.040193 *
---
Signif. codes: 0 *** 0.001 ** 0.01 * 0.05 . 0.1 1

(Dispersion parameter for binomial family taken to be 1)

    Null deviance: 1240.0 on 1499 degrees of freedom
Residual deviance: 1185.6 on 1495 degrees of freedom
AIC: 1195.6

Number of Fisher Scoring iterations: 5
```

---

[6]Remember to install the `Zelig` package the first time you plan to use it.

As in the OLS example, we can reference several different features of the model using the dollar sign notation. To learn what objects can be called in this way, type `objects(logit.1)`.

```
logit.1.coef <- logit.1$coef # Coefficients
logit.1.fv <- logit.1$fitted.values # Expected Probabilities
logit.1.aic <- logit.1$aic # AIC
logit.1.vcv <- vcov(logit.1)
logit.1.se <- sqrt(diag(logit.1.vcv))
logit.1.se
(Intercept)      income    education          age       female
0.375796012 0.021665522 0.090063491 0.004327737 0.151031071
```

Our short tour of estimating OLS and GLM models using R is not designed to make anyone an expert. Rather, our objective was to get readers engaged in using these powerful tools and to show readers that estimating such models and accessing specific aspects of the results is reasonably straightforward in R. This is an essential element of conducting Monte Carlo simulations and analyzing the results.

3.8 BASIC GRAPHICS

The capacity to make high-quality graphics with relative ease is a major strength of R. In the chapters that follow, we will make heavy use of R's graphical capabilities as a means of summarizing information from simulation output.[7] We introduce some basics of creating graphics here. For more information about graphics in R, see Murrell (2005) and numerous sites online that pop up using a search of "R graphics." In addition, all of the R code used to create the graphs and figures in this book is presented in the appendix and is available on the website for the book (`www.sagepub.com/carsey`).

Creating graphs is somewhat different from any of the other areas of R we have covered. A typical graph in R is first created using a function that calls/opens the plot window. This is a separate window that appears on your computer screen with the graph. You can then use additional functions or operations within functions to add elements to that plot. For example, the `hist()` function will produce a histogram of a variable in the plot window. The function `plot()` will produce a two-way scatterplot of two variables.

```
hist(crime$pctmale1424)
plot(crime$imprisonment, crime$crime1960)
```

---

[7]Graphs created in R can be easily produced as several different file types, including PDFs, JPEGs, and TIFFs. This is useful in presenting them in manuscripts and reports. Type `library(help = "grDevices")` to learn more.

There are many ways in which plots can be customized. For example, arguments such as xlab and ylab produce text labels for the *x*-axis and *y*-axis, respectively. Similarly, xlim and ylim allow the user to change the ranges plotted on each axis. A class of arguments called cex allow for changes to text size (numbers greater than one increase the size and numbers less than one decrease it). For example, cex.lab changes the size of the text for axis labels and cex.axis changes the size of the axis tick mark numbers. Type ?hist or ?plot to learn more about arguments to the plotting commands.

There are also several options for special text in plots. The function expression() can be wrapped around any text to make changes to the font (e.g., italics or bold), to add mathematical symbols, or to add Greek letters. The following code shows a few examples. This code also illustrates use of the text() function, which adds text to a specified location on the plot, and the use of superscripts (with brackets) and subscripts (underscore). To see a complete demonstration of the available features, type demo(plotmath). A menu will appear in the plot window that you can scroll through to see several expressions and the necessary code to create them.

```
plot(1:10, 1:10, type = "n", xlab = "", ylab = "") # type = "n" produces
                                                    # a blank plot
title(main = expression(y == Psi*z - sum(beta^gamma)), cex.main = 4)
title(xlab = expression(x %+-% y), cex.lab = 2)
text(3, 4, expression(Delta[K] == 1), cex = 2)
text(8, 8, expression(upsilon_K == epsilon), cex = 2)
```

Bringing all of this together, we used the code below to produce the graphs in Figure 3.1. Note that the functions are the same as before (hist() and plot()), but the graphs present much more information. Additionally, note that the graphs can be created as PDF documents with the pdf() and dev.off() commands.

```
# Histogram
pdf("hist-example.pdf")

par(mar = c(5, 5.25, 3, .5))
hist(crime$pctmale1424, breaks = 20, col = "gray50", xlab = "",
 ylab = expression("Frequency"),
   main = expression("Histogram of % Males Age 14-24"), cex.lab = 1.5,
 cex.main = 1.75, axes = FALSE)
axis(1, cex.axis = 1.25)
axis(2, cex.axis = 1.25, las = 2)
box()

dev.off()

# Scatterplot
pdf("plot-example.pdf")
```

```
par(mar = c(5, 6, 3, .5))
plot(crime$imprisonment, crime$crime1960, ylim = c(0, 2000), pch = 19,
 xlab = "", ylab = "",
   main = expression("Crime Rate by Probability of Imprisonment"),
     cex.main = 1.75, axes = FALSE)
axis(1, cex.axis = 1.25)
axis(2, at = seq(0, 2000, by = 200), cex.axis = 1.25, las = 2)
title(xlab = expression("Ratio of Commitments to Offenses"),
 cex.lab = 1.5)
title(ylab = expression("Number of Offenses per 100,000 People"),
 line = 4.25, cex.lab = 1.5)
box()

dev.off()
```

Figure 3.1   Histogram and Scatterplot Examples

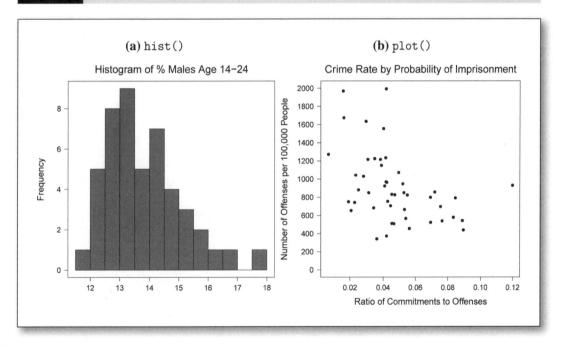

3.9 CONCLUSIONS

This chapter provided a brief introduction to R. We focused on some key basic operations, then presented several commonly used functions, and concluded with an introduction to graphics. While we only scratched the surface of what R offers, we have shown enough to refresh the memories of those with R experience and get those without experience started. If you wish to learn more, see the list of references at the beginning of the chapter. In particular, there is no substitute for reading through the "Introduction to R" manual. Additionally, we recommend that you open the code that accompanies this book and follow along with the examples. Although R can be difficult at first, learning by doing is a good strategy for improving.

In the next chapter, we link the material presented in this chapter and in Chapter 2 to explore random number generation in R and the basic anatomy of a Monte Carlo simulation. We make use of many of the basic R functions we introduced in this chapter, but introduce several new ones as well. We discuss R's capabilities for sampling random numbers from a probability distribution as a means of creating a DGP. This forms the basis for creating simulations. We also discuss how to write efficient, readable code and how to optimize computing resources when creating simulations in R.

4

Random Number Generation

4.1 INTRODUCTION

Drawing one or more random numbers from a probability distribution is fundamental to conducting Monte Carlo simulations. It is the only way we can simulate the stochastic component of a DGP, and getting the stochastic component correctly specified is essential for the proper execution and evaluation of a simulation. In this chapter, we demonstrate the process of drawing random numbers from probability distributions. We also discuss some other critical components of simulations. We cover some additional R programming topics, with a particular focus on repeating R code many times (which we will use to create many simulated samples of data) and using logical statements. After discussing these building blocks of simulation, we then reexamine the statistical simulation example from Chapter 1 in greater detail. We conclude with what we call the general "anatomy" of a script file, discussing what should be included in the code of a simulation and why.

4.2 PROBABILITY DISTRIBUTIONS

As we saw in Chapter 2, R allows you to use a wide variety of probability distributions for four purposes: (1) the CDF, (2) the PDF, (3) the quantile function, and (4) to make random draws from the distribution. Recall from Chapter 2 that the CDF describes the probability that a realization from a given distribution takes on a value less than or equal to some value. The PDF gives the relative likelihood of observing a single value (in the case of a continuous distribution) or the probability of observing a single value (in the discrete case). The quantile function is the inverse of the CDF—it takes a probability specified by the user and returns the corresponding value of the distribution. Finally, the random draw function produces realized random draws from the distribution. All commands that use probability distributions in R consist of a prefix and a suffix. Table 4.1 presents the four prefixes and their usages as well as the suffixes for some commonly used distributions.

| Table 4.1 | Probability Distributions in R |

Prefix	Usage	Suffix	Distribution
p	CDF	norm	normal
d	PDF/PMF	logis	logistic
q	Quantile function (inverse CDF)	t	t
r	Random draw from distribution	f	F
		unif	uniform
		pois	Poisson
		exp	exponential
		chisq	χ^2
		binom	binomial

In what follows, we illustrate the use of these functions with the normal distribution. To compute the probability that a realization of a random variable drawn from a standard normal distribution is less than or equal to 1.645, we use the CDF of the standard normal, which is the pnorm() function, where the only argument we need to provide is the value we wish to evaluate—or 1.645 in this example. With no additional arguments, the pnorm() function defaults to $\mu = 0$ and $\sigma = 1$. To compute the height of the standard normal PDF (e.g., the relative likelihood) at a given value, you would use the dnorm() function. To find the value associated with a probability of 0.95, you would use the qnorm() function. Finally, you would use the rnorm() function to produce 10 random draws from the standard normal distribution.

```
set.seed(082184) # Set the seed for reproducible results
# Use the CDF to calculate the probability a random draw will be less than
# or equal to a given number
pnorm(1.645)
[1] 0.9500151

dnorm(1.5) # Use the PDF to calculate the density
[1] 0.1295176

# Use the inverse CDF to calculate distribution values from quantiles
qnorm(.95)
[1] 1.644854
```

```
rnorm(10) # Random draws
[1]   0.09689246 -1.38491784   0.20534505 0.24484292 -0.58638250 -0.68128660
[7] -0.39018615 -0.09011036 -0.50192922 0.87365513
```

The functions work in a similar way for other distributions. Here is an example using the binomial distribution with the number of trials equal to 50 (e.g., 50 coin flips) and the probability of success set to 0.20 (e.g., 20% chance of getting Heads on any one flip of the coin). To compute the probability of observing 10 or fewer Heads in the 50 coin flips, we use the `pbinom()` function. The function `dbinom()` will produce the probability of observing exactly 17 Heads from our 50 flips. To compute the number of Heads associated with the probability 0.50, use `qbinom()`. Finally, `rbinom()` flips our unfair coin 50 times, computes the number of successes, and repeats that process 10 times. In other words, this line of code takes 10 random draws from the binomial distribution we have defined where each draw consists of 50 flips of our unfair coin and reports the number of heads in each draw.

```
# Use the CDF to calculate the probability of 10 or fewer successes
pbinom(10, 50, .2)
[1] 0.5835594

# Use the PDF to calculate the probability of observing a value of 17
dbinom(17, 50, .2)
[1] 0.008180883

# Use the inverse CDF to calculate distribution values from quantiles
qbinom(.5, 50, .2)
[1] 10

rbinom(10, 50, .2) # Random draws
[1] 7 5 14 13 4 11 9 12 7 12
```

4.2.1 Drawing Random Numbers

We use the random draw functions the most in this book. These functions work well for nearly all applications, but it should be pointed out that they only mimic random processes. The engine driving those commands is one of several algorithms called a random number generator (RNG). These algorithms are actually complex deterministic processes that generate very long strings of *pseudorandom* numbers. For our purposes, pseudorandom numbers will work well, but it is important to appreciate how difficult it is to generate truly random numbers. One example of how to do it is shown by the website `http://www.random.org/`, which produces truly random numbers for free using atmospheric noise.

More important for this book, we can control the numbers that RNGs produce by setting what is called the "seed" of the RNG. You can do this with the `set.`

seed() function, where inside the parentheses you provide an integer. Some recommend using large (e.g., 5 to 7 digit integers).[1] For example, say you ran the following code in R:

```
set.seed(123456)
rnorm(10)
[1]  0.83373317 -0.27604777 -0.35500184  0.08748742 2.25225573 0.83446013
[7]  1.31241551  2.50264541  1.16823174 -0.42616558

set.seed(123456)
rnorm(10)
[1]  0.83373317 -0.27604777 -0.35500184  0.08748742 2.25225573 0.83446013
[7]  1.31241551  2.50264541  1.16823174 -0.42616558

rnorm(10)
[1] -0.99612975 -1.11394990 -0.05573154 1.17443240 1.05321861 0.05760597
[7] -0.73504289  0.93052842  1.66821097 0.55968789
```

Any time you enter the same first two lines, you will get the same "random" numbers. It does not mean that every single time you draw random values you will get the same numbers (note that the third use of rnorm() generates different values). It means that every time you reset the seed to the same value, the same string of "random" numbers will result. Setting the seed is important because it allows for exact replication of your work even when you are using random numbers. If you publish an analysis, you want someone to be able to perfectly reproduce your results. In addition, if you are working on building up your R code to run a simulation, you want to be sure that any changes you make in your code affect the simulation correctly. If you do not set a seed, every time you rerun your simulation you will get different results, and you will not know if those differences stem from a change in your code or just from randomly generating a different set of random numbers.

While it is often useful to set a seed, it is also *extremely* important to use different values of the integer you provide to the set.seed() function for different experiments. You do not want the results of your simulations to be dependent on some feature of the string of pseudorandom numbers that you happen to generate by setting a particular seed.[2] So setting the seed is helpful for replicating

---

[1]Setting the seed in R actually creates a long vector of uniformly distributed integers that are passed to the RNG algorithm for generation of the random numbers you are asking R to produce. R includes many RNGs. For a more complete discussion of this process, see the final section in Chapter 6 of Chambers (2008), Chapter 3 in Rizzo (2008), or Chapter 18 in Jones et al. (2009).

[2]Some programs, like R, reset the internal seed every time the software is launched to prevent repeated use of the same "random" numbers. Other software, such as Stata, sets the same internal seed every time the software is launched, which means you would start with the same sequence of "random" numbers each time in Stata.

results, but it is important to use lots of different integers across your various projects and simulations.[3]

4.2.2 Creating Your Own Distribution Functions

There are many probability distributions available in R, both in its native functions and in user-written packages. See this website for a list: `http://cran.r-project.org/web/views/Distributions.html`. However, should you ever need to use a distribution that is not available in a package, you can create your own using `function()` as discussed in Chapter 3 to create your own function. Depending on your needs, you can write down the CDF, PDF, quantile function, or RNG expression inside the function command. We illustrate this below using the exponential distribution.[4]

The exponential distribution is a positive distribution that describes the time between independent Poisson processes (e.g., the length of time between bus arrivals at a bus stop). It has one parameter, λ, which governs the rate of the process. The PDF of the exponential distribution for a random variable, x, is defined as

$$\lambda \exp(-\lambda x) \tag{4.1}$$

The CDF is defined as

$$1 - \exp(-\lambda x) \tag{4.2}$$

The quantile function (inverse CDF) for $0 \le p < 1$ is

$$-\frac{\log(1-p)}{\lambda} \tag{4.3}$$

These three functions can be written in R with the following code. Note that we set the rate parameter, `lambda`, to 1 by default.

```
# PDF
dexponential <- function(x, lambda = 1){
return(lambda*exp(-lambda*x))
}

# CDF
pexponential <- function(x, lambda = 1){
return(1 - exp(-lambda*x))
}
```

---

[3]Readers should also know that setting the seed and the performance of RGN more generally gets more complicated in parallel processing environments.

[4]Functions already exist in R for the exponential distribution, so this example is purely illustrative.

```
# Quantile Function (inverse CDF)
qexponential <- function(p, lambda = 1){
return(-log(1 - p)/lambda)
}
```

Finally, we can create a function to draw random variates from the exponential distribution by first drawing random numbers from a uniform distribution between 0 and 1, then inserting those numbers into the inverse CDF of the exponential distribution. The logic here is that if a vector of numbers between 0 and 1 are random, the quantiles they produce after being "run through" the formula for the inverse CDF will also be random, but they will now follow that distribution.[5] Accordingly, to create our random number function, rexponential(), we add a call to runif() in place of p in the qexponential() function.

```
# Random Variates
rexponential <- function(n, lambda = 1){
return(-log(1 - runif(n))/lambda)
}
```

The process of creating a distribution function does not need to be particularly elaborate. Here, we simply took the formula for the distribution's CDF, PDF, and quantile functions and copied them into R code. We encourage readers to try creating functions for another distribution in this way because it is a useful way to learn more about probability distributions.

4.3 SYSTEMATIC AND STOCHASTIC

In Chapter 1, we introduced the idea that a DGP includes a systematic component and a stochastic component. In this section, we use these components in greater detail. Remember that the systematic component of a DGP captures the "true" relationship(s) among variables in the population. The stochastic component consists of randomness, or noise. In the frequentist conceptualization of statistical inference, the systematic component is fixed in the population, and thus constant from sample to sample. In contrast, the stochastic component varies from sample to sample, though its distribution remains the same. A complete analysis of some social phenomenon should carefully examine both components of a DGP.

Similarly, simulating some phenomenon involves clearly defining the systematic component of the DGP and the properties of its stochastic component.

---

[5]While relatively straightforward, this is not always a feasible way of using a vector of random uniform numbers to generate a vector of random numbers from another distribution. Problems can arise if the inverse CDF becomes complicated. See Gentle (2003) for a discussion of other methods.

For the rest of this chapter, we return to the statistical simulation from Chapter 1 and offer an extended example that covers each step in more detail. In so doing, we highlight features from probability theory as well as practical aspects of the R code.

4.3.1 The Systematic Component

The goal of statistical inference is to use the data that we have (the sample) to learn something about the data we do not have (the population). In the frequentist perspective, there is some true relationship in the population that we can estimate with our sample. A key challenge in empirical social science research is that we never know the true relationship exactly; we can estimate the relationship, but we never have complete certainty about it. In simulation, we do know the true relationship with certainty. This opens up several possibilities for analyses that are not possible in standard empirical research. For instance, we can illustrate the statistical properties of estimators, evaluate competing estimators, address problems that are too complex to solve analytically, and examine patterns that develop from repeating a process more times than is feasible in the real world. All of these possibilities require control over the DGP.

Below is the beginning of the code for the simulation from Chapter 1, in which we simulated an OLS model with one independent variable. First, we set the seed of the RNG with the set.seed() function. As you may have gathered from the code we have shown to this point, the integer you provide to the set.seed() function is not particularly consequential, though by convention it usually has several digits. To produce the exact numbers from Chapter 1, use 123456.

```
set.seed(123456) # Set the seed for reproducible results
```

Next, we define an object called reps, which is the number of repetitions we will perform in our simulation. Here we set it to 500, which means that we will (eventually) simulate 500 data sets drawn from the DGP we define. Next, we create a matrix of missing values (NA) called par.est with the matrix() function. We will eventually fill this matrix with the coefficient estimates from the simulated data sets. Because of this, we want the par.est matrix to be the right size to store these results. In this case, we are going to store the results of each repetition of our simulation in a row of this matrix. Thus, we set nrow = reps to make sure that we have the same number of rows in this matrix as the number of repetitions we have planned. In this example, we need to save the estimates of the intercept and slope from the OLS regression we estimate for each repetition in the columns of the par.est matrix. Thus, we need two columns for this matrix, which we create by setting ncol = 2 within the matrix() function. We will place the intercept from each run of our simulation in the first column of par.est and estimate of the slope coefficient from each repetition of our simulation in the second column of par.est.

```
reps <- 500 # Set the number of repetitions at the top of the script
par.est <- matrix(NA, nrow = reps, ncol = 2) # Empty matrix to store the
                                             # estimates
```

Now we turn to creating the systematic component of the DGP. We set the true values of the coefficients to 0.20 (the intercept) and 0.50 (the slope coefficient operating on the independent variable). These are formalized in the objects b0 and b1, respectively. The actual numbers we choose are not very important in this case. We simply are creating a benchmark from which to compare estimates that get produced in the simulation.

```
b0 <- .2 # True value for the intercept
b1 <- .5 # True value for the slope
```

Next, we set the size of each simulated sample that we are going to draw, n, to 1,000 and create the values of the independent variable, X, as 1,000 random draws from a uniform distribution. Note that the sample size is *not* the number of times we are going to do the simulation. Rather, it is the number of observations in each of the simulated data sets we will create. Additionally, notice that we are creating X only once—we will not create a new X in each data set. This is to adhere strictly to the OLS assumption that the independent variables are fixed in repeated samples. However, results do not change if a new version of X is drawn with each new data set.

```
n <- 1000 # Sample size
X <- runif(n, -1, 1) # Create a sample of n observations on the
                     # independent variable X
```

We have now defined all of the parts of the systematic portion of the DGP. The next step involves defining the stochastic part of the model. To do so, we need to draw random numbers from the proper probability distribution, then combine those random numbers with our systematic component to produce simulated values of our dependent variable.

4.3.2 The Stochastic Component

We create the dependent variable as a function of the systematic component and a random error. This is accomplished in the following line of code. We generate the object Y (the dependent variable) as a combination of the true intercept (b0) plus the true slope coefficient (b1) multiplied by the independent variable (X). Then, we add random error to Y by using the rnorm() function. In this case, we make 1,000 random draws (because $n = 1,000$) from a standard normal distribution ($\mu = 0$, $\sigma = 1$).

```
Y <- b0 + b1*X + rnorm(n, 0, 1) # The true DGP, with N(0, 1) error
```

We have now generated values for X and Y in a simulated data set of 1,000 observations where the true values of b0 and b1 are defined as 0.2 and 0.5, respectively. Now, we are ready to estimate the OLS regression model. We use the lm() function to regress Y on X.[6] Note that we only include Y and X in the equation (not the error term) because in a real setting we would not know the error term; the only data we would collect would be the dependent variable and independent variable(s). When running an OLS regression on a set of data, you are assuming that the error term is distributed normally with a mean of zero and constant variance (all of which is true in this case because we set it up that way).

```
model <- lm(Y ~ X) # Estimate OLS model
```

We can look at the coefficients using the dollar sign notation. In this example, the estimate of the intercept is 0.2025988 and the estimate of the coefficient on X is 0.4388826. Both seem reasonably "close" to the true values of 0.20 and 0.50, but they are not exactly equal to the true values because we added the random error that distorted the true relationship.[7]

```
model$coef
(Intercept)          X
  0.2025988 0.4388826
```

4.3.3 Repeating the Process

While the example to this point has shown us how to create systematic and stochastic components of a DGP and estimate that DGP, it is somewhat limited because we only did it one time. While it might seem like 0.2025988 and 0.4388826 are "good" estimates of the true parameters, we cannot provide any precise assessments because we do not have any other estimates to which we can make comparisons.

A logical solution would be to repeat the process—remember "in repeated samples." Keeping the same systematic component in place, let's generate a new sample of data (e.g., add a new error term to the systematic part of the DGP to produce a new dependent variable) and estimate the OLS model again.

```
Y <- b0 + b1*X + rnorm(n, 0, 1) # The true DGP, with N(0, 1) error
model <- lm(Y ~ X) # Estimate OLS model
model$coef
(Intercept)          X
  0.2109310 0.4665079
```

---

[6]We do not need to use the data argument because Y and X are not part of any data frame. Rather, they are simply objects that we have created.

[7]To see this illustrated in a different way, try creating Y as a function of only the systematic component by excluding the random error, and then reestimate the regression model: Y <- b0 + b1*X. This produces coefficient "estimates" of 0.20 and 0.50 with standard errors equal to zero.

The result this time is an estimate of 0.2109310 for the intercept and 0.4665079 for the slope coefficient operating on X. The results differ because we drew a new set of random errors.[8] Again, at face value, these estimates seem to be "close" to the true parameters. Compared with the first set of estimates, this second set is slightly further from the truth on the intercept but slightly closer to the true value of the slope coefficient operating on X. Let's repeat the process once more.

```
Y <- a + b*X + rnorm(n, 0, 1) # The true DGP, with N(0, 1) error
model <- lm(Y ~ X) # Estimate OLS model
model$coef
(Intercept)          X
  0.2218581  0.5508824
```

This time we get an intercept estimate that is even further from the truth than the last two, though still reasonably close (0.2218581). Also, in contrast to our first two attempts, the coefficient estimate on X misses the true parameter on the high side (0.5508824) this time.

At this point, we can see the beginnings of a pattern. In all three samples, the estimate for the intercept was "close" to its true value of 0.20 and the estimate for the slope coefficient operating on X was "close" to 0.50. However, the parameter estimates were never exactly equal to their true values, and they were never equal across any of the three trials of our experiment. If we repeat this experiment many more times, however, some additional patterns will emerge. Just how many times is enough is not certain, but most simulation studies include at least 500 to 1,000 repetitions, and some include many more than that. When determining the number of repetitions, you have to balance the increased precision that emerges from using a larger number of repetitions against the amount of time it takes for the simulation to run.[9] We could continue to repeat the three lines of code from above, but that would create an overwhelming amount of code, would make summarizing results difficult, and would make it much more likely that we would make an error. Instead, we will turn next to some basics of programming in R to learn some easy ways to repeat the process with a new stochastic component in each repetition. We will then return to this example near the end of the chapter.

4.4 PROGRAMMING IN R

We will cover a few programming techniques that are useful for the remainder of the book, with a particular focus on what R calls a for loop. As you might

---

[8]We have a new set of errors because we did not set the seed to some number in the first round and then set it to that same seed again for the second round.

[9]Some simulations can be very computer intensive, taking hours or days to run even on very fast machines. We recommend setting the number of repetitions in your simulation to a very low number at first—maybe just 10—when you are just making sure that your code works, then increasing that number substantially for your actual run of the full simulation.

expect, much more is possible than we show here; see Braun and Murdoch (2007) and Jones et al. (2009) for more details.

4.4.1 `for` **Loops**

One option for repeating the same operation many times is to write a `for` loop. For example, let's say we wanted to calculate the first 21 numbers in the Fibonacci sequence. We can use a `for` loop to do this. We start by creating an object called `fibonacci` that is an empty vector of length 21 using the `numeric()` function. Then, we manually fill in the first two numbers (0 and 1) using square brackets.

```
fibonacci <- numeric(21) # This makes an empty vector of length 21
fibonacci[1] <- 0 # We enter the first two numbers manually
fibonacci[2] <- 1
```

Next, the first line of the code below uses the `for()` function to start a counter, represented in this example by the letter `i`. The counter keeps track of what iteration the loop is on. We also need to define what numbers the counter should count. In this case, we want that to be from 3 to 21 because we are going to fill in elements 3–21 of the Fibonacci sequence (recall that we already did the first two above). So the first time through the loop, `i` will be equal to 3. In the next iteration, `i` will equal 4, then 5, then 6, and so on until it reaches 21. Finally, we end the line with a curly bracket. Similar to `function()`, anything inside the curly brackets is part of the `for` loop.

In the second line of the code below, we write down the operations that will be performed inside the loop. In this example, we want the current number in the sequence to be the sum of the previous two numbers (which is the definition of a Fibonacci sequence). We accomplish this with the square bracket notation that allows us to refer to specific locations within an object. We use `fibonacci[i]` to represent the ith element in the object `fibonacci`. We define that element as the sum of `fibonacci[i - 2]`, or the number two back in the sequence from i and `fibonacci[i - 1]`, which is the number one back in the sequence. The entire code looks like this:

```
# This starts the loop by telling R to count from 3 to 21, with the variable
# i representing the number its on in a particular iteration.
for(i in 3:21){

# This tells R to make the current number the sum of the last two numbers
fibonacci[i] <- fibonacci[i - 2] + fibonacci[i - 1]
}
```

Notice again the curly bracket at the end that closes the loop. In a nutshell, a `for` loop repeats the sequence of operations inside the curly brackets as many times as is defined in the parentheses that come immediately after the word `for` that initiates the loop.

Let's take a closer look at how the loop works. We can see that, for example, on the first iteration through the loop, when i is equal to 3, this code is processed as follows:

```
fibonacci[3] <- fibonacci[3 - 2] + fibonacci[3 - 1]
```

This means that the third element in fibonacci is $0 + 1 = 1$, because the first element (fibonacci[3 - 2]) and second element (fibonacci[3 - 1]) are equal to 0 and 1, respectively. On the last iteration, when i is equal to 21, the code is processed as follows:

```
fibonacci[21] <- fibonacci[21 - 2] + fibonacci[21 - 1]
```

This means that element 21 in fibonacci is $2584 + 4181 = 6765$, because the 19th element (fibonacci[21 - 2]) is equal to 2584 and the 20th element (fibonacci[21 - 1]) is equal to 4181. The completed sequence can be seen by typing the object name.

```
fibonacci
 [1]   0    1    1    2    3    5    8   13   21   34  55
[12]  89  144  233  377  610  987 1597 2584 4181 6765
```

4.4.2 Efficient Programming

A for loop can sometimes take a long time to run. However, there are ways to speed things up. We describe two of these solutions below: (1) avoiding for loops altogether and (2) reducing the workload of the for loop.

Avoiding for Loops

Some tasks can be accomplished without for loops, which can speed up the process. Many R operations and functions are "vectorized." An operation that is vectorized takes a vector as input and produces a vector as output, performing the operation to all of the elements of the input vector at once. This is much faster than performing the operation to each element one at a time. We will illustrate that for a simple example. In the following code, we create a very large matrix of 100,000,000 random numbers (1,000 rows by 100,000 columns). Then, we compute the means of every column in two different ways.

In the first approach, we initialize an object called col.means1 to the value NULL. This code creates the object col.means1, but so far it has no properties. Then, we compute the mean of every column using a for loop, going from the first column (i = 1) to the last column (i = 100,000) in order. This method took 19.401 seconds in one run on a standard laptop computer.[10] In the second method,

---

[10]The exact time can vary due to computing power as well as other processes running on your computer. In fact, do not be surprised if the same code takes different amounts of time over the course of several runs, even after setting the seed.

we used the vectorized function in R called colMeans(), which takes the entire matrix as input and computes all of the column means at once. This method took only 0.158 seconds—or less than $\frac{1}{100}$ th of the time the first method took. This may not seem important when we are talking about saving seconds, but this could be very important if you are doing a complex simulation, where the difference between 1 and 100 hours (or days) is substantial.

```
# The large matrix of numbers. Notice the use of scientific notation
large.data <- matrix(rnorm(1e8), nrow = 1000, ncol = 1e5)

# Method 1
start1 <- Sys.time()
col.means1 <- NULL
for(i in 1:ncol(large.data)){
col.means1[i] <- mean(large.data[ , i])
}
end1 <- Sys.time()
end1 - start1
Time difference of 19.401 secs

# Method 2
start2 <- Sys.time()
col.means2 <- colMeans(large.data)
end2 <- Sys.time()
end2 - start2
Time difference of 0.158 secs
```

The lesson from this example is to use vectorized functions in R whenever possible. Using sum(), cumsum(), colSums(), colMeans(), and others like them rather than writing for loops can often save a considerable amount of time. Of course, sometimes for loops cannot be avoided. In that case, great care should be taken to make the loop as efficient as possible. However, as Jones et al. (2009) note, programming time is also important to consider. Saving 2 minutes of computing time through vectorizing your code is not beneficial if it takes 2 hours or 2 days to produce that code.

Reducing Workload

Another way to make your simulation run faster is to reduce the amount of object copying R is required to do as it iterates through your for loop. In the code for the first method above, we initialized the col.means1 object as NULL. As a result, each time through the for loop, R copied the old version of the object, then appended the newest value to the end of it. Forcing R to copy col.means1 every time it goes through the loop adds a little bit of unnecessary time to each iteration. Over the course of 100,000 iterations, that time adds up (and increases as col.means1 gets larger).

An alternative strategy that retains the for loop is to create the object where results from your simulation will be stored and set its size before beginning the loop.

The code below is the same as in the first method, but instead of initializing the object as NULL, we initialize it as a vector of length 100,000 with the numeric() function. Now, in each iteration through the for loop, R will insert the new value into its proper spot in the object col.means3, which has already been created. It does not need to copy the old version of the object and append the newest value every time. Notice that using this approach results in a substantial time improvement; the code ran in 3.056 seconds compared with the original 19.401 seconds—about six times faster. Because it uses a for loop, it is still not as fast as colMeans(), but the code is now a more efficient version of a for loop.

```
# Method 3
start3 <- Sys.time()
col.means3 <- numeric(ncol(large.data))
for(i in 1:ncol(large.data)){
col.means3[i] <- mean(large.data[ , i])
}
end3 <- Sys.time()
end3 - start3
Time difference of 3.056 secs
```

We will use the approach we just demonstrated for much of the book. We do so because we think for loops are typically more intuitive for readers to understand than are vectorized operations. The mental image of repeating a block of code many times comports with the notion of visualizing the phenomenon of repeated samples that is a central motivation for the book. Additionally, our examples in later chapters employ complex manipulations of the stochastic component of the DGP to simulate assumption violations and other problems with statistical estimators. Those features are much easier to include using the for loop approach to programming.

4.4.3 If-Else

Finally, a lot of programming is done by using "if-else" statements. This just means telling R "if Condition A is true, do Action 1; if Condition A is false, do Action 2." One way to do this is with the ifelse() function. Let's say we had a vector of 1,000 numbers between 1 and 100 and we wanted R to find how many were greater than or equal to 23. The following code generates such a vector and uses the ifelse() function to answer this question.

```
set.seed(12854)
a.vector <- round(runif(1000, 1, 100)) # 1000 random integers
                                       # between 1 and 100
# "If the number in a.vector is greater than or equal to 23,
# mark a 1, if not, mark a 0."
big.numbers <- ifelse(a.vector >= 23, 1, 0)

# "How long is the subset of a.vector for which big.number is equal to 1?"
length(subset(a.vector, big.numbers == 1))
[1] 773
```

This code uses a few new functions. First, the round() function rounds numbers to a user-specified number of digits. The default is to round to integers, but there is an argument called digits that can be used to change that (e.g., digits = 2 for two decimal places). We also use >= to signal "greater than or equal to," which is an example of using logical expressions in R. Other logical operators are listed in Table 4.2. These expressions are evaluated to either TRUE or FALSE.

Table 4.2	Logical Operators in R
Operator	**Definition**
<	Less Than
<=	Less Than or Equal To
>	Greater Than
>=	Greater Than or Equal To
==	Equal To
!=	Not Equal To
&	And
|	Or

These logical operators are useful in another new function that appears above: subset(). This function takes a subset of a data object for which a particular condition or set of conditions is met. In this example, we ask R to return the length of the subset of a.vector for which the statement big.numbers == 1 evaluates to TRUE.

4.5 COMPLETING THE OLS SIMULATION

Having learned some programming basics, we now return to the simulation example from Chapter 1 that we described in detail at the beginning of this chapter. We left off with the following lines of code, which combined the systematic component (b0 and b1*X) with the stochastic component (rnorm(n, 0, 1)) to generate the dependent variable, Y, in a single sample. Then, we estimated the parameters of the model with the lm() function.

```
Y <- b0 + b1*X + rnorm(n, 0, 1) # The true DGP, with N(0, 1) error
model <- lm(Y ~ X) # Estimate OLS model
```

To complete the simulation, we would like to repeat this process a large number of times. To do that, we use a `for` loop. Recall that we included the following two lines of code at the top of our file.

```
reps <- 500 # Set the number of repetitions at the top of the script
par.est <- matrix(NA, nrow = reps, ncol = 2) # Empty matrix to store the
                                             # estimates
```

The object `reps` is the number of repetitions we want, or the number of samples we wish to generate. The larger this number, the more precise the results will be, but the longer the simulation will take. It is helpful to run initial simulations at small numbers of iterations, such as 10, 100, or 500, then progress to 1,000 or more once you are confident the code works correctly. Note that by defining the number of repetitions once at the top of the file, you only need to make one edit to your script file when you want to change that number.

The object `par.est` is an empty matrix in which we will store the OLS estimates from the simulation. Initially, each cell is filled with the value NA, which is R's code for missing data. We set the number of rows to the number of repetitions (`reps`) and the number of columns to 2, the number of estimates we plan to save from each iteration of the simulation (in this case, the intercept and slope coefficient operating on X). This code sets the size of the matrix before we begin the `for` loop, which we showed above will speed up the simulation. Finally, note that we fill each cell with NA initially so that we can easily identify a problem in our code later. If the code works correctly, it should replace those NAs with numbers. If any NAs remain at the end, we know there is an error in the code.[11]

Now, we can begin the `for` loop. We want it to repeat a sequence from 1 to `reps` (500 in this case). This is defined in the first line of code below. For each iteration within the loop, we generate a new data set (done on the second line of code), estimate the OLS model on that new data set (the third line of code), and then paste the intercept and slope estimates into their proper location in the `par.est` matrix (the last two lines of code).

```
for(i in 1:reps){ # Start the loop
Y <- b0 + b1*X + rnorm(n, 0, 1) # The true DGP, with N(0, 1) error
model <- lm(Y ~ X) # Estimate OLS model
par.est[i, 1] <- model$coef[1] # Put the estimate for the intercept
                               # in the first column
par.est[i, 2] <- model$coef[2] # Put the estimate for the coefficient on
                               # X in the second column
} # End the loop
```

---

[11]Of course, just because we do not find any NAs after the simulation does not guarantee that the simulation worked correctly. It is just that if we do see some NAs, we know for sure that the code was not correct.

Note how we make use of the counter, i, in the square brackets to help us store our parameter estimates in the proper location within par.est. This tells R exactly where to place the estimates; the intercept estimate goes in Row i, Column 1 and the slope coefficient estimate operating on X goes in Row i, Column 2. Because i increases by 1 in each iteration, this fills every row of the matrix by the time the for loop finishes.[12] Finally, we end the loop with the closed curly bracket.

Now, the matrix par.est is filled with estimates from each simulated sample. We can use the head() function to look at the first six rows of this matrix.[13]

```
head(par.est)
            [,1]        [,2]
[1,]  0.2025988  0.4388826
[2,]  0.2109310  0.4665079
[3,]  0.2218581  0.5508824
[4,]  0.2417893  0.5583468
[5,]  0.1927056  0.5097159
[6,]  0.2133593  0.5549790
```

We can also use the function is.na() to check for any missing values. This function goes through a vector or matrix, evaluating to TRUE whenever it finds an element that is NA and to FALSE otherwise. Because we do not want to see the entire matrix printed out, we can then wrap the unique() function around the is.na() function to print out only the unique values from is.na(). If TRUE comes up as one of the values, we know there is missing data somewhere in the matrix. In this case, we see that FALSE is the only unique value in each of the two columns, signifying no missing data.

```
unique(is.na(par.est))
        [,1]   [,2]
[1,]  FALSE  FALSE
```

Now the simulation is complete. We have defined both the systematic and stochastic components of a DGP, created data from that DGP, drawn a large number of samples with random error each time, estimated our OLS regression model on each sample, and saved the desired results. The result is a matrix with coefficient estimates that we can examine to get a better understanding of how the OLS estimator works. Recall from Chapter 1 that we plotted histograms of the two vectors of parameter estimates (Figure 1.2). We reprint that figure here again.

---

[12]This same task could be accomplished in one line of code because the object model$coef is a vector of length 2, which can be placed in a row as follows: par.est[i,] <- model$ coef. We place each estimate in its appropriate row and column individually for the sake of clarity.

[13]The default option in head() is to print six rows of a matrix or six elements of a vector. This can be changed to another number, such as head(par.est, 4) for the first four rows.

Figure 4.1   Histograms of 500 Simulated β_0 and β_1 Estimates

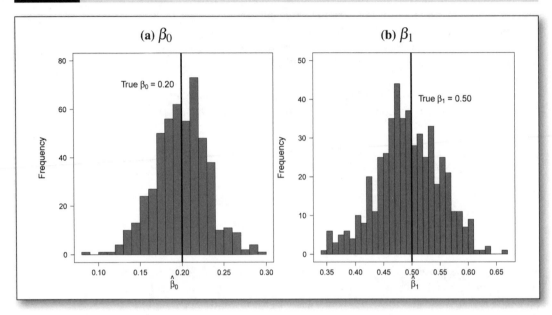

The histograms in Figure 4.1 show us that the parameter estimates appear to be clustered around the true parameter values, distributed roughly symmetrically around those true values, and in fact their distributions appear similar to the normal distribution. There is much more we can examine about OLS regression models using simulations like the one we just conducted—something that is the primary subject of Chapter 5.

4.5.1 Anatomy of a Script File

Before moving on, we review the contents of a typical script file that should be helpful when creating your own simulation code.

1. *Label the file.* The top of the script file should have a title for the file that describes what it does, the name of the author(s), and the date it was last updated.

2. *Clearing the workspace.* Often, it is helpful to clear out any objects that might be left in the R workspace before running a new simulation or other analysis. Suppose you ran one simulation that created an object named "x." Suppose you then run another simulation where you define another object named "X" but later make a typo and refer to lowercase "x" rather than uppercase "X" as intended. If you have not cleared the workspace, your script will try to use the object "x" from your previous simulation. Starting each script file with the line of code `rm(list = ls(all = TRUE))` will eliminate errors like this.

3. *Packages*. It is best to load all of the packages you might need using repeated calls with the `library()` function at the start of your script file.

4. *Set the seed*. Being able to reproduce simulation results (or results for any command using RNG) exactly is important, so the `set.seed()` function should always be at the top of the file. Depending on how many simulations you plan to perform in a single file, you might use the `set.seed()` function several additional times.

5. *Define objects for running the simulation*. At this point, you should create objects associated with running the simulation. These include the number of repetitions you want to include in your simulation and empty vectors and/or matrices in which you can store the results. Doing this near the top makes it easy to change these objects as needed.

6. *Define the systematic component of the DGP*. This part includes coefficients, independent variables, and the sample size. This is one of the most important parts of the simulation because the results can only tell us something if the true DGP is correct. As in the last step, it should be straightforward to make changes to this code as needed.

7. *The loop*. The `for` loop should iterate for a "large" number of times. We have done 500 iterations to this point, but in the next chapter we move to 1,000. The more repetitions you execute, the more precise the results of the simulation will be. Additionally, the stochastic component of the DGP is created inside the loop; this is just as important as the systematic component. Finally, model estimation and storage of results should take place inside the loop.

8. *Analyze the results*. As shown by the size of `par.est` in the basic example in this chapter, Monte Carlo simulations often generate a large amount of data. Summarizing this information is an important part of learning from and communicating simulation results. We address this topic in the pages that follow.

We conclude with three pieces of advice that we think will help you execute your code correctly, facilitate modification of your code, and help you remember what your code does in the future. First, we strongly encourage you to include lots of comments in your script files. Short comments on the same line as a piece of code can help clarify what that line of code is doing. You can also include longer blocks of comments to describe in more detail what a section of your script file is trying to accomplish. Effective use of comments will save countless hours when someone is trying to replicate your results or when you return to a project after stepping away for a day, week, month, or longer.

Second, we strongly encourage you to define basic objects that you will use at the beginning of your script file, and then do all of your programming in reference to those objects rather than in reference to specific numbers. In our example, we defined an object called `reps`, and then made reference to that object when creating our matrix in which we were going to store our results and in defining how many times our `for` loop would run. By doing it this way, if we want to change the number of repetitions within our simulation from 500 to 1,000, we only need to edit the line of code where we defined `reps`. Once that is redefined to equal 1,000, the subsequent line of code that creates the matrix where we store our results will also change to a matrix with 1,000 rows because in that line of code we defined the number of rows to be equal to `reps` rather than to a specific number. Thus, defining things like the number of repetitions, the size of each sample you want to draw, the true values of the population parameters, and other such objects, and then referring to those objects by name later in your code, will make it much easier to adapt your code to new simulations. As a rule of thumb, look for ways in your code to replace specific numbers with objects you can define in advance or attributes you can evaluate. For example, you can often use the `length()` function in R to determine how many observations there are in a vector, which might be a way to determine sample size, the number of parameter estimates you have, or something else that is useful in your code.

Third, you should always extract results directly from R objects rather than retyping them. For example, each time we run an OLS regression, we could look at the results on the screen and then type the coefficient estimates into a results matrix ourselves. This would be a mistake for three reasons: (1) it would be very slow if you ran even a simple regression 500 or 1,000 times. But even if you only ran it once, it would be a mistake because (2) you can introduce error from typos into your results, and (3) R generally does not print results to the screen out to the full precision of the actual estimate. Thus, if a coefficient estimate really goes out to 20 significant digits but R only prints 8 of those to the screen and you only use those, you will introduce truncation error into your analysis. That is why you should always extract any results you want from an R object directly, such as how we did by extracting the intercept and slope coefficient estimates from each OLS regression in our example.

In the next chapter, we show several techniques for summarizing simulation results and provide examples of their use. We focus on the linear regression model, making changes to the example detailed in this chapter. In particular, we demonstrate the implications of several assumption violations of OLS for coefficient estimates and standard errors. This highlights the utility of simulation both as a teaching tool and as a guide for researchers looking to create simulations to evaluate statistical methods in their own work.

5

Statistical Simulation of the Linear Model

5.1 INTRODUCTION

We ended Chapter 4 having completed a basic simulation of a linear model estimated by OLS. Importantly, none of the assumptions of OLS were violated in the DGP we created, so the OLS estimates in those simulated data sets should have been accurate, and Figure 4.1 suggested that they were. However, we have not yet done a full assessment of the results from that simulation, so we do not actually know how well OLS performed in estimating the parameters we created. In fact, we have not even defined criteria on which to judge whether an estimator performed "well" or "poorly." The first goal of this chapter is to define such criteria, focusing on the performance of a model's coefficient estimates and standard errors.

Once we have these criteria in place, the second goal of this chapter is to begin treating a simulation in R as an experiment. Instead of creating a simulation in which all of the OLS assumptions hold, we will change the DGP such that one is violated. This will allow us to assess the consequences of each assumption violation for the OLS estimator. In particular, we will examine the following problems: heteroskedasticity, multicollinearity, measurement error, omitted or irrelevant variables, serial correlation, clustering, and nonnormal errors. Along the way, we will compare OLS with alternative modeling strategies designed to solve some of these problems. This represents one of the key strengths of Monte Carlo simulation. Because we know and have complete control over the true DGP, we can make precise comparisons between two competing estimators.

By the end of this chapter, you should have a very clear understanding of the DGP that OLS regression assumes, how to simulate a wide range of modifications to that DGP, how to systematically evaluate the consequences of those modifications through the use of simulations, and how to use simulation studies to evaluate competing estimators. As a result, this chapter makes a number of important contributions itself. It also provides a solid foundation for Chapter 6, where we consider a wider range of statistical models.

5.2 EVALUATING STATISTICAL ESTIMATORS

To assess how changes to a DGP affect the performance of a statistical estimation method such as OLS, we first need to know how to evaluate estimation methods generally. We begin with a look at three key properties of statistical estimators. Then, we discuss common measures of estimator performance, looking specifically at coefficients and standard errors.

5.2.1 Bias, Efficiency, and Consistency

There are three basic properties of statistical estimators that researchers might want to evaluate using Monte Carlo simulations: (1) bias, (2) efficiency, and (3) consistency. We define these terms below, but in the simulation examples we primarily focus on bias and efficiency in measuring estimator performance.

Bias is about getting the "right answer" on average, across many repeated samples. Formally, an estimator is unbiased if its expected value is equal to the true parameter. Stated a bit more formally, an estimator, $\hat{\theta}$, for the true parameter θ, is unbiased if $E\left(\hat{\theta}\right) = \theta$. This does *not* mean that every single estimate is exactly equal to the truth. Instead, it means that many estimates computed from repeated samples will cluster around the true parameter; the average of the estimates across repeated samples should be (nearly) equal to the truth. This is the source of a classic joke in statistics: "Three statisticians go out hunting. They spot a deer. The first one shoots and misses to the left. The second one shoots and misses to the right. The third one stands up and shouts, 'we got him!'" (quoted in Cohen & Cohen, 2008, p. xviii).

Efficiency refers to the variance around an estimate—the amount of variability in the estimates that an estimator produces from sample to sample. An estimator is efficient if there is little variability across samples and inefficient if there are large fluctuations. Inefficiency alone is sometimes viewed as a less important problem than bias, perhaps because an unbiased but inefficient estimator will still get the right answer on average. However, given that nearly all social science research is conducted using just one sample of data (e.g., one survey sample), researchers should take efficiency just as seriously. As an estimator becomes less efficient, the likelihood that a single estimate is close to the true parameter declines.

Note that an estimator can take on none, one, or both of the properties of bias and efficiency, as illustrated in Figure 5.1. The plots show four targets, with the bull's-eye analogous to the true parameter. Each dot represents a shot at the target, or an estimate computed from one sample of data. In the top left panel, the estimator exhibits unbiasedness because the dots are centered around the bull's-eye; we can imagine that the average of all the dots is equal to the bull's-eye. This is not the case in the top right panel. That target shows a biased estimator. A few of the estimates are near the bull's-eye, but on average they cluster around a point up and to the right of it.

The bottom row shows a change in efficiency. In both of those panels, the dots are tightly packed together compared with the top row. Thus, the estimators in the bottom row are more efficient; there is less variability in their estimates from sample to sample compared with the estimators in the top row. Furthermore, the bottom graphs show biased (left) and unbiased (right) estimators. Of the four panels, the best estimator is the one on the bottom right (unbiased and efficient). Figure 5.1 is a simplified presentation of bias and efficiency. While it correctly illustrates that the two concepts are distinct from each other, in practice researchers often find themselves making choices that result in balancing trade-offs between the two.

Finally, consistency refers to an estimator getting closer and closer to the truth as the sample size increases. This is different from bias, which implies that an estimator averages to the truth even when the sample size is "small." A consistent estimator may or may not be biased, but its main distinguishing feature is that its expected value gets closer and closer to the true value as the sample size increases. Consistency is also related to the notion of variance in an estimator as both are driven by sample size. Taken to the extreme, in a sample with infinite observations, a consistent estimator will be unbiased with a variance equal to zero; it will simply be a spike at the true parameter value.

Figure 5.1 Illustration of Bias and Inefficiency of Parameter Estimates

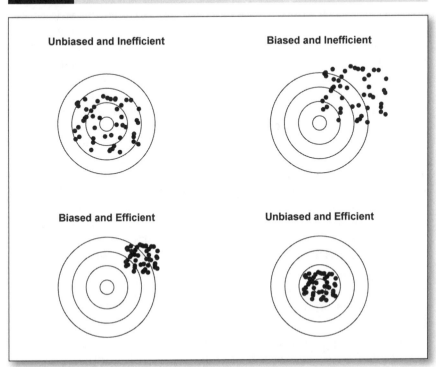

To illustrate the similarities and differences between bias and consistency in a world where sample size varies but is not infinite, consider the following four estimators of the population mean of a variable from a sample of size n. Assume that the observations are sorted in random order. Which estimators are unbiased, consistent, both, or neither?

1. Sum all of the values in the sample, then divide by n.
2. Sum the values of the first 56 observations, then divide by n.
3. Sum the values of the first 56 observations, then divide by 56.
4. Sum all of the values in the sample, then divide by $n - 1$.

The first estimator—which is simply computing the arithmetic mean of the sample—is both *unbiased* and *consistent*. Its expected value is the true population mean. If we could draw many samples and compute Estimator 1 each time, the average of those estimates would be (very close to) the true mean. Furthermore, if we increased n to a larger number, the variability in those estimates would decrease, moving toward zero as n goes to infinity. The second estimator seems a bit odd at first glance; why would we want to add up the values from only the first 56 observations, but then divide that result by n? The answer is that we probably would not because this estimator is *biased* except under the rare condition in which n happens to be 56 (in which case Estimator 2 is equivalent to Estimator 1). If n is less than 56, this estimator is undefined. If n is larger than 56, it will be biased downward (too small, on average). Not only is this estimator biased, it is also *inconsistent*—no matter how large n gets, this estimator will not converge to the true mean.[1]

Estimator 3 is *unbiased*, but *inconsistent*. Because the observations are sorted in random order, the first 56 observations can be thought of as a random subset of the larger sample (assuming again n is larger than 56). Dividing by 56 will produce an unbiased estimate of the sample mean every time. However, notice that the variance of Estimator 3 will never shrink as n increases. Even if we could draw an infinite sample, this estimator tells us to only use the first 56 observations to compute the estimate. Thus, its distribution will never collapse to a spike at the true mean, even if $n = \infty$. Finally, Estimator 4 is *biased*, but *consistent*. Dividing by $n - 1$ makes the estimate of the mean larger than the true mean in a finite sample. However, as n increases, the effect of dividing by one less than the sample size has a smaller and smaller effect. For instance, dividing by 9762 instead of 9763 makes less of an impact on the estimate compared with dividing by 9 instead of 10. Thus, the bias goes to zero as n goes to infinity, and because more information is used as n increases, the estimator is consistent.[2]

---

[1]In fact, unless the true mean is zero, increasing the sample size for Estimator 2 will result in more bias because as n increases, this estimator will get closer and closer to zero.

[2]Careful readers should not confuse this discussion with the standard presentation of estimates for a sample variance, which correctly divide by $n - 1$ to produce an estimate of a population variance based on a random sample. That sample-based formula results in estimates that are unbiased.

5.2.2 Measuring Estimator Performance in R

In a regression model context, it is common to equate bias with the estimates of the coefficients and efficiency with the estimates of their standard errors. At face value, this makes some sense; we want to know if the point estimates are unbiased, and standard errors do provide us with a measure of the expected distribution of the point estimates. In that sense, coefficient estimates and their corresponding standard error estimates are deeply connected. However, simply equating the problem of bias with coefficient estimates and efficiency with standard error estimates misses the fact that both coefficients and standard errors are computed using sample data, which means that both are *estimates* of parameters. The coefficients are estimates of the true marginal effects of the independent variables on the dependent variable, and the standard errors are estimates of the true sampling variability of those coefficients. Either could be biased (e.g., systematically wrong) or inefficient (estimated with less precision than is possible). Importantly, Monte Carlo simulation can be used to evaluate both.

Coefficients

We describe two methods for evaluating coefficient estimates here: (1) absolute bias and (2) mean squared error. Both methods are similar, measuring the average distance between an estimate and its true value.

Absolute Bias

One way to measure coefficient performance is with *absolute bias* (AB), which is sometimes called "error in estimation." For the Estimator $\hat{\theta}$, the error in estimation can be computed as $|\hat{\theta} - \theta|$, or "the distance between an estimator and its target parameter" (Wackerly, Mendenhall, & Scheaffer, 2002, p. 373). Because we repeat an analysis multiple times in a Monte Carlo simulation, we can compute the AB each time. As a result, we need a way to summarize these calculations. This is commonly done by computing the mean of the AB.

We illustrate this process by returning to the OLS simulation from Chapter 4. Note that in this case we change the number of repetitions to 1,000 to get more precise results (i.e., `reps <- 1000`). After running the simulation, the matrix `par.est` contains 1,000 estimates of β_0 (Column 1) and 1,000 estimates of β_1 (Column 2). To compute error in estimation, we use the formula for AB from above. Note that these commands are automatically vectorized, so the operations are performed on all of the estimates at once.

```
# Basic OLS Example from Chapters 1 and 4, now with 1000 reps
set.seed(123456) # Set the seed for reproducible results

reps <- 1000 # Set the number of repetitions at the top of the script
par.est <- matrix(NA, nrow = reps, ncol = 2) # Empty matrix to store the
                                             # estimates
b0 <- .2 # True value for the intercept
b1 <- .5 # True value for the slope
```

```
n <- 1000 # Sample size
X <- runif(n, -1, 1) # Create a sample of n observations on the
                     # independent variable X
for(i in 1:reps){ # Start the loop
Y <- b0 + b1*X + rnorm(n, 0, 1) # The true DGP, with N(0, 1) error
model <- lm(Y ~ X) # Estimate OLS model
vcv <- vcov(model) # Variance-covariance matrix
par.est[i, 1] <- model$coef[1] # Put the estimate for the intercept
                               # in the first column
par.est[i, 2] <- model$coef[2] # Put the estimate for the coefficient on
                               # X in the second column
} # End the loop


# Coefficients
# Absolute Bias
ab.beta0 <- mean(abs(par.est[ , 1] - b0))
ab.beta0
[1] 0.02466789


ab.beta1 <- mean(abs(par.est[ , 2] - b1))
ab.beta1
[1] 0.04389335
```

Our results show that the mean AB for our estimates of β_0 was about 0.025, and the same measure was about 0.044 for β_1. These numbers do not have much meaning on their own—it is hard to say whether we have evidence of "large" or "small" AB in this case. Instead, measures like these take on more meaning when compared with another method of estimating these parameters. At that point, we could then conclude which method resulted in a lower AB in the parameter estimates. We will explore this idea further below.

Mean Squared Error

Another option that is more commonly used is the *mean squared error* (MSE). The MSE of a point estimate is the expectation of its squared deviation from the truth. Again using the Estimator $\hat{\theta}, MSE = E\left[\left(\hat{\theta}-\theta\right)^2\right]$ (Wackerly et al., 2002, p. 367). MSE is a function of both the relative efficiency and bias of an estimator. This can be seen through an alternative formula for expressing MSE, which is $V(\hat{\theta})+[B(\hat{\theta})]^2$, where $V(\hat{\theta})$ is the estimator's variance and $B(\hat{\theta})$ is its bias (Wackerly et al., 2002, p. 367).[3] Returning to our simulation, the MSE for each parameter can be computed as follows.

```
# MSE
mse.beta0 <- mean((par.est[ , 1] - b0)^2)
mse.beta0
[1] 0.0009851733
```

---

[3]Because both variance and bias go into MSE, isolating only one of those two components would involve subtracting out the other.

```
mse.beta1 <- mean((par.est[ , 2] - b1)^2)
mse.beta1
[1] 0.003031893
```

Again, the results are not extremely informative in isolation, but rather are more useful when comparing two or more methods of estimating the parameters. When making those comparisons, we would generally define the estimator that minimized AB or MSE as performing better. In terms of which measure to use, the differences between them are relatively minor and both will nearly always give you the same pattern of results. MSE is more commonly used because it offers a balance between bias and efficiency.[4] As such, MSE may be preferable.[5] We illustrate both in the examples that follow.

Before moving on, we want to emphasize again that the actual numbers produced from AB or MSE are not all that informative by themselves. In fact, they are easy to change by making changes to the DGP. Thus, these measures are really only useful in a relative sense. We do not know if an MSE of 0.003031893 for β_1 is "good" or "bad" until we compare it with the MSE of β_1 after we have made a change to the simulation. We will examine several such changes and how they affect these measures later in this chapter. For now, we move to assessing the estimates of standard errors in simulated data.

Standard Errors

Assessing whether a standard error is "correct" is a bit more difficult to conceptualize at first glance compared with evaluating coefficients. Remember that a standard error is an estimate of the variability in a parameter estimate. Thus, we calculate standard errors because they give us an estimate of how certain we are about a given coefficient estimate. As a result, we generally would like standard errors to be small because that indicates greater precision in our coefficient estimates. However, it is *not* accurate to say that the smallest standard error is necessarily the "best." In fact, our estimate of a standard error could be too small, leading us to a false level of confidence in the precision of our coefficient estimates. Furthermore, while we could calculate the true standard error in a very simple example such as the standard error of a single mean, it becomes more difficult when we add complexity to sets of parameters being estimated and

---

[4]Actually, both AB and MSE incorporate both bias and relative efficiency in their calculation because greater variability in parameter estimates results in larger average distances for either measure. MSE, by squaring those distances, places somewhat greater emphasis on variability than does AB, though bias still plays a dominant role in both measures.

[5]MSE as a measure can also be applied to evaluating an individual regression model, where the comparisons are *not* between multiple estimates of the coefficients but rather between the observed and predicted values of the dependent variable. In that case, MSE refers to the mean of the squared regression model residuals. Since OLS is designed by construction to minimize the sum of the squared errors, the MSE measure closely parallels OLS, suggesting why it may be more common.

evaluated. Fortunately, there are several options for measuring standard error performance using simulations. We describe two of them here: (1) the standard deviation method and (2) coverage probabilities.[6] The main goal of each one is to evaluate how well a given method for computing standard errors produces standard errors that reflect the true variability of the coefficient estimates.

Before describing these methods, it is necessary to add code to our simulation example to store the standard errors in the output along with the coefficient estimates. To do this, we first add two additional columns to our matrix of results by changing the `ncol =` argument of the `matrix()` function from `ncol = 2` to `ncol = 4`.

Then, inside the `for` loop, we use the `vcov()` function to create an object we named `vcv`, which is the estimated variance–covariance matrix of the coefficient estimates. Finally, also inside the `for` loop, we compute the standard errors of $\hat{\beta}_0$ and $\hat{\beta}_1$ by taking the square root of the elements on the main diagonal of `vcv`.[7] Our revised simulation code looks like this:

```
set.seed(123456) # Set the seed for reproducible results

reps <- 1000 # Set the number of repetitions at the top of the script
par.est <- matrix(NA, nrow = reps, ncol = 4) # Empty matrix to store the
                                             # estimates
b0 <- .2 # True value for the intercept
b1 <- .5 # True value for the slope
n <- 1000 # Sample size
X <- runif(n, -1, 1) # Create a sample of n observations on the # independent variable X

for(i in 1:reps){ # Start the loop
Y <- b0 + b1*X + rnorm(n, 0, 1) # The true DGP, with N(0, 1) error
model <- lm(Y ~ X) # Estimate OLS model
vcv <- vcov(model) # Variance-covariance matrix
par.est[i, 1] <- model$coef[1] # Put the estimate for the intercept
                               # in the first column
par.est[i, 2] <- model$coef[2] # Put the estimate for the coefficient on
                               # X in the second column
par.est[i, 3] <- sqrt(diag(vcv)[1]) # SE of the intercept
par.est[i, 4] <- sqrt(diag(vcv)[2]) # SE of the coefficient on X
} # End the loop
```

Now, the matrix `par.est` has 1,000 estimates of β_0 (Column 1), 1,000 estimates of β_1, 1,000 estimates of the standard error of β_0 (Column 3), and 1,000 estimates of the standard error of β_1 (Column 4). We can now apply our two methods of evaluating the estimates of the standard errors to the results stored in those last two columns of `par.est`.

---

[6]Others include nominal rejection rates, which are similar to coverage probabilities, and overconfidence (see Beck & Katz, 1995).

[7]In this approach, we only use the `vcov()` function once, when creating the object vcv. This makes the code slightly more efficient than if we used `vcov()` every time a standard error was computed (two times in each loop × 1,000 iterations = 2,000 times).

Standard Deviation

With the standard errors saved, our first approach for assessing standard error performance is the standard deviation method. Because the simulation process mimics the repeated samples phenomenon, the amount of variability in the simulated coefficient estimates should reflect the true amount of variability from sample to sample. This means that the standard errors calculated each time we estimated our OLS model should be very close to the standard deviation of the 1,000 simulated coefficient estimates. Specifically, we can compare the mean of our 1,000 estimated standard errors with the observed standard deviation of our 1,000 coefficient estimates. The code below conducts that comparison.

```
# Standard Deviation
sd.beta0 <- sd(par.est[ , 1]) # SD of the intercept estimates
mean.se.beta0 <- mean(par.est[ , 3]) # Mean SE of the intercept
sd.beta0
[1] 0.0313973
mean.se.beta0
[1] 0.03161351

sd.beta1 <- sd(par.est[ , 2]) # SD of the coefficient on X estimates
mean.se.beta1 <- mean(par.est[ , 4]) # Mean SE of the coefficient on X
sd.beta1
[1] 0.05501627
mean.se.beta1
[1] 0.05487065
```

Notice that for both β_0 and β_1 the numbers are quite close. This means that *on average* the standard error is accurately reflecting the true coefficient variability. Just how close is close enough? We are not aware of any hard-and-fast rule here. In our example, it is pretty similar out to the third or fourth decimal point—we feel confident in calling this very close. If we found out that the mean of our estimated standard errors was half the size of the standard deviation of our simulated coefficients, we would feel confident in saying that is not close at all. A possible rule of thumb would be to report on whether or not you would reach a different conclusion about the statistical significance or substantive importance of an estimated coefficient if you inflated/deflated the standard error you calculated from your sample by the same proportion that your simulation study suggests that calculated standard errors might be too large or too small based on this kind of simulation comparison. Of course, if you are going to go that far, you will see in Chapter 8 that you might just go ahead and employ a resampling alternative to estimating standard errors, such as the bootstrap method.

Also, remember that the numbers 0.03161351 and 0.05487065 produced from the simulation we just ran are means across 1,000 estimates of the standard error. In Figure 5.2, we plot histograms of the 1,000 standard errors estimated for each coefficient.

Figure 5.2 shows us that the standard error estimates from the simulations follow a distribution of values that are centered on the true variability (i.e., the standard deviation of the simulated coefficients). This is analogous to the coefficient

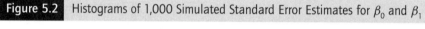

Figure 5.2 Histograms of 1,000 Simulated Standard Error Estimates for β_0 and β_1

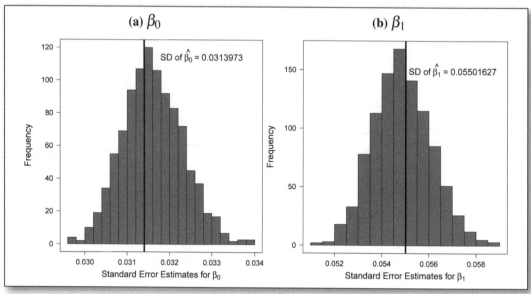

estimates being distributed around the true values we set in the DGP (see Figure 1.2). Figure 5.2 reinforces the point that, just like a coefficient, the standard error of a coefficient produced in a sample of data is itself just an estimate of that statistic and, as such, is subject to variability from sample to sample. Here we see that the way OLS calculates standard errors gets those estimates correct on average, but some individual estimates miss on the low side and some miss on the high side. When you just have a single sample of data, you cannot know when you run an OLS regression and compute standard errors for the coefficients whether your particular sample is on the low or high side strictly due to random sampling error.

Coverage Probabilities

Another option for assessing standard error performance is through the evaluation of confidence intervals and their coverage probabilities. Consider the meaning of a 95% confidence interval: If the same formula is used to compute a 95% confidence interval in repeated samples, the confidence interval will enclose the true parameter in 95% of the samples, on average. This definition is somewhat difficult to comprehend because researchers generally do not have a large number of samples. Rather, in a typical analysis, we get one sample of data and therefore see only one confidence interval for a given statistic.[8]

---

[8] The temptation is to interpret a confidence interval estimated from a single sample of data in probabilistic terms—to say something like "there is a 95% chance that my confidence interval contains the true value." However, this is *not* correct. Any one confidence interval either does or does not include the true value. All you can say from a classical frequentist perspective is that in repeated samples, 95% of the confidence intervals you would calculate would contain the true value of a parameter.

However, we can make the definition more clear by taking advantage of the fact that in a simulation we do see repeated samples. A *coverage probability* is the proportion of simulated samples for which the estimated confidence interval includes the true parameter. In this way, computing a coverage probability is akin to assessing whether the method for computing confidence intervals (and, thus, standard errors) is living up to its definition. If whatever method we are using to compute a confidence interval is "correct," we should observe a 95% confidence interval derived from that method that includes the true parameter in 95% of the simulated samples. If this number is less than 95%, our method of producing standard errors is computing estimates of those standard errors that are too small, on average. If it is larger than 95%, we know that the standard errors our method calculates are too large, on average. Of course, we do not need to limit ourselves to 95% confidence intervals to make use of the concept of a coverage probability. For example, we could select a 50% confidence interval, which we would then expect to return a coverage probability of 0.50. In fact, focusing only on 95% confidence intervals (or the even higher 99% threshold) might make it harder to detect methods that are systematically overestimating them because there is not much room to be wrong between 95% and 100%.

Figure 5.3 illustrates the coverage probability concept graphically. The graphs plot the estimates of β_0 (Panel a) and β_1 (Panel b) for 100 of the simulated samples from the basic OLS simulation (plotting all 1,000 makes visibility difficult). Dots represent the specific coefficient estimates, and vertical lines represent 95% confidence intervals constructed as they normally would be from the corresponding standard error estimates. Confidence intervals shown in light gray are those for which the estimated 95% confidence interval includes the true value of the parameter, while the confidence intervals shown in dark gray are the ones that do not include the true parameter. Notice that 5 of the 100 β_0 estimates and 6 of the 100 β_1 estimates do not include the true parameter. Put differently, 95% of the confidence intervals include the true parameter in Panel (a) and 94% of them do so in Panel (b). This is good evidence that the standard errors are accurately capturing the true variability in the estimates from sample to sample.

Having defined and illustrated what a coverage probability is, we turn next to computing the coverage probabilities for the entire set of estimates. First, we create a function called `coverage()` to compute coverage probabilities. This function takes as its arguments the vector of coefficient estimates, their standard errors, the true parameter value, a confidence level (the default is 95%), and the model degrees of freedom (the default is ∞).[9] It returns a vector of 1s and 0s

---

[9]The degrees of freedom parameter is used in computing the confidence interval for each coefficient estimate. The specified confidence level and degrees of freedom go into the quantile function of the t distribution (`qt()`) to determine the critical value to multiply with the standard error. The result then gets added and subtracted from the estimated coefficient to form the confidence bounds. We set the default degrees of freedom to ∞ because the t distribution with infinite degrees of freedom is equivalent to the normal. This is typically fine for "large" sample sizes, but not for small sample sizes. As we show below, an easy way to insert the correct degrees of freedom is to enter the object that stores the sample size (in our examples, n) minus the rank of the estimated model, which is stored in the object `$rank`. For example, n − model$rank in the basic OLS simulation will produce 1000 − 2 = 998 (sample size of 1000 minus two estimated parameters).

signifying whether each estimate's confidence interval includes the true parameter or not along with the mean of that vector, which is the proportion of 1s. That proportion measures the coverage probability. The function also returns a matrix with the confidence interval created for each coefficient estimate, the coefficient estimates themselves, and a set of simulation error bounds, which we describe below. We also make use of several additional functions within R in this code.[10]

```
coverage <- function(b, se, true, level = .95, df = Inf){ # Estimate,
                                                            # standard error,
                                                            # true parameter,
                                                            # confidence level,
                                                            # and df
    qtile <- level + (1 - level)/2 # Compute the proper quantile
    lower.bound <- b - qt(qtile, df = df)*se # Lower bound
    upper.bound <- b + qt(qtile, df = df)*se # Upper bound
    # Is the true parameter in the confidence interval? (yes = 1)
    true.in.ci <- ifelse(true >= lower.bound & true <= upper.bound, 1, 0)
    cp <- mean(true.in.ci) # The coverage probability
    mc.lower.bound <- cp - 1.96*sqrt((cp*(1 - cp))/length(b)) # Monte Carlo error
    mc.upper.bound <- cp + 1.96*sqrt((cp*(1 - cp))/length(b))
    return(list(coverage.probability = cp, # Return results
                true.in.ci = true.in.ci,
                ci = cbind(lower.bound, upper.bound),
                mc.eb = c(mc.lower.bound, mc.upper.bound)))
}
```

We can now use the function to compute coverage probabilities for the estimates in the simulation. Note that we do not specify the `level` argument, which gives us the default of 0.95.

```
cp.beta0 <- coverage(par.est[ , 1], par.est[ , 3], b0, df = n - model$rank)
cp.beta0$coverage.probability
[1] 0.941

cp.beta1 <- coverage(par.est[ , 2], par.est[ ,4], b1, df = n - model$rank)
cp.beta1$coverage.probability
[1] 0.951
```

The result is two coverage probabilities very near 95% (0.941 for β_0, 0.951 for β_1). These are unlikely to be exactly 0.95 because we only have a finite number of estimates, but they will converge toward 0.95 as the number of repetitions increases because we know in this example that we have not violated any of the assumptions of OLS regression.

As we noted above, we can compute bounds around those coverage probabilities to account for simulation error that emerges because we only conducted our

---

[10]Note the use of `list()` inside `return()` to return multiple objects from the function and `cbind()` to bind the two vectors `lower.bound` and `upper.bound` together in a matrix.

Figure 5.3	Coefficient Estimates and 95% Confidence Intervals of β_0 and β_1 for 100 Simulated Samples

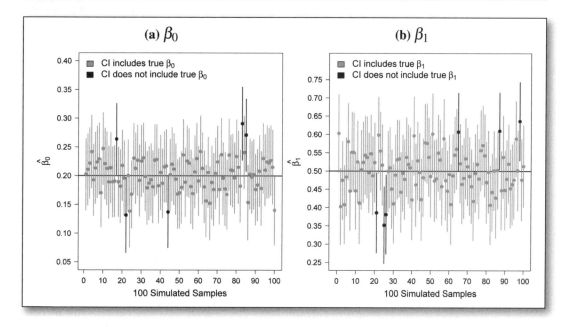

simulation for a fixed number of repetitions. To do this, we make use of the fact that whether a confidence interval includes the true parameter follows a binomial distribution (i.e., a series of trials that have two possible outcomes: "yes" or "no"). To compute a confidence interval around a binomial proportion (such as the proportion that come up "yes"), we can use the normal approximation to the binomial distribution. Under the normal approximation, the 95% simulation error bound for a coverage probability, p, and number of repetitions, r, is

$p \pm 1.96 \times \sqrt{\frac{p(1-p)}{r}}$. The coverage() function that we created above computes

this automatically.[11] The error bounds for these coverage probabilities are as follows:

- β_0: $0.941 \pm 1.96 \times \sqrt{\dfrac{0.941(1-0.941)}{1000}} = [0.926, 0.956]$

- β_1: $0.951 \pm 1.96 \times \sqrt{\dfrac{0.951(1-0.951)}{1000}} = [0.938, 0.964]$

---

[11]There are several other ways of forming a binomial confidence interval and many of them are better than the normal approximation for values near 0 or 1. We use the normal approximation for simplicity, but see Agresti and Coull (1998) for more on other methods.

In both cases, the error bounds include 0.95. Also, notice that because the analyst controls the number of repetitions (r in this notation), then with all else equal, the error bounds can be made smaller and smaller just by increasing the number of repetitions in the simulation. Overall, these coverage probabilities tell us that the OLS standard errors are performing correctly. Again, this is not a surprise here given that all of the OLS assumptions hold in this example. In the next section, we turn to simulations as experiments, in which we make changes to the DGP that affect these and other measures of model performance.

5.3 SIMULATIONS AS EXPERIMENTS

Now that we have the tools to evaluate simulation results, our next task is to add some complexity to the DGP we want to evaluate. We illustrate this by exploring a series of variations on our basic OLS simulation. We then evaluate the results and compare them with our previous results when all of the OLS assumptions held. Specifically, we examine the consequences of heteroskedasticity, multicollinearity, measurement error, omitted or irrelevant variables, serial correlation, clustered data, and nonnormal errors. Thus, each of the simulations to come is really a test of how well OLS performs at providing unbiased and efficient estimates of coefficients and their standard errors when the actual DGP being used to simulate the data differs from a DGP that meets all of the assumptions of OLS. The consequences of each of these violations is well understood in theory. Our goal is to use these examples to help readers see more readily the consequences of these violations and to provide a foundation for doing more general Monte Carlo simulations for estimators other than OLS.

5.3.1 Heteroskedasticity

OLS assumes that the variance of the dependent variable (Y) conditional on the model (e.g., the Xs and βs) is constant. Stated more simply, OLS assumes that the variance of the residuals is constant. The term for constant variance is homoskedasticity. In contrast, heteroskedasticity is a term that means nonconstant variance. Thus, the presence of heteroskedasticity in the residuals of an OLS regression constitutes a violation of an OLS assumption. More specifically, heteroskedasticity presents problems for OLS when the variance of the residuals is a function of one or more independent variables.[12] As most statistics courses and textbooks discuss, nonconstant error variance is an efficiency problem because the model does not predict the dependent variable as reliably at certain values of the independent variables (e.g., Gujarati & Porter, 2008). We can use simulation to illustrate this more clearly.

---

[12]We want to emphasize that we are talking about the *variance* in the residual being a function of one or more of the independent variables; not the residuals themselves. Correlation/ association between the independent variables and the residuals *is* a problem—it is just not *this* problem.

To simulate heteroskedasticity, we make a few changes to our code from the basic OLS simulation. First, we create a new object in which to store the results. Adding `.ncv` to the name stands for "nonconstant variance."

```
par.est.ncv <- matrix(NA, nrow = reps, ncol = 4) # Empty matrix to store the
                                                 # estimates
```

To produce heteroskedasticity, we need to simulate a residual for the DGP that does not have a constant variance. In particular, we want to simulate a DGP where that residual variance is a function of one (or more) independent variables. We accomplish this in our code by replacing the "1" in the standard deviation of the error term with exp $(X \times \gamma)$. We use the exponential distribution because the exponential of any number will always be positive, which is helpful because there is no such thing as a negative variance. The other part of the formula is our independent variable of interest (X) multiplied by some parameter (in this case, represented by γ). In this example, we then set the parameter γ (gamma in the R code) to 1.5. This is an arbitrary choice, so we encourage you to explore the impact of changing the value of γ on the results produced by the simulation.[13] Most important, this setup renders the error variance a function of X. In this case, larger values of X will be associated with larger variance in the error term of the DGP compared with smaller values of X. Finally, notice that we create the object `sigma.est` as an empty vector in which we store the estimates of σ, the residual standard deviation of the estimated model, for each iteration of our simulation. We will use this in a second heteroskedasticity simulation below.

```
# Heteroskedasticity (Simulation 1 of 3)
set.seed(100484) # Set the seed for reproducible results

reps <- 1000 # Set the number of repetitions at the top of the script
par.est.ncv <- matrix(NA, nrow = reps, ncol = 4) # Empty matrix to store the
                                                 # estimates
sigma.est <- numeric(reps) # Empty vector to store sigma
b0 <- .2 # True value for the intercept
b1 <- .5 # True value for the slope
n  <- 1000 # Sample size
X  <- runif(n, -1, 1) # Create a sample of n observations on the # independent variable X
gamma <- 1.5 # Heteroskedasticity parameter

for(i in 1:reps){ # Start the loop
Y <- b0 + b1*X + rnorm(n, 0, exp(X*gamma)) # Now the error variance is a
                                           # function of X plus random noise
model <- lm(Y ~ X) # Estimate OLS model
sigma.est[i] <- summary(model)$sigma # Store sigma
vcv <- vcov(model) # Variance-covariance matrix
par.est.ncv[i, 1] <- model$ coef[1] # put the estimate for the intercept
```

---

[13]You should be able to predict the results if you set γ to zero. Try it and see if you were right.

```
                                        #in the first column
par.est.ncv[i, 2] <- model$ coef[2] # Put the estimate for the coefficient on
                                       # X in the second column
par.est.ncv[i, 3] <- sqrt(diag(vcv)[1]) # SE of the intercept
par.est.ncv[i, 4] <- sqrt(diag(vcv)[2]) # SE of the coefficient on X
} # End the loop
```

Figure 5.4 illustrates the change we have made using one sample of the simulated data. The graph plots X on the x-axis and Y on the y-axis with the OLS regression line running through the points. Notice that the spread of the points increases dramatically as X increases.

Now that we have seen the basic idea behind changing a DGP in a simulation, we can examine the consequences of this change for the coefficient estimates. We do this by comparing their distributions with those from the basic OLS simulation with no assumptions violated. Before proceeding, we need to make an adjustment to our basic OLS simulation to make a "fair" comparison. Remember from the last simulation that we saved the estimate of σ in each model in the object sigma.est. As it turns out, the average $\hat{\sigma}$ in that simulation was about 1.87 (type mean(sigma.est) to see this). In the basic OLS simulation from above,

| Figure 5.4 | Heteroskedasticity Created by Simulating the Error Term Standard Deviation as a Function of X |

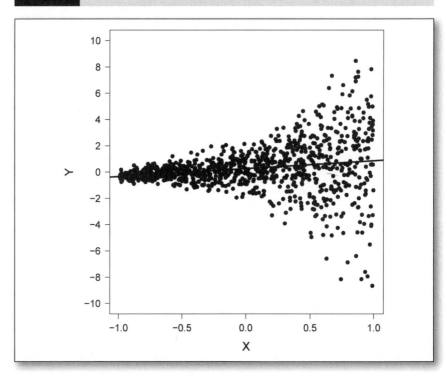

we set the standard deviation of the error term to 1, which, not surprisingly, produces an average $\hat{\sigma}$ value over 1,000 repetitions very close to 1. Thus, if we
simply compare the basic OLS simulation with this heteroskedasticity simulation,
two parameters will actually be changing: (1) the overall variance of the error
term and (2) heteroskedasticity. Thus, if we see differences between the two simulations, we may not be able to say whether they emerge due to heteroskedasticity or just from the difference in the average size of σ. We want to make a
comparison where only heteroskedasticity is changing.

To do this, we conduct another simulation in which we create two DGPs,
represented by two dependent variables. The first, Y1, is created with heteroskedasticity in the exact same manner as the previous simulation. The second, Y2,
is created with homoskedasticity and a standard deviation of the error term equal
to the average $\hat{\sigma}$ from the heteroskedastic simulation (≈ 1.87).[14] Now, we know
that the overall variance of the error term does not change, on average, between
these two DGPs. The only difference between them is that one includes heteroskedasticity (Y1) and one does not (Y2). After creating the heteroskedastic
and homoskedastic DGPs, we then estimate an OLS model with each one
(model1 and model2, respectively). We store the coefficient estimates from
each model and the standard errors from the model of the heteroskedastic DGP
(model1).

```
# Heteroskedasticity (Simulation 2 of 3)
# Compare to homoskedasticity with sigma set to the average value
# of the estimates of sigma from the last simulation
sigma <- mean(sigma.est)

set.seed(100484) # Set the seed for reproducible results

reps <- 1000 # Set the number of repetitions at the top of the script
par.est.ncv <- matrix(NA, nrow = reps, ncol = 6) # Empty matrix to store the
                                                 # estimates
b0 <- .2 # True value for the intercept
b1 <- .5 # True value for the slope
n <- 1000 # Sample size
X <- runif(n, -1, 1) # Create a sample of n observations on the
                     # independent variable X
gamma <- 1.5 # Heteroskedasticity parameter

for(i in 1:reps){ # Start the loop
Y1 <- b0 + b1*X + rnorm(n, 0, exp(X*gamma)) # Y1: Heteroskedasticity
Y2 <- b0 + b1*X + rnorm(n, 0, sigma) # Y2: Homoskedasticity, same average
                                     # sigma as Y1
model1 <- lm(Y1 ~ X) # Estimate OLS models
```

---

[14]Note that we do not simply type 1.87 into the code, but rather use mean(sigma.
est) because it is more precise.

```
model2 <- lm(Y2 ~ X)
vcv <- vcov(model1) # Variance-covariance matrix (model 1)
par.est.ncv[i, 1] <- model1$coef[1] # Put the estimate for the intercept
                                    # in the first column (model 1)
par.est.ncv[i, 2] <- model1$coef[2] # Put the estimate for the coefficient on
                                    # X in the second column (model 1)
par.est.ncv[i, 3] <- model2$coef[1] # Put the estimate for the intercept
                                    # in the first column (model 2)
par.est.ncv[i, 4] <- model2$coef[2] # Put the estimate for the coefficient on
                                    # X in the second column (model 2)
par.est.ncv[i, 5] <- sqrt(diag(vcv)[1]) # SE of the intercept (model 1)
par.est.ncv[i, 6] <- sqrt(diag(vcv)[2]) # SE of the coefficient on X (model 1)
} # End the loop
```

Now, we can compare the estimates from the two DGPs. To do this, we switch from histograms to kernel density estimates. A kernel density is essentially a smoothed histogram represented by a line. We do this to allow for better visibility when comparing two distributions. Figure 5.4 plots the density of coefficient estimates for β_0 and β_1 both with and without heteroskedasticity.

Notice that in each panel of Figure 5.5 the density of estimates both with and without heteroskedasticity show unbiasedness—the peaks of the distributions are centered at the true parameter values. However, while the spread of the distributions of β_0 are virtually identical in Panel (a), there is a noticeable difference in the spread of the distributions of β_1 in Panel (b). In the case of β_0 (Panel a), the estimates are no more or less efficient under heteroskedasticity. However, the β_1 estimates generated under heteroskedasticity (Panel b) have less density concentrated near the true value and more density farther away. This is graphical evidence of the efficiency problem that heteroskedasticity creates. When the variance of the error term is a function of an independent variable (i.e., is not constant), any single estimate of a coefficient on that independent variable is less likely to be close to the true parameter compared with when the error variance is constant. This phenomenon does not extend to the intercept term because it does not operate on any independent variable.

Having shown that heteroskedasticity can create greater variance in the coefficient estimates, our next question is whether or not the estimated standard errors for those coefficients effectively capture this greater variance or whether heteroskedasticity causes problems there as well. We can use the coverage() function to evaluate this.

```
cp.beta0.ncv <- coverage(par.est.ncv[ , 1], par.est.ncv[ , 5], b0,
 df = n - model1$rank)
cp.beta0.ncv$coverage.probability
[1] 0.957
cp.beta0.ncv$mc.eb
[1] 0.9444268 0.9695732
```

```
cp.beta1.ncv <- coverage(par.est.ncv[ , 2], par.est.ncv[ , 6], b1,
  df = n - model1$rank)
cp.beta1.ncv$coverage.probability
[1] 0.852


cp.beta1.ncv$mc.eb
[1] 0.8299907 0.8740093
```

Notice first that, similar to the graph in Figure 5.5, Panel (a), the standard error of β_0 is unaffected by heteroskedasticity, with a coverage probability of 0.957 and a 95% error bound of [0.944, 0.970]. However, the coverage probability of 0.852 for β_1 with a 95% error bound of [0.830, 0.874] indicates that the OLS estimates of its standard error are too small, on average. This is not surprising because we created a DGP with nonconstant error variance as a function of X. The conventional standard error assumes constant variance, which does not hold in this case. Thus, the conventional method for calculating standard errors is not appropriate when heteroskedasticity is present.[15] In other words, heteroskedasticity results in greater variance in the estimates of β_1, but the conventional method of computing the standard error of β_1 fails to capture this.

IMPACTS HYPOTHESIS TESTING... MAY CONCLUDE A PARAMETER IS S.S. WHEN IT REALLY ISN'T !!!

Figure 5.5 The Effects of Heteroskedasticity on the Distribution of β_0 and β_1 Estimates

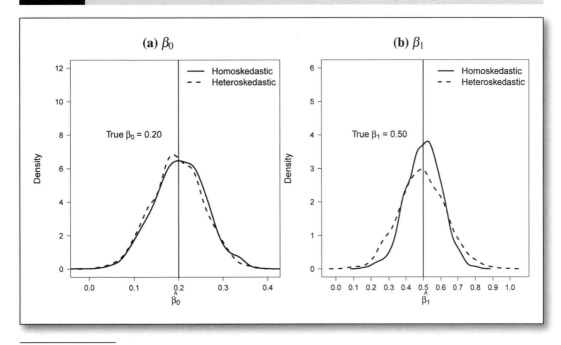

---

[15]In this case, OLS computes "small" standard errors, but they are not correct—smaller standard errors are not always better.

So far our simulation has shown that adding heteroskedasticity to the DGP in the form of a positive increase in the variance of the residual as X increases does not bias our estimates of either β_0 or β_1. However, it does result in less efficient estimates for β_1 that is not captured properly by the conventional method of computing the standard error of β_1. You should explore other values for γ and other forms of heteroskedasticity to see if this always happens.

This leads to the question of whether there is a solution to the problem of getting the wrong standard error estimate for β_1, and, if so, how we can use our simulation methods to evaluate it. A common fix for heteroskedasticity is to estimate what are called "robust" standard errors (see Long & Ervin, 2000; White, 1980). The term *robust* implies that the method is capable of generating standard error estimates even in the face of a possible assumption violation—in this case, heteroskedasticity. The robust variance–covariance matrix, which uses the model residuals to better approximate coefficient variability, can be estimated with the `vcovHC()` function in the `sandwich` package. We can rerun the simulation, substituting this line of code for `vcov()` to determine whether robust standard errors actually "work" as they are intended. For simplicity, we will do this by modifying the first heteroskedasticity simulation because we do not need the homoskedastic DGP here.

```
# Heteroskedasticity: Robust SEs (Simulation 3 of 3)
# Just simulate the version with heteroskedasticity, assess performance of
# robust standard errors
library(sandwich)

set.seed(100484) # Set the seed for reproducible results

reps <- 1000 # Set the number of repetitions at the top of the script
par.est.ncv <- matrix(NA, nrow = reps, ncol = 4) # Empty matrix to store the
                                                 # estimates
b0 <- .2 # True value for the intercept
b1 <- .5 # True value for the slope
n <- 1000 # Sample size
X <- runif(n, -1, 1) # Create a sample of n observations on the
                     # independent variable X
gamma <- 1.5 # Heteroskedasticity parameter

for(i in 1:reps){ # Start the loop
Y <- b0 + b1*X + rnorm(n, 0, exp(X*gamma)) # Now the error variance is a
                                           # function of X plus random noise
model <- lm(Y ~ X) # Estimate OLS model
vcv <- vcovHC(model) # Robust variance-covariance matrix
par.est.ncv[i, 1] <- model$ coef[1] # Put the estimate for the intercept
                                     # in the first column
par.est.ncv[i, 2] <- model$coef[2] # Put the estimate for the coefficient on
                                    # X in the second column
par.est.ncv[i, 3] <- sqrt(diag(vcv)[1]) # SE of the intercept
par.est.ncv[i, 4] <- sqrt(diag(vcv)[2]) # SE of the coefficient on X
} # End the loop
```

We can then compute the coverage probability for β_1 using the robust standard error. Doing so produces the following result.

```
cp.beta1.ncv.robust <- coverage(par.est.ncv[ , 2], par.est.ncv[ , 4], b1,
  df = n - model$rank)
cp.beta1.ncv.robust$coverage.probability
[1] 0.938
cp.beta1.ncv.robust$mc.eb # Simulation error
[1] 0.923053 0.952947
```

The coverage probability improves to 0.938, with simulation error bounds of [0.923, 0.953]. Because these bounds include 0.95, we conclude that robust standard errors do, in fact, account for coefficient variability under heteroskedasticity (as we have simulated it here).

This is our first complete example of using Monte Carlo simulation to evaluate the performance of a statistical estimator when we intentionally altered the population DGP so as not to conform to one of the assumptions of that estimator. Additionally, we evaluated the performance of a different estimation method designed to overcome that assumption violation. For many, this would constitute the complete set of steps in a Monte Carlo simulation, with the possible exception of repeating the simulation many times across a range of some parameter, such as using different degrees of heteroskedasticity to explore the consequences of relatively minor versus major violations of this assumption.

5.3.2 Multicollinearity

Another common efficiency problem is multicollinearity, or correlation between independent variables. Technically, only perfect collinearity between two or more of the independent variables violates an OLS assumption, while any multicollinearity short of that is better thought of as an empirical challenge rather than an assumption violation. Still, when two (or more) independent variables are correlated with each other, the variability in the coefficient estimates operating on those independent variables increases, which leads to increases in the standard errors. As a result, separating the unique effects of each independent variable on the dependent variable becomes more difficult. We show an example of this below. We "turn off" the heteroskedasticity from the last simulation by setting the standard deviation of the error term back to 1. To introduce multicollinearity, we add a second independent variable to the DGP (X_2), with a true coefficient of $\beta_2 = 0.75$.

In the heteroskedasticity example, we conducted the simulation with only one value of γ. Instead of conducting this multicollinearity simulation at just one value of correlation between X_1 and X_2, we do it for a range of correlations from 0 to 0.99. This allows for a more comprehensive assessment of the effects of multicollinearity. To do so, we add another `for` loop, subscripted with j, that iterates through 11 different correlation values from 0 to 0.99, defined in the object `mc.level`. In other words, the simulation of 1,000 repetitions is done 11 times, one time for each of the 11 different correlations between the independent variables. This produces a total of $11 \times 1,000 = 11,000$ simulated data sets.

We add the correlation to the DGP by drawing X_1 and X_2 from a multivariate normal distribution using the `rmvnorm()` function that is available in the `mvtnorm` package. Instead of defining one mean and one standard deviation as we do with `rnorm()` when we generate a single random normal variable, `mvtnorm()` takes a vector of means and a variance–covariance matrix as its arguments. In this case, we set the means of both independent variables to 0, their variances each equal to 1, and then we change their covariance to each value in `mc.level` as the `for` loop indexed by `j` iterates.[16] Again, because we add this second loop that iterates over 11 different levels of correlation between X_1 and X_2, we are no longer just simulating one DGP 1,000 times. Rather, we are simulating 11 DGPs, each for 1,000 times.

Finally, at each level of correlation, we store the standard deviation of the estimates for β_1 and β_2 and place them in the matrix `sd.betas`. Note that we are not saving each individual estimate of β_1 and β_2 in this case, but rather just one summary statistic for each coefficient to represent the simulation at each correlation value. The code is given below.[17]

```
# Multicollinearity
library(mvtnorm)
set.seed(121402) # Set the seed for reproducible results

reps <- 1000 # Set the number of repetitions at the top of the script
par.est.mc <- matrix(NA, nrow = reps, ncol = 4) # Empty matrix to store the
                                                # estimates
b0 <- .2 # True value for the intercept
b1 <- .5 # True value for the slopes
b2 <- .75
n <- 5000 # Sample size

# Levels of multicollinearity
mc.level <- c(0, .1, .2, .3, .4, .5, .6, .7, .8, .9, .99)
# Matrix to store SD of the coefficient estimates
sd.betas <- matrix(NA, nrow = length(mc.level), ncol = 2)

for(j in 1:length(mc.level)){ # Start the j loop
X.corr <- matrix(c(1, mc.level[j], mc.level[j], 1), nrow = 2, ncol = 2)
X <- rmvnorm(n, mean = c(0, 0), sigma = X.corr) # Create two correlated
X1 <- X[ , 1]                                   # independent variables
X2 <- X[ , 2]

for(i in 1:reps){ # Start the i loop
Y <- b0 + b1*X1 + b2*X2 + rnorm(n, 0, 1) # The true DGP, with N(0, 1) error
```

[16]By setting the variance of each independent variable to 1, the covariance and correlation between them are equal. This simplifies our simulation, but could be changed to explore its consequences.

[17]We use the `cat()` function to print out text on the screen after each iteration through the `j` loop. This tells us how much of simulation is complete.

```
model <- lm(Y ~ X1 + X2) # Estimate OLS model
vcv <- vcov(model) # Variance-covariance matrix
par.est.mc[i, 1] <- model$coef[2] # Put the estimate for the coefficient on
                                  # X1 in the first column
par.est.mc[i, 2] <- model$coef[3] # Put the estimate for the coefficient on
                                  # X2 in the second column
par.est.mc[i, 3] <- sqrt(diag(vcv)[2]) # SE of the coefficient on X1
par.est.mc[i, 4] <- sqrt(diag(vcv)[3]) # SE of the coefficient on X2
} # End the i loop
sd.betas[j, ] <- c(sd(par.est.mc[ , 1] - b1), sd(par.est.mc[ , 1]))
cat("Just completed correlation =", mc.level[j],
"(", j, "of", length(mc.level), ")", "\n")
} # End the j loop
```

We first ran the code as it is above with $n = 1,000$, then changed n to $5,000$ and ran it again. Figure 5.6 shows the results for β_1 (which are similar to those of β_2). In Panel (a), which shows the $n = 1,000$ simulation results, the standard deviation of β_1 increases as the correlation between the independent variables increases. However, notice that the rate of increase is not linear; instead, it is a small increase from correlations of 0 to 0.70, then larger increases from 0.70 to 0.99. This tells us that efficiency loss as a result of multicollinearity is relatively minor for most of the range of correlation levels, but becomes a more serious problem when independent variables are highly correlated.[18]

Panel (b) of Figure 5.6 shows us the results for $n = 5,000$. The same pattern as in Panel (a) emerges again in Panel (b), but it is less severe; the standard deviation of the β_1 estimates at a correlation of 0.99 is less than half of the value it was when $n = 1,000$. This demonstrates one major solution for multicollinearity: collect more data. The multicollinearity is a problem because it reduces the amount of information available to estimate your coefficients. Increasing the sample size compensates for this by adding more information in the form of more data points back into the analysis.

This example illustrates how simulation can help us understand the magnitude of effects. While we could show this result analytically, using a simulation allows us to see how particular changes in the DGP based on different levels of multicollinearity affect the level of efficiency loss. In other words, the simulation provides greater intuition about the consequences of multicollinearity by explicitly linking it to the DGP and illustrating its impact across any level of multicollinearity a user might want to consider.

5.3.3 Measurement Error

Our next example explores the consequences of measurement error in an independent variable. This is analogous to having an imperfect proxy variable for X in place

---

[18]Note that simply checking the bivariate correlation among independent variables is not sufficient to diagnose multicollinearity when there are three or more independent variables in the model. Researchers should compute variance inflation factors (VIFs) for each independent variable. See Gujarati and Porter (2008).

of a true measure of the concept itself. In statistics courses and textbooks, we learn that measurement error in an independent variable causes bias to regression coefficients because it produces correlation between the independent variable and the error term. Unlike heteroskedasticity and multicollinearity, however, this is a much harder problem to detect within a single sample of data. While the underlying problem is one of correlation between the independent variable as measured and the error term that results from assuming that the independent variable is measured without error, you cannot simply run a regression and then calculate the correlation between the suspect independent variable and the observed residual. That observed correlation will be zero by construction because of this OLS assumption. However, we can illustrate the consequences of measurement error in an independent variable through simulation.

As before, we begin with the basic OLS simulation with no assumption violations. We use this starting point to generate the data for Y just as before—based on fixed model parameters, an independent variable called X that does *not* include measurement error, and our typical normally distributed residual. Our strategy in creating measurement error is to generate another version of the independent variable that simply adds random noise drawn from a normal distribution to X. We will call this object Xp, which you might think of as "*X* plus" random measurement error. Then, we substitute Xp for X into the OLS regression model that we estimate repeatedly in our simulation. We generate Y based on the true DGP, but we run our repeated OLS regressions by regressing Y on Xp instead of X. We do this for several levels of measurement error so that we can understand how

| Figure 5.6 | The Effect of Correlation Between X_1 and X_2 on the Standard Deviation of β_1 Estimates for $n = 1,000$ and $n = 5,000$ |

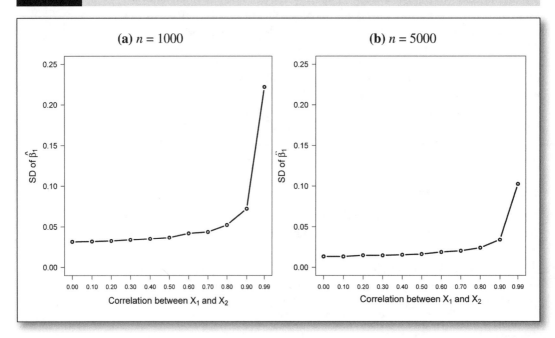

increases in measurement error affects bias in coefficient estimates. We generate an object called e.level, which is the standard deviation of the random noise we add to X to produce Xp. As e.level increases, measurement error becomes a more serious problem. We also create an empty matrix called ab.merror to store the AB from each estimate of β_1.

At each iteration through the j loop, a new standard deviation of the measurement error becomes part of the construction of Xp. Importantly, notice that Xp gets included in the lm() function inside the i loop. After estimating the model, we compute the AB for the estimated coefficient and store it in the object ab.1. After the code iterates through the i loop 1,000 times, ab.1 gets placed in a column of the matrix ab.merror and the simulation begins again with a new measurement error standard deviation.

```
# Measurement Error
set.seed(385062) # Set the seed for reproducible results

reps <- 1000 # Set the number of repetitions at the top of the script
b0 <- .2 # True value for the intercept
b1 <- .5 # True value for the slope
n <- 1000 # Sample size
X <- runif(n, -1, 1) # Create a sample of n observations on the
                     # independent variable X

# Level of measurement error (SD of random noise)
e.level <- c(0, .1, .2, .3, .4, .5, .6, .7, .8, .9, 1)
# Empty matrix to store absolute bias
ab.merror <- matrix(NA, nrow = reps, ncol = length(e.level))

# Empty array to store the estimates
par.est.merror <- array(NA, c(reps, 2, length(e.level)))

for(j in 1:length(e.level)){ # Start the j loop
ab.1 <- numeric(reps)
par.est <- matrix(NA, nrow = reps, ncol = 2) # Empty matrix to store the
                                             # estimates
Xp <- X + rnorm(n, 0, e.level[j]) # X measured with error

for(i in 1:reps){
Y <- b0 + b1*X + rnorm(n, 0, 1)
model <- lm(Y ~ Xp)
par.est[i, 1] <- model$coef[1] # Put the estimate for the intercept
                               # in the first column
par.est[i, 2] <- model$coef[2] # Put the estimate for the coefficient on
                               # X in the second column
ab.1[i] <- abs(model$coef[2] - b1)
}

par.est.merror[ , , j] <- par.est
ab.merror[ , j] <- ab.1
cat("Completed e =", e.level[j], "\n")
gc() # Clear out RAM for better performance
}
```

We plot the results from this code in Figure 5.7. Panel (a) plots the distributions of the β_1 estimates for two values of the measurement error standard deviation: 0 (no measurement error) and 1 (the maximum value in this particular simulation). The graph shows that when there is no measurement error (solid line), the estimates of β_1 show no bias—the distribution is centered on the true parameter. In contrast, the distribution of the β_1 estimates with measurement error (dashed line) shows considerable bias. The mean of those estimates is 0.13, well below the true parameter of 0.50.[19]

In Panel (b) of Figure 5.7, the x-axis plots the standard deviation of the measurement error and the y-axis plots the AB of every simulated data set. The black lowess line shows the trend in AB. As the standard deviation of the measurement error increases (i.e., more noise added to X), AB increases. This graph shows that bias gets worse as measurement error increases, though not at a linear rate. The largest increase in bias comes in the middle of the x-axis, with smaller increases at the extreme values. This pattern is not an accident. Rather, it stems from the ratio of true variance in X relative to measurement error and how quickly the bias

| **Figure 5.7** | The Effect of Measurement Error in X on β_1 Estimates |

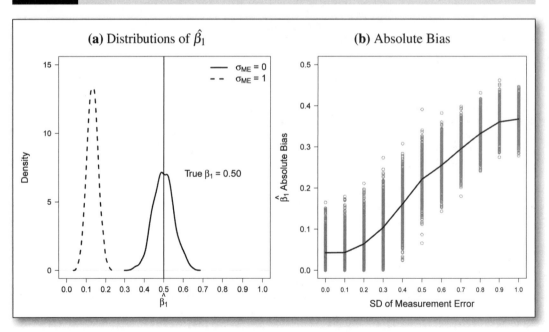

---

[19]Interestingly, the biased estimates show better efficiency—the spread of the dashed line is smaller than that of the solid line. This is because in this particular simulation, the variance of the independent variable we use in the regressions, Xp, increases as measurement error increases. When all else is equal, the variability in slope coefficient estimates decreases as variance in the independent variable on which they are operating increases.

introduced by measurement error pushes the estimates of β_1 toward zero. We encourage you to explore these and other features of this simulation.

As a final comment, you might have noticed something slightly different in this simulation. Specifically, we used a true DGP with no assumption violations to generate our values for the dependent variable and made our change in the simulation later in how we estimated our regression models. We want to make three comments as a way of summarizing where we are thus far. First, what we did in this simulation is best thought of as changing the DGP that produces our observed independent variable rather than the DGP that produces our observed dependent variable. Remember, the assumptions of OLS speak to both. In that sense, what we did here is similar to our other simulations in that we compared the result of an OLS analysis where every aspect of the overall DGP met OLS assumptions with an analysis where one (and only one) of those assumptions did not hold.

Second, you might have begun to think at this point that it is not "fair" in some sense to expect OLS to perform well when we are purposely violating an OLS assumption. In this example, we know that Xp was a version of X that contained random error, yet we used it anyway. In other words, we should not be surprised that OLS has problems when we used the "wrong" version of the independent variable. Our response is that you are right—expecting OLS to automatically perform well when its assumptions do not hold is misguided. However, we only know this because we control the DGP in a simulation. In applied work, you only have your sample of data with which to work. That is why understanding, detecting, and evaluating the consequences of assumption violations is so important.

Last, we would generalize the previous point to say that it is more than just using the "wrong" measure of an independent variable. Rather, the simulation showed that if you estimate a statistical model of any type that does not comport with the DGP, you should not expect to produce results that help you uncover the true DGP. The best solution to these kinds of problems is to figure out a better model to estimate, where "better" is defined as being a more accurate representation of the underlying DGP.

5.3.4 Omitted Variable

Another problem related to the systematic part of the DGP is omitting a relevant independent variable that is part of the true DGP from the statistical model that is estimated. While this might stem from any number of causes, one source of this problem is when a researcher does not know a particular variable belongs in the specification or cannot collect that variable. If the omitted independent variable is uncorrelated with all of the independent variables that are included, then leaving it out will usually have only a small impact on model efficiency. However, if the omitted independent variable is correlated with one or more of the independent variables that are included, this will result in bias to the coefficient estimates.

Similar to the multicollinearity and measurement error simulations, we examine the omitted variable problem across a range of correlations between the included and excluded independent variables. We generate the DGP with two independent variables (X_1 and X_2), correlated at 11 different values from 0 to 0.99. We generate the dependent variable with both X_1 and X_2 in the true equation, but we only include X_1 in estimation of the model.[20] We then collect the estimates for β_1 along with the MSE of those estimates before incrementing to the next level of correlation between the independent variables and repeating the simulation.

```
# Omitted Variable
library(mvtnorm)
set.seed(37943) # Set the seed for reproducible results

reps <- 1000 # Set the number of repetitions at the top of the script

b0 <- .2 # True value for the intercept
b1 <- .5 # True value for the slopes
b2 <- .75
n <- 1000 # Sample size

# Level of IV correlation
cor.level <- c(0, .1, .2, .3, .4, .5, .6, .7, .8, .9, .99)

# Empty matrix to store the estimates
par.est.ov <- matrix(NA, nrow = reps, ncol = length(cor.level))
# Empty matrix to store mean squared error
mse.ov <- matrix(NA, nrow = length(cor.level), ncol = 1)

for(j in 1:length(cor.level)){ # Start the j loop
for(i in 1:reps){ # Start the loop
X.corr <- matrix(c(1, cor.level[j], cor.level[j], 1), nrow = 2, ncol = 2)
X <- rmvnorm(n, mean = c(0, 0), sigma = X.corr) # Create two correlated
X1 <- X[ , 1]                                   # independent variables
X2 <- X[ , 2]
Y <- b0 + b1*X1 + b2*X2 + rnorm(n, 0, 1) # The true DGP, with N(0, 1) error
model <- lm(Y ~ X1) # Estimate OLS model
par.est.ov[i, j] <- model$coef[2] # Put the estimate for the coefficient on
                                  # X1 in column j
} # End the i loop
mse.ov[j] <- mean((par.est.ov[ , j] - b1)^2)
cat("Completed cor =", cor.level[j], "\n")
} # End the j loop
```

---

[20]Notice that we generate the independent variables inside the i loop in this example. We do this so that the average correlation across the 1,000 samples is equal to what we define. For example, at a theoretical correlation of zero, we want the average correlation across the 1,000 samples to be (very near) zero. If we did not regenerate the independent variables inside the i loop, only one correlation value would be drawn at each theoretical value that would either be too high or too low due to random chance.

We present the results in Figure 5.8. Panel (a) gives the density estimates of the 1,000 β_1 estimates simulated at a correlation of zero between X_1 and X_2 and the 1,000 estimates at $r_{X_1X_2} = 0.99$. The distribution of estimates at $r_{X_1X_2} = 0$ is centered right at 0.50, indicating no bias. This demonstrates that omitting a variable that is not correlated with an included variable does not affect parameter estimates in the case of OLS (though this is not true for all estimators). In contrast, the distribution of estimates when $r_{X_1X_2} = 0.99$ shows a considerable amount of bias. In fact, recall from the code that the coefficient on the omitted variable is set to 0.75. The mean of the distribution with $r_{X_1X_2} = 0.99$ is 1.242, which is 0.50 (true β_1) + 0.742. Thus, at near-perfect correlation with the omitted variable, almost all of the true effect of that omitted variable is incorrectly attributed to X_1 through the biased estimate of β_1.

Panel (b) of Figure 5.8 plots the MSE of the β_1 estimates as the correlation between independent variables increases. The strong positive relationship seen in Panel (a) is formalized here; as the correlation between X_1 and X_2 increases, the MSE associated with the estimates of β_1 (when X_2 is omitted) increases. Furthermore, this increase occurs at an increasing rate: going from $r_{X_1X_2} = 0$ to $r_{X_1X_2} = 0.10$ produces an increase in MSE of 0.006, while an increase from 0.80 to 0.90 leads to an MSE increase of 0.094.

Like all of our examples, we encourage you to explore how changing aspects of this simulation changes the nature of the results. What if the correlation between X_1 and X_2 is negative rather than positive? What if the true value of the

Figure 5.8   The Effect of Omitted Variable Correlation With X_1 on β_1 Estimates

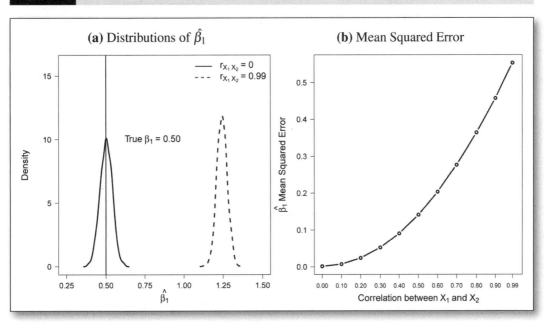

coefficient operating on X_2 in the DGP is negative rather than positive? What if there is a third variable that is included in the model but it is not correlated with the omitted variable? What if you increase your sample size for each draw in the simulation? This kind of exploration will help you see the real nature of your DGP and how your chosen statistical estimator performs.

5.3.5 Serial Correlation

Another problem that can arise with an OLS model is serial correlation—where one or more of a model's errors influence one or more other errors. This is most often considered in the context of time-series analysis where past values of the error term influence current values. However, there can also be spatial/proximity-based correlation among the errors. We will focus on the time-series example here.

The presence of serial correlation by itself is an efficiency problem, similar to what we saw with heteroskedasticity.[21] R has a wide variety of functions for time-series analysis, and one we can use in simulation is `arima.sim()`. We can use this function to simulate time-series processes. We will use it to create an AR(1) process,[22] which is serial correlation in which the value of the error term in the last period influences the current value, but values beyond one period back do not have any additional unique effect on the current value. There are many possible solutions and strategies for dealing with serial correlation, the choice of which should depend on what you understand the underlying DGP to be. In this example, we will focus on the popular modeling strategy of including a lagged value of the dependent variable in the model as an independent variable.

To conduct this simulation, we create an object called `ac`, to represent the AR(1) parameter (this is often labeled ρ in textbooks), which we assign to the value 0.75 (it can vary between 0 and 1, with larger values indicating stronger serial correlation). We replace the typical `rnorm()` function used to construct our error term with `arima.sim()`. The arguments `list(order = c(1, 0, 0), ar = ac)` produce the AR(1) process.[23] Notice also that we set the sample size to 50 in this example. We do so because that is more typical of time-series models in social science (e.g., 50 years of annual data). After generating Y, we first estimate the model as usual, ignoring the serial correlation. Then, we estimate it again, this time including a lagged value of Y in the specification. This second model requires some new manipulation.[24]

---

[21]However, if the appearance of serial correlation is caused by a problem like an omitted variable or some other improper model specification, the real problem of misspecification should be addressed before worrying about serial correlation.

[22]"AR" stands for autoregressive.

[23]You can type `?arima.sim` in R for more details.

[24]In particular, we create a data object called `lag.data` using the `ts.intersect()` function, which binds together Y, X, and the lagged value, `lag.Y`.

```
# Serial Correlation
set.seed(125842) # Set the seed for reproducible results

reps <- 1000 # Set the number of repetitions at the top of the script
par.est.sc <- matrix(NA, nrow = reps, ncol = 2) # Empty matrix to store the
                                                # estimates
b0 <- .2 # True value for the intercept
b1 <- .5 # True value for the slopes
n <- 50 # Sample size
ac <- .75 # AR(1) parameter

X <- runif(n, -1, 1) # Create a sample of n observations on the
                     # independent variable X

for(i in 1:reps){
# AR(1) process in the error term
Y <- b0 + b1*X + arima.sim(list(order = c(1, 0, 0), ar = ac), n = n)
# Without including a lag of Y
model <- lm(Y ~ X)

# With lagged Y
lag.data <- ts.intersect(cbind(Y, X), lag(Y, k = 1))
colnames(lag.data) <- c("Y", "X", "lag.Y")
model.lag <- lm(Y ~ X + lag.Y, data = lag.data)
par.est.sc[i, 1] <- model$coef[2]
par.est.sc[i, 2] <- model.lag$coef[2]
}
```

Figure 5.9 gives us the distribution of estimates for β_1 for each estimator. The result is a trade-off between bias and efficiency. Notice that the OLS models that included lag.Y (solid line) is the most efficient of the two—the peak of the distribution of the estimated values for β_1 for this model is the higher, and it has less spread compared with the distribution of the β_1 estimates for the model that does not include lag.Y. However, also notice that its peak is slightly off from the true value. In contrast, the distribution of the estimates of β_1 from the OLS regressions that did not include lag.Y as an independent variable is centered right on 0.50. However, the spread of the estimates of β_1 for the model that did not include lag.Y is somewhat larger, indicating less efficiency. This simulation showed that including a lagged value of the dependent variable as an independent variable in the model improves efficiency because it captures serial correlation in the residual, but at the cost of some bias. This bias emerges because the lagged value of Y has a random component to it—by definition, Y consists of a systematic and a stochastic component—that affects the model in the same way that random measurement error in an independent variable does; it leads to some level of bias.[25]

---

[25] For a detailed examination of this issue that uses simulation, see Keele and Kelly (2006).

Figure 5.9	The Distribution of β_1 Estimates With and Without Lagged Y

5.3.6 Clustered Data

In the last example, we saw nonindependence among the errors based on time—serial correlation. In this example, we examine the consequences of another form of nonindependence—clustering. This occurs when the errors among groups of observations are correlated with each other. For example, patients are grouped in hospitals and students are grouped in schools. If there is something about those patients (students) that makes them similar to each other within hospitals (schools) in some way even after considering a set of independent variables, then clustering remains in the residuals. Clustered data also arises when there are repeated measures from the same actor. For example, analyses of the votes made by members of Congress or the Supreme Court are clustered by member because each vote is an observation and each member votes on many bills or cases. Similarly, time-series cross-section (TSCS) data—in which several time series for different units (e.g., countries, cities, individual survey respondents) are joined together—can be thought of as clustered data.[26]

---

[26]For more on TSCS, including studies using simulation to evaluate methods such as panel-corrected standard errors (PCSE), see Beck and Katz (1995), Kristensen and Wawro (2003), and Wilson and Butler (2007).

A large literature shows that this data structure can have important consequences for both coefficient estimates and standard errors of statistical models.[27]
In particular, it can produce inefficiency, and sometimes bias in coefficient estimates, and lead to estimates of standard errors that are too small. We can illustrate
these properties through simulation. In this example, we simulate clustered data
and then compare the following strategies for handling it:

- Naïve OLS (i.e., ignoring the problem)
- OLS with "fixed effects" (indicator variables for each group)
- Adjusting the OLS standard errors
- Multilevel modeling (MLM)

In the first part of the simulation, we compare standard OLS, OLS with fixed
effects, and MLM coefficient estimates. In the second part, we compare OLS
standard errors, a version of robust standard errors that handles clustering, and
MLM standard errors. We begin by generating clustered data in the DGP. We
create an object called c.label that groups observations into clusters. We set
the sample size to 1,000 and the number of clusters, nc, to 50. In other words,
there are 1,000 individuals (e.g., patients, voters, or students) and 50 clusters
(hospitals, states, or schools). We set the object p to 0.50. This parameter, which
can vary between 0 and 1, sets the degree to which the data are clustered by con-
trolling the relative amounts of between-cluster variance and within-cluster variance (in this case, the two are equal, see Harden, 2011).

We use the rmvnorm() function to generate two individual-level variables
(i.e., variables that are unique to each observation) labeled effect1 and
effect2, and two cluster-level variables (variables that are the same within
clusters but vary across clusters) labeled effect3 and effect4. The covariances between these pairs of variables are set to 0, the variances of effect1
and effect3 are set to 1, and the variances of effect2 and effect4 are set
to p and $1 - p$. We then create an independent variable, X, to use in our models
as the sum of effect1 and effect3. Next, we create an error term, error,
to use in our models as the sum of effect2 and effect4. This produces an
error term in which half of the variance comes from the cluster-level and half
from the individual level.[28] By construction, the error term is uncorrelated with
the independent variable.

We use our independent variable and our error term to generate the dependent
variable as before. Then, we estimate the model where Y is a linear function of
X three different ways, using (1) OLS, (2) OLS with fixed effects, and (3)
MLM.[29] We store the coefficient estimates from each of those three estimators

---

[27]See, for example, Wooldridge (2002), Steenbergen and Jones (2002), Gelman and Hill (2007),
Green and Vavreck (2008), Arceneaux and Nickerson (2009), and Harden (2011, 2012a).

[28]This can be controlled by changing the value of p.

[29]We use the lme4 package for MLM (Bates et al., 2011).

and their standard errors. We also estimate robust cluster standard errors (RCSE) for the OLS coefficients. We will explain more about what RCSEs are below.[30] There is a lot going on in this code, but most of it you have seen before. Take your time working through it to make sure you can see what is happening.

```
# Clustered Data
library(mvtnorm)
library(lme4)
# Function to compute robust cluster standard errors (Arai 2011)
rcse <- function(model, cluster){
require(sandwich)
M <- length(unique(cluster))
N <- length(cluster)
K <- model$rank
dfc <- (M/(M - 1)) * ((N - 1)/(N - K))
uj <- apply(estfun(model), 2, function(x) tapply(x, cluster, sum))
rcse.cov <- dfc * sandwich(model, meat = crossprod(uj)/N)
return(rcse.cov)
}


set.seed(28704) # Set the seed for reproducible results

reps <- 1000 # Set the number of repetitions at the top of the script
par.est.cluster <- matrix(NA, nrow = reps, ncol = 3) # Empty matrix to store
                                                     # the estimates
se.est.cluster <- matrix(NA, nrow = reps, ncol = 4) # Empty matrix to store
                                                    # the standard errors
b0 <- .2 # True value for the intercept
b1 <- .5 # True value for the slope
n <- 1000 # Sample size
p <- .5 # Rho
nc <- 50 # Number of clusters
c.label <- rep(1:nc, each = n/nc) # Cluster label

for(i in 1:reps){ # Start the loop
i.sigma <- matrix(c(1, 0, 0, 1 - p), ncol = 2) # Level 1 effects
i.values <- rmvnorm(n = n, sigma = i.sigma)
effect1 <- i.values[ , 1]
effect2 <- i.values[ , 2]

c.sigma <- matrix(c(1, 0, 0, p), ncol = 2) # Level 2 effects
c.values <- rmvnorm(n = nc, sigma = c.sigma)
effect3 <- rep(c.values[ , 1], each = n/nc)
effect4 <- rep(c.values[ , 2], each = n/nc)
```

----

[30]We do this with a function called `rcse()`, which is based on a function originally written by Arai (2011) and given in the replication code for this chapter. See Williams (2000) or Harden (2011) for more details on RCSE.

```
X <- effect1 + effect3 # X values unique to level 1 observations
error <- effect2 + effect4

Y <- b0 + b1*X + error # True model

model.ols <- lm(Y ~ X) # Model estimation
model.fe <- lm(Y ~ X + factor(c.label))
model.mlm <- lmer(Y ~ X + (1|c.label))

par.est.cluster[i, 1] <- model.ols$coef[2] # Coefficients
par.est.cluster[i, 2] <- model.fe$coef[2]
par.est.cluster[i, 3] <- fixef(model.mlm)[2]

vcv.ols <- vcov(model.ols) # Variance-covariance matrices
vcv.rcse <- rcse(model.ols, c.label)
vcv.fe <- vcov(model.fe)
vcv.mlm <- vcov(model.mlm)

se.est.cluster[i, 1] <- sqrt(diag(vcv.ols)[2]) # Standard errors
se.est.cluster[i, 2] <- sqrt(diag(vcv.rcse)[2])
se.est.cluster[i, 3] <- sqrt(diag(vcv.fe)[2])
se.est.cluster[i, 4] <- sqrt(diag(vcv.mlm)[2])
} # End the loop

# Coverage probabilities
ols.cp <- coverage(par.est.cluster[ , 1], se.est.cluster[ , 1], b1,
 df = n - model.ols$rank)
rcse.cp <- coverage(par.est.cluster[ , 1], se.est.cluster[ , 2], b1,
 df = n - model.ols$rank)
fe.cp <- coverage(par.est.cluster[ , 2], se.est.cluster[ , 3], b1,
 df = n - model.fe$rank)
mlm.cp <- coverage(par.est.cluster[ , 3], se.est.cluster[ , 4], b1,
 df = n - length(fixef(model.mlm)))
```

Figure 5.10 shows the results. Panel (a) gives the distributions of the estimates of β_1 for OLS, OLS with fixed effects, and MLM. It is difficult to distinguish the OLS with fixed effects distribution from that of MLM because the estimates are very similar.[31] However, there is a clear distinction between those two and naïve OLS, which ignores the clustering. While all three estimators are unbiased under this scenario, the OLS estimates show considerably more variance (and less efficiency) than do the other two. Thus, there is a clear advantage to using an estimator that addresses the clustered structure of the data in coefficient estimation.

Panel (b) of Figure 5.10 plots the coverage probabilities (with simulation error bounds) for the OLS standard errors, RCSE, the OLS with fixed effects standard errors, and MLM standard errors. The OLS standard errors show a

---

[31]We encourage interested readers to consider how the DGP might be changed such that OLS with fixed effects and MLM show more difference from one another.

Figure 5.10 Comparison of Estimators for Clustered Data

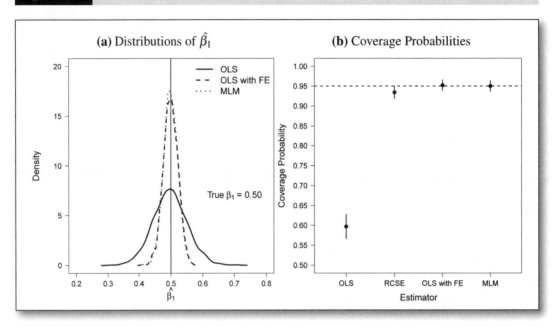

severe downward bias (i.e., their estimated values are too small). The 95% confidence intervals only cover the true coefficient in about 60% of the simulated estimates. This happens because the OLS estimator assumes the errors are iid, but in this case they are not. Due to the "cluster effect" in the error term, there is less information in the data than the estimator assumes; the "effective sample size" is less than the true sample size. [32] RCSE show improvement over the conventional OLS standard errors with a coverage probability of 0.933, but notice that even this method is biased slightly downward (simulation error bounds of [0.918, 0.948]).[33] Finally, the standard errors associated with OLS with fixed effects and MLM are both unbiased (coverage probabilities of 0.952 and 0.949, respectively).

5.3.7 Heavy-Tailed Errors

In our final simulation in this chapter, we examine the consequences of violating the normality assumption. There are many ways in which this assumption could be violated, but in the interest of space we will focus on only one here.

[32]An extreme example of this would be if we made 10 copies of each observation in a sample size of 100. This would create a data set with 1,000 observations, but there would be no unique information in the data beyond the 100 true observations.

[33]We will discuss a cluster-level bootstrapping option that further improves on RCSE in Chapter 8.

Specifically, we will look at the consequences for OLS when the true error distribution has heavier tails than the normal distribution. Distributions with heavy tails are important to social scientists because they are more likely to generate observations that are outliers compared with what one would expect from the normal distribution. In this example, we compare the performance of OLS with that of median regression (MR), which assumes that the error term follows a Laplace distribution. The Laplace has heavier tails than the normal, as shown in Figure 5.11, which plots the normal and Laplace PDFs relative to each other.

How does assuming that the error term follows a Laplace distribution affect estimation? As any typical statistics textbook explains, the sample median serves as a more robust measure of central tendency than does the sample mean when outlying observations are present. Similarly, MR, which conditions the median of the dependent variable on the independent variables, can serve as an alternative to the conditional-mean framework of OLS in the presence of outliers.[34] By minimizing the sum of absolute residuals rather than squared residuals like OLS, MR is not disproportionately influenced by outliers.[35] Indeed, while outliers can have a

| Figure 5.11 | Normal and Laplace PDFs |

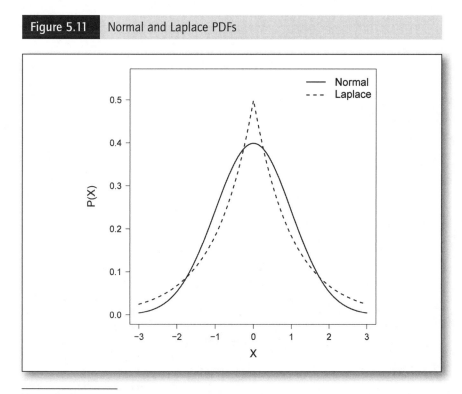

---

[34]MR is a special case of quantile regression (QR) with the median as the conditional quantile of interest (Koenker & Bassett, 1978).

[35]Although OLS is known for its robustness to violations of basic assumptions, improvement is feasible when the tails of the error term are heavier than a normal distribution. These improvements can make important differences in results (Harden & Desmarais, 2011).

substantial effect on OLS estimates, their impact on those of MR is negligible. As a result, MR is a more efficient estimator than OLS under these circumstances. As an additional benefit, MR allows the analyst to handle heavy-tailed data without giving special treatment to outliers or just deleting them.

To illustrate this, we simulate a model with normal errors and one with Laplace errors using the `rlaplace()` function from the `VGAM` package. The Laplace distribution has two parameters that are analogous to μ and σ of the normal distribution: (1) a location parameter defined as any real number, a, and (2) a scale parameter that must be positive, b. We set these to $a = 0$ and $b = 1$. After creating a DGP with normal errors and a DGP with Laplace errors, we then estimate models on both types of data using OLS and MR (using the `rq()` function from the `quantreg` package).[36]

```
# Heavy Tailed Errors
library(VGAM)
library(quantreg)
set.seed(3856) # Set the seed for reproducible results

reps <- 1000 # Set the number of repetitions at the top of the script
par.est.htail <- matrix(NA, nrow = reps, ncol = 4) # Empty matrix to store
                                                   # the estimates
b0 <- .2 # True value for the intercept
b1 <- .5 # True value for the slope
n <- 1000 # Sample size
X <- runif(n, -1, 1) # Create a sample of n observations on the
                     # independent variable X

for(i in 1:reps){ # Start the loop
Y.norm <- b0 + b1*X + rnorm(n, 0, 1) # The true DGP, with N(0, 1) error
Y.lap <- b0 + b1*X + rlaplace(n, 0, 1) # The true DGP, with Laplace(0, 1) error
model.ols.norm <- lm(Y.norm ~ X) # Estimate OLS model
model.mr.norm <- rq(Y.norm ~ X, tau = .5) # Estimate MR model
model.ols.lap <- lm(Y.lap ~ X) # Estimate OLS model
model.mr.lap <- rq(Y.lap ~ X, tau = .5) # Estimate MR model

par.est.htail[i, 1] <- model.ols.norm$coef[2] # Put the OLS estimate
                                              # in the first column (normal)
par.est.htail[i, 2] <- model.mr.norm$coef[2] # Put the MR estimate
                                             # in the second column (normal)
par.est.htail[i, 3] <- model.ols.lap$coef[2] # Put the OLS estimate
                                             # in the first column (Laplace)
par.est.htail[i, 4] <- model.mr.lap$coef[2] # Put the MR estimate
                                            # in the second column (Laplace)
} # End the loop
```

---

[36]As the code illustrates, MR is estimated with the `rq()` function in a similar manner to how the `lm()` function estimates OLS. The argument `tau` is used to specify the quantile of interest (0.50 in the case of the median).

```
# Compute MSE
mse.ols.norm <- mean((par.est.htail[ , 1] - b1)^2)
mse.mr.norm <- mean((par.est.htail[ , 2] - b1)^2)
mse.ols.lap <- mean((par.est.htail[ , 3] - b1)^2)
mse.mr.lap <- mean((par.est.htail[ , 4] - b1)^2)
```

The densities of the MR and OLS estimates are plotted in Figure 5.12. Panel (a) shows the results from the DGP with normal errors and Panel (b) shows the Laplace error results. In Panel (a), OLS is more efficient, with a higher density of estimates near the true parameter value than MR. The OLS MSE for the β_1 estimates is 0.003 while the MR MSE is 0.005. In contrast, MR is considerably more efficient than OLS in Panel (b); the MR MSE is 0.003 compared with 0.006 for OLS. These results are expected because the DGP underlying Panel (a) is designed to conform to the OLS assumption while the underlying DGP used in Panel (b) was designed to conform to the DGP that MR assumes.

This leads to the question of when MR or OLS is a better choice in a given sample of data. Harden and Desmarais (2011) propose a sample-based procedure called the CVDM test that uses a technique called cross-validation to choose between the two estimators.[37] This test evaluates which of the DGPs assumed by

Figure 5.12 The Distribution of $\beta1$ Estimates With OLS and MR Under Normal and Laplace Error Terms

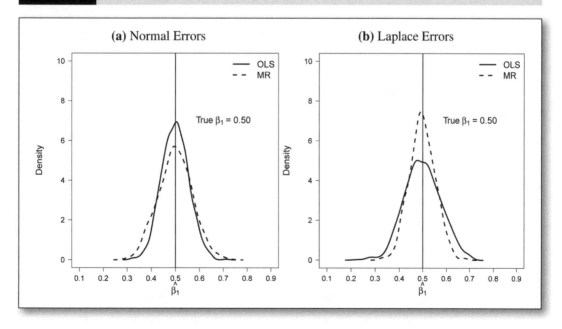

---

[37]CVDM stands for "cross-validated difference in means." See Chapter 9 for more on cross-validation.

each estimator is more likely to have produced a majority of the data points in a given sample. We can use simulation to determine whether the CVDM test works. Specifically, we can simulate data, run the test on each simulated sample, then assess how often the test selects the correct estimator (remember that we know the correct estimator because we know the DGP).

To do this, we again make a modification to the familiar OLS simulation from this chapter.[38] In this case, we draw the error term from an exponential power (EP) distribution (see Mineo & Ruggieri, 2005). With the EP distribution, the parameter p determines the relative MSE of OLS to MR. When $p = 1$, the EP distribution is equivalent to the Laplace distribution, and when $p = 2$ it is equivalent to the normal distribution. As we know from Figure 5.12, MR is the better choice (lower MSE) when the error distribution is Laplace (i.e., $p = 1$), and OLS is the more efficient choice when the errors are normal ($p = 2$). Thus, as p increases, MR MSE increases while OLS MSE decreases. We run the simulation several times at many different values of p. This produces some simulations in which MR is the better estimator of the true DGP and some where OLS is the better estimator of the true DGP. This allows us to assess whether the CVDM test selects correctly. Additionally, this design allows us to assess the performance of the CVDM test even when the distribution is neither normal nor Laplace (i.e., when $1 < p < 2$, see Mineo & Ruggieri, 2005). This is important because applied researchers never know the true distribution of the underlying DGP that produced their data. Thus, it is crucial that the test is not adversely affected by distributional misspecification.

We conduct the simulations for 50 values of p ranging from 1 to 2. MR performance should decline as p increases while OLS performance should improve. At each value of p, we create 1,000 data sets with $n = 50$, then estimate OLS and MR models and conduct the CVDM test in each one.[39] Then, we calculate the OLS and MR MSE as well as the proportion of times the test selects OLS across those 1,000 data sets. This produced a total of 50 values of $p \times 1,000$ data sets per value of $p = 50,000$ total simulated data sets.

```
# CVDM Test
library(normalp)
source("CVDM.r")

set.seed(130425) # Set the seed for reproducible results

reps <- 1000 # Set the number of repetitions at the top of the script
par.est.cvdm <- matrix(NA, nrow = reps, ncol = 2) # Empty matrix to store
                                                  # the estimates
cvdm.stat <- numeric(reps) # Vector to store the CVDM test statistic
```

---

[38]This simulation is adapted from Harden and Desmarais (2011).

[39]We use a small sample size to save computation time. For results at other sample sizes, see Harden and Desmarais (2011) or try changing the sample size in the code yourself. The code for the CVDM test is in the file "CVDM.r."

```
b0 <- .2 # True value for the intercept
b1 <- .5 # True value for the slope
n <- 50 # Sample size
X <- runif(n, -1, 1) # Create a sample of n observations on the
                     # independent variable X

p <- seq(1, 2, length = 50) # Parameter for the EP distribution
cvdm.select <- numeric(length(p)) # Empty vector to store the % of times
                                  # the CVDM test selects OLS
mse.ols <- numeric(length(p)) # Empty vectors to store MSE
mse.mr <- numeric(length(p))

for(j in 1:length(p)){ # Start the j loop
gc() # Clear out RAM

for(i in 1:reps){ # Start the i loop
Y <- b0 + b1*X + rnormp(n, p = p[j]) # The true DGP, EP error
model.ols <- lm(Y ~ X) # Estimate OLS model
model.mr <- rq(Y ~ X, tau = .5) # Estimate MR model

par.est.cvdm[i, 1] <- model.ols$coef[2] # Put the OLS estimate
                                         # in the first column
par.est.cvdm[i, 2] <- model.mr$coef[2] # Put the MR estimate
                                        # in the second column
# Store the CVDM test statistic
cvdm.stat[i] <- CVDM(Y ~ X, data = data.frame(Y, X))$cvjt
cat("Completed p =", j, "i =", i, "\n")
} # End the i loop

mse.ols[j] <- mean((par.est.cvdm[ , 1] - b1)^2) # MSE at each value of p
mse.mr[j] <- mean((par.est.cvdm[ , 2] - b1)^2)
# Compute the % of times the test selects OLS (cvdm.stat > 0)
cvdm.select[j] <- length(subset(cvdm.stat, cvdm.stat > 0))/reps
} # End the j loop
```

Figure 5.13 displays results from the simulations. Each point on the graph represents one set of the 1,000 simulated data sets. The x-axis plots the relative MSE of OLS to MR (i.e., MSE of OLS divided by MSE of MR). When this is equal to one, OLS and MR perform equally well. When it is less than one, OLS performed better, and when it is larger than one, MR performed better. The y-axis plots the percentage of times in those 1,000 data sets that the CVDM test selects OLS. If the test performed perfectly, the points should fall at 100% on the y-axis when relative MSE is less than one (i.e., always select OLS when OLS MSE is smaller than MR MSE) and 0% when relative MSE is larger than one (i.e., never select OLS when OLS MSE is larger). Gray sections of the graphs indicate areas in which the test makes an incorrect selection more than 50% of the time.

Figure 5.13 CVDM Test Performance at *n* = 50

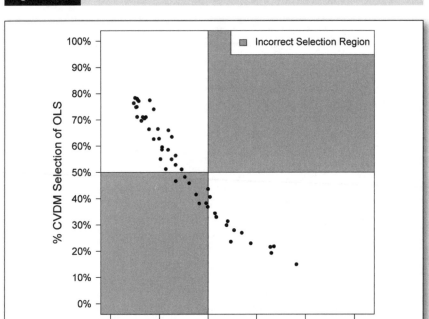

In general, the test selects the estimator with lower MSE much more often than not, though the graph shows that it does not perform perfectly. As Harden and Desmarais (2011) demonstrate, test performance improves dramatically as the sample size increases.

More important for our purposes, this example demonstrates another utility of simulation. Previously we have used simulation to evaluate the impact of estimating OLS with data that did not conform to one of the assumptions of OLS. In several instances, we went further to use simulation to evaluate some proposed fixes to these problems largely within the OLS framework. In this simulation, we compared two different estimators of the conditional central tendency of a dependent variable, and then used simulation not to evaluate those estimators themselves, but rather to evaluate a test proposed in the literature designed to help researchers choose between the two estimators. Evaluating the performance of a statistical test is a very common and very powerful use of Monte Carlo simulation. While we do not do so here, this simulation could be extended to evaluation of the CVDM test's performance under different conditions (e.g., sample size, number of independent variables, or others) to generalize our assessment of its performance on a wider range of actual data sets.

5.4 CONCLUSIONS

We covered a lot of ground in this chapter. We imagine (and hope) that readers will go back through different sections of this chapter more than once. We began with an overview of the evaluation of statistical estimators and discussed how to measure estimator performance in a simulation context. We then put these measures and principles from the first chapters to use conducting simulations with the linear model. These simulations have illustrated key principles about the linear model, with a particular focus on OLS assumption violations. We have also seen how simulation can be used to compare competing estimators and its usefulness in evaluating whether a sample-based statistical test performs well.

The linear model is good for illustrating these principles because it is widely studied, based on strong statistical theory, widely taught in applied quantitative methods courses, and relatively easy to simulate. However, there is a wide range of statistical models that are or should be in most social scientists' toolkits. We focus on several GLMs in the next chapter, including those for binary, count, and duration-dependent variables. We show that the same basic simulation principles we have developed so far can also be used for those models. Because some of our simulations will be getting more demanding, we also discuss some computational issues that arise with simulation. You may have already noticed that some of the simulations in this chapter (such as the last one) can take a long time to run. We provide some strategies for dealing with this problem.

6

Simulating Generalized Linear Models

6.1 INTRODUCTION

In the previous chapter, we dug much deeper into simulations, choosing to focus on the standard linear model for all the reasons we discussed. However, most social scientists study processes that do not conform to the assumptions of OLS. Thus, most social scientists must use a wide array of other models in their research. Still, they could benefit greatly from conducting simulations with them. In this chapter, we discuss several models that are extensions of the linear model called generalized linear models (GLMs). We focus on how to simulate their DGPs and evaluate the performance of estimators designed to recover those DGPs. Specifically, we examine binary, ordered, unordered, count, and duration GLMs. These models are not quite as straightforward as OLS because the dependent variables are not continuous and unbounded. As we show below, this means we need to use a slightly different strategy to combine our systematic and stochastic components when simulating the data. None of these examples are meant to be complete accounts of the models; readers should have some familiarity beforehand.[1]

After showing several GLM examples, we close this chapter with a brief discussion of general computational issues that arise when conducting simulations. You will find that several of the simulations we illustrate in this chapter take much longer to run than did those from the previous chapter. As the DGPs get more demanding to simulate, the statistical estimators become more computationally demanding, and the simulation studies we want to conduct increase in complexity, we can quickly find ourselves doing projects that require additional resources. We consider when it is advantageous to use research computing clusters and/or parallel processing. We also show a basic example of parallel processing. We look at how to distribute the workload of a simulation across multiple cores of a computer (this can be done on most modern desktops or laptops). As we will see, this can considerably reduce the time it takes to complete a simulation.

---

[1] For lengthier treatments of these models see Faraway (2006), Gelman and Hill (2007), Greene (2011), King (1998), or Long (1997).

6.2 SIMULATING OLS AS A PROBABILITY MODEL

Although OLS is typically taught through its analytic solution using matrix algebra, it can also be estimated by ML, which makes more clear the connections between OLS, GLMs, and probability theory. ML is a general method of estimating the unknown parameters of a statistical model using a sample of data.[2] We assume that the outcome we are interested in studying follows some probability distribution that has one or more unknown parameters that we want to estimate. In the OLS case, we assume a normal distribution with parameters μ and σ. Instead of thinking of the error term as taking on a normal distribution, we now think of the dependent variable as being normally distributed, and we think of the independent variables informing estimates of μ and/or σ.

To see this more clearly, consider the OLS model as we have seen it to this point. The dependent variable (Y) is a function of an intercept (β_0), coefficients operating on independent variables (β and X, respectively), and an error term that follows a normal distribution by assumption (ε).

$$
\begin{aligned}
Y &= \beta_0 + \beta X_1 + \beta_2 X_2 + \cdots + \varepsilon \\
&\quad \varepsilon \sim \mathcal{N}(0, \sigma)
\end{aligned}
\tag{6.1}
$$

Another way to define this same model is to write Y as following a normal distribution.

$$
\begin{aligned}
Y &\sim \mathcal{N}(\mu, \sigma) \\
\mu &= \beta_0 + \beta_1 X_1 + \beta_2 X_2
\end{aligned}
\tag{6.2}
$$

In this representation, we see that Y is normally distributed with the mean (μ) and a constant standard deviation (σ). The second line of the model expresses μ as equal to the sum of the coefficients multiplied by the independent variables (often called the "linear predictor"). In other words, the dependent variable is explicitly written as following a probability distribution with its mean set to a linear combination of coefficients and independent variables rather than having such a distribution "attached" to the end of the equation via an error term.

This is important to point out because the dependent variables in other types of models are assumed to follow other distributions. Thus, creating a DGP for these kinds of dependent variables is not as straightforward as adding random noise to the end of an equation. For example, to simulate a binary dependent variable model (e.g., logistic regression), we need to produce a dependent variable that takes on only the values of 0 or 1. We cannot do this by simply adding `rnorm()` to the end of the equation. Instead, we will use a function to link the systematic portion of the model to the probability parameter of the Bernoulli distribution, which we then use to generate a series of Bernoulli trials (e.g., "coin flips"), producing the 0s and 1s for our observed dependent variable. In the case of OLS, this

---

[2]In fact, ML can be thought of as a general theory of inference (see King, 1998).

function is called the "identity," which means we leave the model's linear predictor unchanged to produce the normal distribution's μ parameter.

The main consequence of making this change for simulation studies is that we will generate the DGP in R in a slightly different way. Recall that our simulations to this point have included some variant of the following lines, used to produce the dependent variable, Y.[3]

```
b0 <- .2 # True value for the intercept
b1 <- .5 # True value for the slope
n <- 1000 # Sample size
X <- runif(n, -1, 1) # Create a sample of n observations on the
                     # independent variable X

Y <- b0 + b1*X + rnorm(n, 0, 1) # The true DGP, with N(0, 1) error
```

We can produce this exact same result by writing the code for the last line as follows. This produces Y using only the rnorm() command with the systematic component of the model substituted for μ.

```
Y <- rnorm(n, b0 + b1*X, 1) # The true DGP, Y ~ N(mu, sigma)
```

You can substitute this second line in the first version in the basic OLS simulation from Chapter 1 to check their equivalence. We did so. Below is the first six rows of the results matrix produced using the original code to generate Y (the first block of code above). Recall that the first and second columns are the estimates of β_0 and β_1, respectively, and the third and fourth columns are the standard errors of β_0 and β_1, respectively. Recall also that we defined b0 = 0.2, b1 = 0.5, and X is drawn from a uniform distribution bounded by -1 and 1.

```
head(par.est)
          [,1]       [,2]       [,3]       [,4]
[1,] 0.2025988 0.4388826 0.03167166 0.05497156
[2,] 0.2109310 0.4665079 0.03173455 0.05508072
[3,] 0.2218581 0.5508824 0.03124873 0.05423750
[4,] 0.2417893 0.5583468 0.03227737 0.05602289
[5,] 0.1927056 0.5097159 0.03146897 0.05461976
[6,] 0.2133593 0.5549790 0.03166222 0.05495519
```

The results using the new approach from the code above are identical. We encourage you to try this to see it for yourself.

```
head(par.est)
          [,1]       [,2]       [,3]       [,4]
[1,] 0.2025988 0.4388826 0.03167166 0.05497156
[2,] 0.2109310 0.4665079 0.03173455 0.05508072
```

---

[3]Note that this is NOT the complete code needed for the simulation.

```
[3,]  0.2218581  0.5508824  0.03124873  0.05423750
[4,]  0.2417893  0.5583468  0.03227737  0.05602289
[5,]  0.1927056  0.5097159  0.03146897  0.05461976
[6,]  0.2133593  0.5549790  0.03166222  0.05495519
```

In the rest of the simulations in this book, we will use this new approach to generate the dependent variable explicitly from a given probability distribution.

6.3 SIMULATING GLMS

Having seen the DGP assumed by OLS constructed explicitly from its assumed probability distribution, we now turn to simulating other types of DGPs and evaluating different statistical models designed to recover them. In each one, we use the same basic strategy. We link the systematic component of the model—which we keep the same as in Chapter 5—to the mean of a probability distribution, then draw our dependent variable from that distribution. We can then evaluate the results as we have done in previous chapters.

6.3.1 Binary Models

We start with binary models, where the dependent variable can take on two outcomes, usually coded 1 or 0. For example, a large literature in political science examines the determinants of voter turnout. Individual-level turnout involves one of two options: a person voted (1) or did not vote (0), which researchers then model as a function of several independent variables. Two of the most common models are the logistic regression (logit) and probit models. We simulate both below.

To create the DGP for a binary model, we need the systematic component of the DGP to influence whether an observation is a 1 or 0 on the dependent variable, but we still want to incorporate an element of randomness (e.g., the stochastic component). To do this, we use the `rbinom()` function to produce each observation's value for the dependent variable as a single Bernoulli trial (e.g., a coin flip). The systematic component of the model affects the probability of observing a 1. Importantly, this probability is different for each observation, based on its values of the independent variables. The stochastic component of the model comes from the fact that the systematic component only effects the probability of observing a 1, but does not determine it entirely. Even if the probability of an observation getting a 1 is 0.99, there is still a chance that a single realization will come up 0. The difference between the logit and probit models lies in exactly how the probabilities are computed.

Logit

The logit model we simulate is written as follows:

$$\Pr(Y = 1) = \text{logit}^{-1}(\beta_0 + \beta_1 X) \tag{6.3}$$

To compute the probability of observing a 1 (p) with logit, we use the inverse logit function (logit^{-1}), which is

$$\frac{\exp(p)}{1+\exp(p)} \tag{6.4}$$

Putting this all together, we can rewrite Equation 6.3 as

$$\Pr(Y=1) = \frac{\exp(\beta_0+\beta_1 X)}{1+\exp(\beta_0+\beta_1 X)} \tag{6.5}$$

Several packages in R have functions to do this computation, or we can create our own.

```
inv.logit <- function(p){
return(exp(p)/(1 + exp(p)))
}
```

This function takes the systematic component of the model and translates it into probabilities varying between 0 and 1. Each observation gets its own probability because each observation has different values on the independent variable(s). Here is an example for six observations. First, we define the true parameters b0 and b1, and the independent variable, X.

```
b0 <- .2 # True value for the intercept
b1 <- .5 # True value for the slope
n <- 1000 # Sample size
X <- runif(n, -1, 1) # Create a sample of n observations on the
                     # independent variable X
```

The first line below reports the first six observed values of X. The second line reports the expected probability that Y = 1 for those six values, given b0 = 0.2 and b1 = 0.5 in the population DGP.

```
head(X)
[1] 0.39876948 -0.17150942 -0.49228411 0.19624512 -0.03102461 -0.30160264

head(inv.logit(b0 + b1*X))
[1] 0.5985398 0.5285303 0.4884665 0.5739835 0.5459916 0.5122972
```

The next step is putting these probabilities into the rbinom() function to produce the dependent variable. The first argument is the number of random draws, which we set to the sample size because we want a draw of either 1 or 0 for each observation. The second argument is the number of trials. We set this number to 1 because each of the n observations in our data set is one single Bernoulli trial (one coin flip). Finally, the third argument is the probability of observing a 1 for each observation; we place our systematic component here. Again, this influences the chances of each observation coming up 1, but does not determine its value entirely.

```
Y <- rbinom(n, 1, inv.logit(b0 + b1*X)) # The true DGP Bernoulli trials
```

As a check to see that Y only takes on values of 0 or 1, you can use the `table()` function in R to produce a frequency table, like this:

```
table(Y)
Y
  0   1
477 523
```

In this particular example, where n was set equal to 1,000, we ended up with 477 values of 0 and 523 values of 1. If you repeat the code (without setting the seed), you would expect to get a slightly different number of 0s and 1s just due to random chance.

How we generate the dependent variable is the only major difference so far between this simulation and the OLS simulations we have done in the earlier chapters. To evaluate the logit model as an estimator of our parameters, we tell R to estimate a logit model instead of OLS using the `glm()` function rather than the `lm()` function. The full simulation code is below, including the inverse logit function and coverage probability function (see Chapter 5).

```
# Logit
# Inverse Logit Function
inv.logit <- function(p){
return(exp(p)/(1 + exp(p)))
}

# CP Function
coverage <- function(b, se, true, level = .95, df = Inf){ # Estimate,
                                                   # standard error,
                                                   # true parameter,
                                                   # confidence level,
                                                   # and df
qtile <- level + (1 - level)/2 # Compute the proper quantile
lower.bound <- b - qt(qtile, df = df)*se # Lower bound
upper.bound <- b + qt(qtile, df = df)*se # Upper bound
# Is the true parameter in the confidence interval? (yes = 1)
true.in.ci <- ifelse(true >= lower.bound & true <= upper.bound, 1, 0)
cp <- mean(true.in.ci) # The coverage probability
mc.lower.bound <- cp - 1.96*sqrt((cp*(1 - cp))/length(b)) # Monte Carlo error
mc.upper.bound <- cp + 1.96*sqrt((cp*(1 - cp))/length(b))
return(list(coverage.probability = cp, # Return results
        true.in.ci = true.in.ci,
        ci = cbind(lower.bound, upper.bound),
        mc.eb = c(mc.lower.bound, mc.upper.bound)))
}
```

```
set.seed(32945) # Set the seed for reproducible results

reps <- 1000 # Set the number of repetitions at the top of the script
par.est.logit <- matrix(NA, nrow = reps, ncol = 4) # Empty matrix to store
                                                   # the estimates
b0 <- .2 # True value for the intercept
b1 <- .5 # True value for the slope
n <- 1000 # Sample size
X <- runif(n, -1, 1) # Create a sample of n observations on the
                     # independent variable X

for(i in 1:reps){ # Start the loop
Y <- rbinom(n, 1, inv.logit(b0 + b1*X)) # The true DGP, Bernoulli trials
model <- glm(Y ~ X, family = binomial (link = logit)) # Estimate logit model
vcv <- vcov(model) # Variance-covariance matrix
par.est.logit[i, 1] <- model$coef[1]  # Put the estimate for the
                                      # intercept in the first column
par.est.logit[i, 2] <- model$coef[2]  # Put the estimate for the coefficient
                                      # on X in the second column
par.est.logit[i, 3] <- sqrt(diag(vcv)[1]) # SE of the intercept
par.est.logit[i, 4] <- sqrt(diag(vcv)[2]) # SE of the coefficient on X
} # End the loop
```

We can then assess results of this logit simulation in the same way that we did for the OLS simulation we conducted in Chapter 5 (e.g., plot histograms or density curves of the estimates, compute AB, MSE, or coverage probabilities). Figure 6.1 plots the distributions of the coefficient estimates. We can verify that our simulation worked because both sets of estimates are centered at the true parameter values. Additionally, the coverage probabilities show no problems: 0.956 (β_0) and 0.958 (β_1). Of course, now you could return to the DGP for this simulation and explore how any alterations to it affect the logit estimator's ability to accurately and efficiently recover the parameters of the underlying DGP.

Probit

In the probit model, the probability of observing a 1 is assumed to come from the normal CDF instead of the inverse logit. To simulate a probit model, we simply replace the inv.logit() function with pnorm() function (recall that this computes the normal CDF) in our DGP. Then, we must set the link function to probit in the glm() function to estimate the probit model rather than the logit model.

```
# Probit
set.seed(3295255) # Set the seed for reproducible results

reps <- 1000 # Set the number of repetitions at the top of the script
par.est.probit <- matrix(NA, nrow = reps, ncol = 4) # Empty matrix to store
                                                    # the estimates
```

```
b0 <- .2 # True value for the intercept
b1 <- .5 # True value for the slope
n <- 1000 # Sample size
X <- runif(n, -1, 1) # Create a sample of n observations on the
                     # independent variable X

for(i in 1:reps){ # Start the loop
Y <- rbinom(n, 1, pnorm(b0 + b1*X)) # The true DGP, Bernoulli trials
model <- glm(Y ~ X, family = binomial (link = probit)) # Estimate probit model
vcv <- vcov(model) # Variance-covariance matrix
par.est.probit[i, 1] <- model$coef[1]  # Put the estimate for the
                                        # intercept in the first column
par.est.probit[i, 2] <- model$coef[2]  # Put the estimate for the coefficient
                                        # on X in the second column
par.est.probit[i, 3] <- sqrt(diag(vcv)[1]) # SE of the intercept
par.est.probit[i, 4] <- sqrt(diag(vcv)[2]) # SE of the coefficient on X
} # End the loop
```

Figure 6.1 Histograms of 1,000 Simulated Logit β_0 and β_1 Estimates

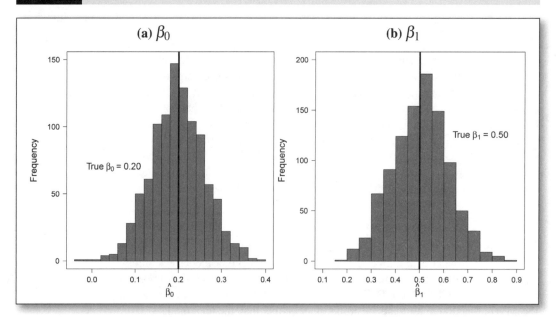

We can then assess results as usual. Again, we see that the means of the estimates are very close to the true values, and the coverage probabilities are near 0.95. Now that you know how to simulate a proper DGP for the probit model, you can explore how changes to that DGP affect the results produced by your simulation.

```
mean(par.est.probit[ , 1]) # Mean of intercept estimates
[1] 0.2007092
mean(par.est.probit[ , 2]) # Mean of coefficient on X estimates
[1] 0.4996981
# Coverage probability for the intercept
coverage(par.est.probit[ , 1], par.est.probit[ , 3], b0,
 df = n - model$rank)$coverage.probability
[1] 0.957
# Coverage probability for the coefficient on X
coverage(par.est.probit[ , 2], par.est.probit[ , 4], b1,
 df = n - model$rank)$coverage.probability
 [1] 0.942
```

6.3.2 Ordered Models

The ordered models we consider here represent extensions of the binary models we presented in the last section. Ordered models allow for more than two categories on the dependent variable to be observed, but with a rank ordering to those categories. An example could be a survey question that asks respondents how often they feel angry about their job, with answer choices "never," "seldom," "often," or "every day." This variable has four categories with a clear ordering. We can use an ordered logit or ordered probit model to estimate the effect of an independent variable on the probability of a respondent falling into the available categories.

To simulate an ordered model, we use a *latent variable* interpretation of the dependent variable.[4] The idea behind this interpretation is that we would prefer to measure the dependent variable of interest on a continuous scale and then model it as a linear function of one or more independent variables. However, the measure we have of the dependent variable only records whether respondents fall into one of several categories. We call the unobserved continuous measure Y^*. The observed dependent variable, Y, represents categories that each cover a range of this unobserved latent variable. Formally, labeling the cutpoints between the k categories τ_k, Y is defined as follows.[5]

$$Y = \begin{cases} 1 & \text{if } Y^* < \tau_1 \\ 2 & \text{if } \tau_1 \leq Y^* < \tau_2 \\ 3 & \text{if } \tau_2 \leq Y^* < \tau_3 \\ 4 & \text{if } \tau_3 \leq Y^* < \tau_4 \\ . \\ . \\ . \\ k & \text{if } Y^* \geq \tau_K \end{cases} \qquad (6.6)$$

---

[4]This same interpretation could also apply to the logit and probit models that we described in the previous section. See Long (1997) for an excellent presentation of the latent variable approach.

[5]Different texts use different Greek letters or other symbols to refer to these cutpoints, including μ, ς, and c. We follow Long's (1997) use of τ below. The R command polr() that we use in estimation refers to the cutpoints as zeta.

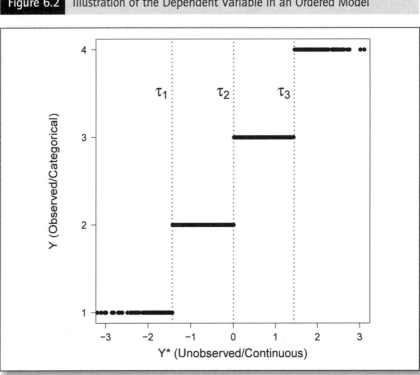

Figure 6.2   Illustration of the Dependent Variable in an Ordered Model

Figure 6.2 provides an example with simulated data. We plot Y^* on the x-axis and the four categories of Y on the y-axis. The three vertical dashed lines mark the three cutpoints that divide the values of Y^* into the four categories of Y. Notice that as Y^* increases, Y also increases, but there is some loss in precision— observations within the same category of Y have different values for Y^*.

In this example, we will simulate an ordered probit model, which assumes that the unobserved Y^* is normally distributed.[6] In this example, we will simulate one common systematic component of the model across all categories, which means that the effect of a change in X on the probability of a respondent moving from one category on Y to the next remains the same across all categories.[7] Just like the simulations for binary logit and probit, our task is to construct a DGP that

---

[6]We could use this same procedure to simulate ordered logit using the logistic distribution.

[7]By "same," we do not mean that the probability of being in any of the categories must be equal to each other—they do not. Rather, the best way to think about this assumption is that Y^* is assumed to be a linear function of X. This fulfills the proportional odds assumption (also called the "parallel regressions" assumption) of standard ordered models (see Long, 1997).

captures the probability of Y^* falling in a particular category given the location defined by the systematic component of a model plus its stochastic component. For the latent variable framework we present, what we need to do is generate random samples of Y^* and then assign those simulated values of Y^* to different categories of Y based on where those Y^* values are relative to the cutpoints. That means we need a method of defining those cutpoints.

Because Y^* is a latent variable—a variable we do not directly observe or measure—it has no defined scale. Thus, before we can estimate the model, we need to establish a scale for it. Specifically, we need to define a location and a variance for Y^*. To define the variance, we first need to define the probability distribution we assume for it, which for ordered models is typically either the normal or logistic distribution. We know by definition that the variance for the standard normal is equal to 1, while the variance for the standard logistic is equal to $\frac{\pi^2}{3}$. Thus, the variance of the stochastic portion Y^* will be either 1 (for a normal) or $\frac{\pi^2}{3}$ (for a logistic), which could be multiplied by some constant if you wanted to introduce more or less variance in the stochastic portion of Y^*. In fact, we were making these assumptions about the variance of the stochastic term when we estimated binary logit and probit models in the previous sections.

The location of Y^* can be set in a number of ways, two of which are most common. First, we could set one of the cutpoints equal to zero and then estimate the model's intercept term (β_0) and the rest of the cutpoints relative to the cutpoint fixed at zero. In fact, this is the default built into most binary logit and probit estimation routines in statistical software, including those we used above. In binary logit and probit, there is only one cutpoint anyway, so setting it to zero and estimating the intercept is common because that looks familiar to users of OLS and many other GLMs.

The second common alternative that many software programs use, including the R function we will use below, is to fix the intercept term at zero and then produce estimates of all of the cutpoints relative to that intercept. There is no right or wrong answer regarding which strategy to use—not even a better or worse. The intercept and the cutpoints cannot be estimated in absolute terms—they can only be estimated relative to each other. In other words, the model is not identified in a statistical sense without restricting one of these to zero. Importantly, the choice of which one to set at zero will not affect the *relative* estimates of the others. Most important, the choice of whether we set β_0 to zero or one of the τ parameters to zero has absolutely no effect on the estimate of our slope parameters, and it has absolutely no effect on our estimates of the probability of an observation falling into a given category of Y. In this simulation, we will set the intercept to zero and estimate the different cutpoints.

Because our statistical estimator is going to fix β_0 to zero and produce estimates of the cutpoints, we need a way to define those cutpoints in our DGP so that we can check to see if our estimator accurately recovers them. To determine the values of the cutpoints in the DGP, we need to define them relative to the probability distribution that Y^* follows. In other words, we need to know the expected population mean and variance of Y^* before we simulate the DGP for Y. We take advantage of a couple of shortcuts here to make the problem more tractable.

Remember that Y^* is the sum of a systematic and a stochastic component. As such, both the mean and the variance of Y^* will come from the means and variances of these two components. For this simulation, we will consider the ordered probit model, which means we know the stochastic component of the model will follow a normal distribution with a mean of zero and a constant variance. For this simulation, we are going to draw our values for X from a normal distribution as well (rather than the uniform distribution we have been using). Because the values of the β coefficients in the DGP are fixed, the systematic component of our DGP will also be normally distributed with a mean of $\beta_0 + \beta_1 X$ and a constant variance. If two random variables are each normally distributed, their sum will also be normally distributed, with the mean and variance defined as follows:

$$A \sim N(\mu_A, \sigma_A^2)$$
$$B \sim N(\mu_B, \sigma_B^2)$$
$$AB = A + B$$
$$AB \sim N(\mu_A + \mu_B, \sigma_A^2 + \sigma_B^2)$$

Thus, in this simulation, Y^* will be normally distributed with an expected mean equal to the mean of the systematic portion of the model, $\beta_0 + \beta_1 X$ plus zero (because the expected mean of the error is zero) and a variance equal to the variance of $\beta_0 + \beta_1 X$ plus whatever we set for the variance of the stochastic component of the model.

This allows us to use the quantiles associated with a normally distributed variable with a defined mean and variance to generate cutpoints for our DGP. Specifically, the qnorm() function in R will produce a quantile from a normal distribution for a defined probability, mean, and variance. For example, if you want to know the cutpoint on a normal distribution that separates the lower 25% of the distribution from the upper 75% of the distribution, and that normal distribution has a mean of 5 and a standard deviation of 7, you would type

```
qnorm(.25, mean = 5, sd = 7)
[1] 0.2785717
```

This returns a value of just over 0.278. Now, we can finally do a simulation of an ordered probit model. In this example, we generate a dependent variable that will have four categories. Our DGP will assume that 10% of the observations fall in the first category, 40% fall in the second category, another 40% fall in the third category, and the last 10% fall in the fourth category.[8] We will use a single independent variable again, and we will set the intercept equal to zero in the DGP because the statistical estimator we use below will fix the intercept to zero and estimate the cutpoints. We will evaluate our simulation based on its ability to

---

[8]This distribution is defined for the DGP. Of course, the observed distribution of observations across the four categories will vary from sample to sample due to randomness.

recover the slope coefficient and the cutpoints. This first block of code defines several values and variables, including β_0, β_1, X, and our three cutpoints.

```
# Ordered Models
library(MASS)
set.seed(8732) # Set the seed for reproducible results

reps <- 1000 # Set the number of repetitions at the top of the script
par.est.oprobit <- matrix(NA, nrow = reps, ncol = 2) # Empty matrices to store
taus.oprobit <- matrix(NA, nrow = reps, ncol = 3) # the estimates
b0 <- 0 # True value for the intercept
b1 <- .5 # True value for the slope
n <- 1000 # Sample size
X <- rnorm(n, 0, 1) # Create a sample of n observations on the
                    # independent variable X

XB <- b0 + b1*X # Systematic component
sd.error <- 1 # SD of the error of the unobserved Y*
# Define the true cutpoints
tau1 <- qnorm(.1, mean = mean(XB), sd = sqrt(var(XB) + sd.error^2))
tau2 <- qnorm(.5, mean = mean(XB), sd = sqrt(var(XB) + sd.error^2))
tau3 <- qnorm(.9, mean = mean(XB), sd = sqrt(var(XB) + sd.error^2))
```

Next, inside the `for` loop we generate the object `Y.star`, the unobserved dependent variable. We create this using the `rnorm()` function in the same way as if we were simulating an OLS model.[9] Then, we generate the observed dependent variable, `Y`, such that observations of Y^* falling below the first cutpoint, τ_1, get coded as 1, those between τ_1 and τ_2 get coded as 2, those between τ_2 and τ_3 get coded as 3, and those above τ_3 get coded as 4. We do this in R by using the square brackets and the logical operators from Table 4.2. For example, the code `Y[Y.star < tau1] <- 1` means "for observations in which `Y.star` is less than the object `tau1`, code `Y` as a 1."

```
for(i in 1:reps){ # Start the loop
Y.star <- rnorm(n, XB, sd.error) # The unobserved Y*
Y <- rep(NA, n) # Define Y as a vector of NAs with length n
Y[Y.star < tau1] <- 1 # Set Y equal to a value according to Y.star
Y[Y.star >= tau1 & Y.star < tau2] <- 2
Y[Y.star >= tau2 & Y.star < tau3] <- 3
Y[Y.star >= tau3] <- 4
```

Then, we need to tell R to estimate an ordered probit model, which we can do with the `polr()` function from the MASS package.

```
model <- polr(as.ordered(Y) ~ X, method = "probit", Hess = TRUE)
```

---

[9]If we wanted to simulate ordered logit, we would use the `rlogis()` function.

We add a few options to this code. First, we wrap the `as.ordered()` function around the dependent variable to tell R that it should treat it as an ordered variable. Additionally, notice that the `polr()` function takes the argument `method`, which we set to `"probit"` for an ordered probit model (type `?polr` for other options). Finally, `Hess = TRUE` tells R that we want to produce the standard errors. The complete simulation code is below. Note that we also create an empty matrix called `par.est.oprobit` to store the estimates of β_1 and its standard error, and a second empty matrix called `taus.oprobit` to store the estimates of the cutpoints from the simulation.

```
# Ordered Models
library(MASS)
set.seed(8732) # Set the seed for reproducible results

reps <- 1000 # Set the number of repetitions at the top of the script
par.est.oprobit <- matrix(NA, nrow = reps, ncol = 2) # Empty matrices to store
taus.oprobit <- matrix(NA, nrow = reps, ncol = 3)   # the estimates
b0 <- 0 # True value for the intercept
b1 <- .5 # True value for the slope
n <- 1000 # Sample size
X <- rnorm(n, 0, 1) # Create a sample of n observations on the
                    # independent variable X


XB <- b0 + b1*X # Systematic component
sd.error <- 1 # SD of the error of the unobserved Y*
# Define the true cutpoints
tau1 <- qnorm(.1, mean = mean(XB), sd = sqrt(var(XB) + sd.error^2))
tau2 <- qnorm(.5, mean = mean(XB), sd = sqrt(var(XB) + sd.error^2))
tau3 <- qnorm(.9, mean = mean(XB), sd = sqrt(var(XB) + sd.error^2))


for(i in 1:reps){ # Start the loop
Y.star <- rnorm(n, XB, sd.error) # The unobserved Y*
Y <- rep(NA, n) # Define Y as a vector of NAs with length n
Y[Y.star < tau1] <- 1 # Set Y equal to a value according to Y.star
Y[Y.star >= tau1 & Y.star < tau2] <- 2
Y[Y.star >= tau2 & Y.star < tau3] <- 3
Y[Y.star >= tau3] <- 4
# Estimate ordered model
model <- polr(as.ordered(Y) ~ X, method = "probit", Hess = TRUE)
vcv <- vcov(model) # Variance-covariance matrix
par.est.oprobit[i, 1] <- model$coef[1]  # Put the estimate for the coefficient
                                         # on X in the second column
par.est.oprobit[i, 2] <- sqrt(diag(vcv)[1]) # SE of the coefficient on X
taus.oprobit[i, ] <- model$zeta
cat("Just completed iteration", i, "\n")
} # End the loop
```

We can check the results by computing the mean of the vector of simulated estimates of β_1, the means of the estimated cutpoints (τ_1, τ_2, and τ_3), and the coverage probability for the standard error of β_1. All of these quantities are very close to their true values.

```
mean(par.est.oprobit[ , 1]) # Mean of coefficient on X estimates
[1] 0.5020573

# Compare the actual taus to the means of the tau estimates
data.frame(True = c(tau1, tau2, tau3),
 Estimated = apply(taus.oprobit, 2, mean))
          True     Estimated
1 -1.429516141  -1.430006071
2  0.006193689   0.009096949
3  1.441903520   1.445353416

# Coverage probability for the coefficient on X
coverage(par.est.oprobit[ , 1], par.est.oprobit[ , 2], b1,
 df = n - length(c(coef(model), model$zeta)))$coverage.probability
[1] 0.944
```

6.3.3 Multinomial Models

Multinomial models also have dependent variables that consist of more than two categories, but there is no inherent rank–order relationship between the categories. For example, a prospective homeowner may receive financial assistance for a down payment on the home from a family member, a community grant program, or an employer. There is no ordering from "less" to "more" among these outcomes as there are with ordered variables. A model such as multinomial logit (MNL) or multinomial probit (MNP) can be used to estimate the probability of observing one of the outcomes given the independent variables.[10] In this section, we will focus on MNL.

A distinguishing feature of MNL is that for K possible outcomes, it estimates $K - 1$ sets of coefficients on the independent variable(s)—treating one category as a baseline and estimating sets of coefficients comparing each of the other categories with that baseline category. One way to conceptualize MNL is as a series of logit models connected together, one for each outcome (hence the multiple sets of coefficients).[11] Recall that our inverse logit function produced expected probabilities of observing a 1 with the logit model by computing $\dfrac{\exp(\beta_0 + \beta_1 X)}{1 + \exp(\beta_0 + \beta_1 X)}$.

---

[10]See Kropko (2008) for a simulation study that compares MNL to MNP.

[11]A distinguishing feature of this model is the IIA assumption, which stands for "independence of irrelevant alternatives." Briefly, this means that the relative probabilities between two outcome categories do not change if another outcome category is introduced. Consider a group of people deciding on which restaurant to choose for lunch. If the chance of selecting Restaurant A over Restaurant B changes when Restaurant C becomes a possibility, IIA is violated.

We can compute expected probabilities for multiple logit models by adding multiple systematic components to that formula. For example, consider a dependent variable, Y, with three outcomes (A, B, or C) and Category C as the baseline category. The probability of Outcome A can be written as follows.[12]

$$\Pr(Y = A) = \frac{\exp(\beta_{0A} + \beta_{1A} X)}{1 + \exp(\beta_{0A} + \beta_{1A} X) + \exp(\beta_{0B} + \beta_{1B} X)} \tag{6.7}$$

Notice that there are different coefficients for Outcome A (β_{0A}, β_{1A}) and Outcome B (β_{0B}, β_{1B}). The probability of Outcome B is defined similarly.

$$\Pr(Y = B) = \frac{\exp(\beta_{0B} + \beta_{1B} X)}{1 + \exp(\beta_{0A} + \beta_{1A} X) + \exp(\beta_{0B} + \beta_{1B} X)} \tag{6.8}$$

Finally, we take advantage of the fact that the probabilities of the three outcomes must sum to 1 (i.e., the three outcomes are mutually exclusive and exhaustive). That means the probability of Outcome C is relatively straightforward.

$$\Pr(Y = C) = 1 - \Pr(Y = A) - \Pr(Y = B) \tag{6.9}$$

To simulate this type of dependent variable, we need to make a few changes to our code. First, we need to set true values of the coefficients for two of the outcomes (remember, one outcome is used as a baseline category). Instead of just b0 and b1, we create b0A and b1A for Outcome A and b0B and b1B for Outcome B.

```
# Unordered Models
library(Zelig)
set.seed(45262) # Set the seed for reproducible results

reps <- 1000 # Set the number of repetitions at the top of the script
par.est.mnl <- matrix(NA, nrow = reps, ncol = 4) # Empty matrix to store
                                                 # the estimates
b0A <- .2 # True values for the intercepts
b0B <- -.2
b1A <- .5 # True values for the slopes
b1B <- .75
n <- 1000 # Sample size
X <- runif(n, -1, 1) # Create a sample of n observations on the
                     # independent variable X
```

Next, outside the for loop we compute the probabilities from these coefficients using Equations 6.7 to 6.9. This can be done outside the for loop because these

---

[12]The "1" appears in the denominator because the linear predictor of the baseline category (C) is set to zero, and $\exp(0) = 1$.

probabilities only represent the systematic component of the model (which is the same in every repetition of the simulation), not the stochastic component.

```
# Compute the probabilities of each outcome based on the DGP
pA <- exp(b0A + b1A*X)/(1 + exp(b0A + b1A*X) + exp(b0B + b1B*X))
pB <- exp(b0B + b1B*X)/(1 + exp(b0A + b1A*X) + exp(b0B + b1B*X))
pC <- 1 - pA - pB
```

The next step is to combine the systematic and stochastic components inside the `for` loop to create the dependent variable. To do this, we use the `sample()` function inside a separate `for` loop that iterates through every observation in the sample. For each observation, we draw a "sample" of length 1 from the letters A, B, and C with replacement (i.e., each observation gets an A, B, or C for the dependent variable). Importantly, we make use of the `prob` argument within the `sample()` function to define the probabilities of getting an A, B, or C for each observation. We use the `for` loop to iterate through each observation because these probabilities are unique to each observation based on the independent variable(s) from the systematic portion of the model.

```
for(i in 1:reps){ # Start the loop
Y <- rep(NA, n) # Define Y as a vector of NAs with length n
for(j in 1:n){ # Create the dependent variable in another loop
Y[j] <- sample(c("A", "B", "C"), 1, replace = TRUE,
prob = c(pA[j], pB[j], pC[j]))
}
```

For example, the code below shows the result of `sample()` for the first observation and the 983rd observation in the last data set in the simulation below. The probabilities of each outcome are about 0.41 (Outcome A), 0.30 (Outcome B), and 0.29 (Outcome C) for Observation #1. In this case, Outcome A was drawn. The probabilities of each outcome for Observation #983 are 0.39, 0.25, and 0.36, respectively. In that case, Outcome B was chosen even though it had the lowest probability of the three options.

```
# Observation 1
c(pA[1], pB[1], pC[1])
[1] 0.4127436 0.3001694 0.2870870
Y[1]
[1] "A"

# Observation 983
c(pA[983], pB[983], pC[983])
[1] 0.3931114 0.2503725 0.3565161
Y[983]
[1] "B"
```

The next step is to estimate the model and store the results as usual. The complete simulation code is below. Several packages will estimate MNL, including

Zelig. Similar to ordered models, it is helpful to wrap as.factor() around the dependent variable name to tell R that it is a factor variable (not ordered). Additionally, notice the use of the coefficients() function to store the coefficient estimates from the model.

```
# Unordered Models
library(Zelig)
set.seed(45262) # Set the seed for reproducible results

reps <- 1000 # Set the number of repetitions at the top of the script
par.est.mnl <- matrix(NA, nrow = reps, ncol = 4) # Empty matrix to store the
                                                 # estimates
b0A <- .2 # True values for the intercepts
b0B <- -.2
b1A <- .5 # True values for the slopes
b1B <- .75
n <- 1000 # Sample size
X <- runif(n, -1, 1) # Create a sample of n observations on the
                     # independent variable X
# Compute the probabilities of each outcome based on the DGP
pA <- exp(b0A + b1A*X)/(1 + exp(b0A + b1A*X) + exp(b0B + b1B*X))
pB <- exp(b0B + b1B*X)/(1 + exp(b0A + b1A*X) + exp(b0B + b1B*X))
pC <- 1 - pA - pB

for(i in 1:reps){ # Start the loop
Y <- rep(NA, n) # Define Y as a vector of NAs with length n
for(j in 1:n){ # Create the dependent variable in another loop
Y[j] <- sample(c("A", "B", "C"), 1, replace = TRUE,
prob = c(pA[j], pB[j], pC[j]))
  }

# Estimate a MNL model
model <- zelig(as.factor(Y) ~ X, model = "mlogit",
  data = data.frame(Y, X), cite = FALSE)
vcv <- vcov(model) # Variance-covariance matrix
par.est.mnl[i, 1] <- coefficients(model)[3] # Coefficient on X, outcome 1
par.est.mnl[i, 2] <- coefficients(model)[4] # Coefficient on X, outcome 2
par.est.mnl[i, 3] <- sqrt(diag(vcv)[3]) # SE of coefficient on X, outcome 1
par.est.mnl[i, 4] <- sqrt(diag(vcv)[4]) # SE of coefficient on X, outcome 2
cat("Just completed iteration", i, "\n")
} # End the loop
```

As before, we can then examine the results to check that our estimates come close to the true DGP. Generally, the results look good, though the mean of the estimate on β_{1B} is a bit off the true value of 0.75 (mean of 0.757). Of course, this is due to random chance. We ran the simulation again with the number of repetitions set to 10,000 and came up with a mean of 0.75.

```
# Mean of coefficients on X estimates
mean(par.est.mnl[ , 1]) # Outcome 1
[1] 0.5011012
mean(par.est.mnl[ , 2]) # Outcome 2
[1] 0.7565751

# Coverage probabilities for the coefficients on X
# Outcome 1
coverage(par.est.mnl[ , 1], par.est.mnl[ , 3], b1A,
 df =n - length(coef(model)))$coverage.probability
[1] 0.949
# Outcome 2
coverage(par.est.mnl[ , 2], par.est.mnl[ , 4], b1B,
 df = n - length(coef(model)))$coverage.probability
[1] 0.958
```

6.4 EXTENDED EXAMPLES

The examples we have shown so far in this chapter have been relatively similar to each other and to the OLS examples from the previous chapters. We create the DGP of a particular estimator, generate data from that DGP many times, estimate the model on each simulated data set, then check to see if we accurately recovered the true DGP through the estimator. We kept things relatively simple in each simulation by not violating any of the assumptions of the models we explored. We encourage interested readers to expand and refine these simulations for other analyses, possibly exploring changes to the DGPs and observing how the various models perform. However, simulation is also a valuable tool for better understanding problems that arise in real data and comparing the ability of competing estimators to handle them. We show examples of this below.

6.4.1 Ordered or Multinomial?

Ordered and multinomial models are similar in the sense that the dependent variables are each composed of a finite number of categories. The difference is that ordered models assume there truly is an ordered structure to those categories, while the DGP of the multinomial model is assumed to have no inherent ordering. This leads to the question of consequences for violating these assumptions. What would happen if we estimated a multinomial model on a dependent variable that is truly ordered or an ordered model on a dependent variable that is truly unordered?

In his book *Regression Models for Categorical and Limited Dependent Variables*, Long (1997) provides the following answer to these questions:

> If a dependent variable is ordinal and a model for nominal variables [e.g., multinomial logit] is used, there is a loss of efficiency since information is being ignored. On the other hand, when a method for ordinal variables [e.g., ordered logit] is applied to a nominal dependent variable, the resulting estimates are biased or even nonsensical (p. 149).

We can validate Long's assertions with a simulation. We will create two different DGPs with one independent variable—one DGP in which the dependent variable is ordered and one in which it is unordered—then estimate an ordered logit and a multinomial logit on each of these dependent variables (four models in total). For each of the four models, we will compute the change in expected probability for each category associated with moving from the minimum to the maximum value of the independent variable (e.g., the marginal effect of X).[13]

The first part of the code is given below. It is adapted from the last two examples, but in this case, both the ordered and unordered dependent variables are created with three numeric categories (1, 2, and 3). We create both with numeric categories so that we can estimate an ordered model on each. If we generated the unordered dependent variable as "A," "B," and "C," the ordered model would produce an error. Also, we create the object d.pp, which is a group of matrices (called an array), to store changes in expected probabilities estimated from the models (see below).

```
# Ordered vs. MNL
library(Zelig)
set.seed(99999)

reps <- 1000 # Set the number of repetitions at the top of the script
d.pp <- array(NA, c(4, 3, reps)) # Empty array to store
                                 # simulated change in probabilities

# Ordered logit model DGP
b0 <- 0 # True value for the intercept
b1 <- .5 # True value for the slope
n <- 1000 # Sample size
X <- runif(n, -1, 1) # Create a sample of n observations on the
                     # independent variable X

# MNL model DGP
b0A <- .2 # True values for the intercepts
b0B <- -.2
b1A <- .5 # True values for the slopes
b1B <- .75
n <- 1000 # Sample size

# Compute the probabilities of each outcome based on the DGP
pA <- exp(b0A + b1A*X)/(1 + exp(b0A + b1A*X) + exp(b0B + b1B*X))
pB <- exp(b0B + b1B*X)/(1 + exp(b0A + b1A*X) + exp(b0B + b1B*X))
pC <- 1 - pA - pB
```

---

[13]We cannot directly compare coefficients between ordered and unordered models because the former produces one set of coefficients and the other produces multiple sets of coefficients (one for each category minus the baseline category).

```
for(i in 1:reps){
# Ordered dependent variable
Y.star <- rlogis(n, b0 + b1*X, 1) # The unobserved Y*
# Define the true cutpoints
tau1 <- quantile(Y.star, .25)
tau2 <- quantile(Y.star, .75)
Y.o <- rep(NA, n) # Define Y as a vector of NAs with length n
Y.o[Y.star < tau1] <- 1 # Set Y equal to a value according to Y.star
Y.o[Y.star >= tau1 & Y.star < tau2] <- 2
Y.o[Y.star >= tau2] <- 3
# Ordered data
o.data <- data.frame(Y.o, X) # Put the data in a data frame

# Unordered dependent variable
Y.m <- rep(NA, n) # Define Y as a vector of NAs with length n
for(j in 1:n){ # Create the dependent variable in another loop
Y.m[j] <- sample(1:3, 1, replace = TRUE, prob = c(pA[j], pB[j], pC[j]))
}
# Unordered data
m.data <- data.frame(Y.m, X) # Put the data in a data frame
```

Next, we need to estimate an ordered logit and an MNL on *both* dependent variables. We use the `zelig()` command for both types of models.[14] The object names reflect the type of model and whether that model makes the "correct" assumption about the DGP. For example, `o.correct` is an ordered logit model of the dependent variable that is truly ordered. In contrast, `m.incorrect` is an MNL model of the dependent variable that is truly ordered.

```
# Estimate the models with the ordered dependent variable
o.correct <- zelig(as.ordered(Y.o) ~ X, model = "ologit",
  data = o.data, cite = FALSE)
m.incorrect <- zelig(as.factor(Y.o) ~ X, model = "mlogit",
  data = o.data, cite = FALSE)

# Estimate the models with the multinomial dependent variable
m.correct <- zelig(as.factor(Y.m) ~ X, model = "mlogit",
  data = m.data, cite = FALSE)
o.incorrect <- zelig(as.ordered(Y.m) ~ X, model = "ologit",
  data = m.data, cite = FALSE)
```

Recall that ordered models assume that one set of coefficients characterizes the effect of the independent variables on the dependent variable, regardless of the category (the proportional odds or parallel regressions assumption). In contrast, multinomial models estimate a different set of coefficients for all but one of the categories. As a result, the coefficients from the two types of models are not directly comparable to each other.

---

[14]The `zelig()` command uses `polr()` to conduct the estimation, but makes computing changes in expected probabilities easier.

However, we can compare changes in the expected probability of each category computed from each model. The `Zelig` package allows this to be done with the `setx()` and `sim()` commands. We discuss these commands in more detail in Chapter 9, but for now the basic idea is that we can set the independent variable to some values (in this case, the minimum and maximum), and simulate the change in expected probability for each category moving between those two values. We store these values in the array `d.pp`. Recall from above that an array is a group of matrices. In this case, the object contains 1,000 matrices (one for each repetition in the simulation) with four rows and three columns each. In each iteration of the `for` loop, a matrix in `d.pp` is filled with the change in expected probability of each of the three categories (columns) for each of the four models (rows).[15]

```
# Set X to its minimum and maximum for each model
x.oc <- setx(o.correct, X = min(X)) # For o.correct
x.oc1 <- setx(o.correct, X = max(X))

x.mi <- setx(m.incorrect, X = min(X)) # For m.incorrect
x.mi1 <- setx(m.incorrect, X = max(X))

x.mc <- setx(m.correct, X = min(X)) # For m.correct
x.mc1 <- setx(m.correct, X = max(X))

x.oi <- setx(o.incorrect, X = min(X)) # For o.incorrect
x.oi1 <- setx(o.incorrect, X = max(X))

# Compute the change in expected probabilities of falling in each category
# when moving from the minimum to the maximum of X
sim.oc <- sim(o.correct, x = x.oc, x1 = x.oc1)$qi$fd
sim.mi <- sim(m.incorrect, x = x.mi, x1 = x.mi1)$qi$fd
sim.mc <- sim(m.correct, x = x.mc, x1 = x.mc1)$qi$fd
sim.oi <- sim(o.incorrect, x = x.oi, x1 = x.oi1)$qi$fd
d.pp[1, , i] <- apply(sim.oc, 2, mean)
d.pp[2, , i] <- apply(sim.mi, 2, mean)
d.pp[3, , i] <- apply(sim.mc, 2, mean)
d.pp[4, , i] <- apply(sim.oi, 2, mean)
cat("Just completed iteration", i, "of", reps, "\n")
}
```

The final step is to compare the changes in expected probabilities. We know that those computed from the models `o.correct` and `m.correct` are, in fact, correct, because in each one the estimator's assumptions about the DGP match the truth. To assess Long's (1997) claim, we need to compare the results from `o.incorrect` and `m.incorrect` to `o.correct` and `m.correct`,

---

[15]Specifically, the objects `sim.oc`, `sim.mi`, `sim.mc`, and `sim.oi` hold 100 simulated changes in the expected probability for each category. We use the `apply()` command to compute the mean change in each of the three categories. See Chapter 9 for more details on this method, which we call "QI (quantities of interest) simulation."

respectively. In the last section of the code, we compute the means and standard deviations of the 1,000 sets of changes in the expected probability of each category (remember the `for` loop ran for 1,000 iterations). These quantities allow us to assess bias and efficiency, respectively.

```
# Compute the average change in probability
# for each of the four models
dpp.means <- rbind(apply(d.pp[1, , ], 1, mean),
  apply(d.pp[2, , ], 1, mean), apply(d.pp[3, , ], 1, mean),
  apply(d.pp[4, , ], 1, mean))
```

```
# Compute the SD of the change in probability
# for each of the four models
dpp.sds <- rbind(apply(d.pp[1, , ], 1, sd),
  apply(d.pp[2, , ], 1, sd), apply(d.pp[3, , ], 1, sd),
  apply(d.pp[4, , ], 1, sd))
```

We present these results in Table 6.1. The top half of the table gives the means of the 1,000 simulated changes in expected probability for each category computed by each model/dependent variable combination. The bottom half of the table reports the standard deviations of those simulated changes.

Table 6.1	Means and Standard Deviations of the Simulated Changes in Expected Probability for Each Category With Ordered Logit and MNL Models		

Category:	1	2	3
Means			
Ordered DV, Ordered Model	−0.1820	−0.0015	0.1835
Ordered DV, MNL Model	−0.1800	−0.0040	0.1840
Unordered DV, MNL Model	0.0718	0.1852	−0.2570
Unordered DV, Ordered Model	0.1668	−0.0107	−0.1561
Standard Deviations			
Ordered DV, Ordered Model	0.0364	0.0013	0.0370
Ordered DV, MNL Model	0.0442	0.0522	0.0453
Unordered DV, MNL Model	0.0508	0.0472	0.0459
Unordered DV, Ordered Model	0.0443	0.0056	0.0421

Note: The top half of the table gives the means of the 1,000 simulated changes in expected probability for each category computed by each model/dependent variable combination. The bottom half of the table reports the standard deviations of those simulated changes.

Beginning with the means, notice that when the dependent variable is truly ordered, the ordered model and MNL model produce changes in the expected probability of each category that are nearly identical. In contrast, when the dependent variable is truly unordered, the two models diverge considerably; the incorrect ordered model does not return the same changes in expected probabilities that the correct MNL model does. Moving to the standard deviations, notice that they are larger with the MNL model under both dependent variable scenarios. This is not surprising given that the MNL model estimates more parameters than does the ordered model, and thus uses more degrees of freedom.

In short, the results validate Long's (1997) claim. When the dependent variable is truly ordered, but a multinomial model is incorrectly used, no bias results (similar means), but there is a loss of efficiency (larger standard deviations for MNL). This is because the multinomial model is simply not using all of the available information (i.e., the ordered structure of Y), and so it estimates parameters that it does not need (coefficients for each category). In contrast, when an ordered model is applied to a truly unordered dependent variable, the corresponding changes in expected probabilities are biased because the estimator tries to impose an ordered structure that is not really there.

6.4.2 Count Models

We next move to a few examples of simulations with count models. Count models are used for dependent variables that take on positive integer values. Examples include the number of births at a hospital in a day or the number of patents awarded during some period. Count models allow the analyst to model such variables as a function of independent variables. A typical starting point for estimating the parameters of a count model is Poisson regression.

The Poisson Model

Recall from Chapter 2 that the Poisson distribution has one parameter, λ, which is both the mean and variance of the distribution. Poisson regression links the systematic portion of the model to a Poisson distribution through λ. It assumes the natural log of the dependent variable's expected value can be modeled by the sum of the independent variables multiplied by their coefficients.

$$\log[E(Y|X)] = \beta_0 + \beta_1 X_1 + \beta_2 X_2 \qquad (6.10)$$

Exponentiating both sides yields an expected mean of the dependent variable of

$$E(Y|X) = \exp(\beta_0 + \beta_1 X_1 + \beta_2 X_2) \qquad (6.11)$$

As with other examples from this chapter, the coefficients can be estimated by ML (see King, 1998). We can simulate such a model using the rpois() function. To produce the dependent variable, we set λ to the exponentiated systematic component of the model (because the dependent variable cannot be negative), as in `rpois(n, lambda = exp(b0 + b1*X))`. Everything else is exactly as we have seen before.

```
# Poisson
set.seed(3759) # Set the seed for reproducible results

reps <- 1000 # Set the number of repetitions at the top of the script
par.est.pois <- matrix(NA, nrow = reps, ncol = 4) # Empty matrix to store the
                                                  # estimates
b0 <- .2 # True value for the intercept
b1 <- .5 # True value for the slope
n <- 1000 # Sample size
X <- runif(n, -1, 1) # Create a sample of n observations on the
                     # independent variable X

for(i in 1:reps){ # Start the loop
Y <- rpois(n, exp(b0 + b1*X)) # The true DGP
model <- glm(Y ~ X, family = "poisson") # Estimate Poisson model
vcv <- vcov(model) # Variance-covariance matrix
par.est.pois[i, 1] <- model$coef[1] # Put the estimate for the intercept
                                    # in the first column
par.est.pois[i, 2] <- model$coef[2] # Put the estimate for the coefficient on
                                    # X in the second column
par.est.pois[i, 3] <- sqrt(diag(vcv)[1]) # SE of the intercept
par.est.pois[i, 4] <- sqrt(diag(vcv)[2]) # SE of the coefficient on X
} # End the loop

# Means of the coefficient estimates
mean(par.est.pois[ , 1]) # Intercept
[1] 0.2002308
mean(par.est.pois[ , 2]) # Coefficient on X
[1] 0.4988037

# Coverage probabilities
# Intercept
coverage(par.est.pois[ , 1], par.est.pois[ , 3], b0,
 df = model$rank)$coverage.probability
[1] 0.952
# Coefficient on X
coverage(par.est.pois[ , 2], par.est.pois[ , 4], b1,
 df = model$rank)$coverage.probability
[1] 0.948
```

The equivalence of the mean and variance in the Poisson distribution is an important limitation of the Poisson regression model because count processes in the social world often unfold such that the variance is larger than the mean, a phenomenon called overdispersion.[16] Several options exist to handle this problem, including the negative binomial model.

---

[16]Technically, what is most important is the comparison of the *conditional* mean and *conditional* variance. If the independent variables can account for the difference between the mean and variance of *Y*, the Poisson model is appropriate.

Comparing Poisson and Negative Binomial Models

The negative binomial (NB) is a more flexible approach to modeling count data because it can accommodate overdispersion through the estimation of a second parameter that allows the variance to be different from the mean. The NB model can be thought of as a "mixture" model because it combines the Poisson density with another density—the Gamma (see Cameron & Trivedi, 1998). Notice from the last simulation that we perfectly determined λ by setting it equal to the systematic component of the model. With NB, we set λ equal to the systematic portion plus a random component. This gives it a mean, μ, which is equal to the systematic component and a separate variance, υ.

$$\mu = \exp(\beta_0 + \beta_1 X_1 + \beta_2 X_2) \tag{6.12}$$

$$\upsilon = \mu + \frac{\mu^2}{\theta} \tag{6.13}$$

where θ is a dispersion parameter. The main point to keep in mind is that because there is a separate parameter for the variance, the NB is not adversely affected by overdispersion.

To illustrate the impact of overdispersion, we simulate overdispersed data, estimate Poisson and NB models, then compare the results. To simulate overdispersed count data we use the `rnbinom()` function, which takes the arguments `size`, which is the dispersion parameter in Equation 6.13, and `mu`, which is the mean. We set the dispersion parameter to 0.50 and the mean to the systematic component of the model. To see the difference in the data generated with and without overdispersion, compare the two panels of Figure 6.3. Panel (a) plots one simulated data set from the simulation above, which uses `rpois()` to produce Y. Panel (b) comes from data simulated with `rnbinom()`. In each graph, a solid line is placed at the mean of Y and a dashed line is placed at its variance. Notice that in Panel (a) the mean and variance are virtually identical, but in Panel (b) the variance is nearly six times the mean. Our next step is to assess the consequences of this difference for the Poisson and NB estimators.

The simulation code is below. We simulate Y with `rnbinom()`, then estimate the Poisson and NB models with `glm()` and `glm.nb()`, respectively. The `glm.nb()` function comes from the MASS package. We store the coefficients and standard errors for β_1.

```
# Poisson vs. Negative Binomial
library(MASS)
set.seed(763759) # Set the seed for reproducible results

reps <- 1000 # Set the number of repetitions at the top of the script
par.est.pnb <- matrix(NA, nrow = reps, ncol = 4) # Empty matrix to store the
                                                 # estimates
b0 <- .2 # True value for the intercept
```

```
b1 <- .5 # True value for the slope
n <- 1000 # Sample size
X <- runif(n, -1, 1) # Create a sample of n observations on the
                     # independent variable X

for(i in 1:reps){
Y <- rnbinom(n, size = .5, mu = exp(b0 + b1*X)) # Generate data with
                                                # overdispersion
model.p <- glm(Y ~ X, family = "poisson") # Estimate Poisson model
model.nb <- glm.nb(Y ~ X) # Estimate NB model
vcv.p <- vcov(model.p) # Variance-covariance matrices
vcv.nb <- vcov(model.nb)
par.est.pnb[i, 1] <- model.p$coef[2] # Store the results
par.est.pnb[i, 2] <- model.nb$coef[2]
par.est.pnb[i, 3] <- sqrt(diag(vcv.p)[2])
par.est.pnb[i, 4] <- sqrt(diag(vcv.nb)[2])
cat("Completed", i, "of", reps, "\n")
}
```

| Figure 6.3 | Dependent Variables From Poisson and Negative Binomial DGPs |

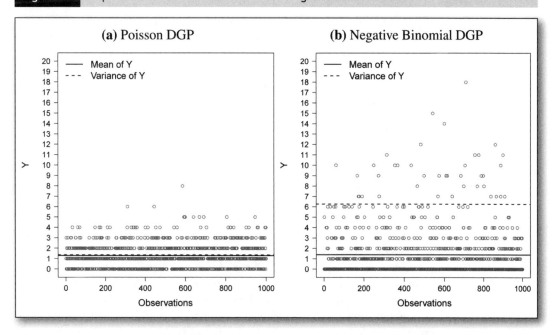

Textbook discussions of count models tell us that the Poisson model's coefficient estimates are consistent if overdispersion is the only problem, but that the standard errors are too small (Faraway, 2006). We can check this by computing the means of the simulated estimates, MSE, and coverage probabilities.

```
# Means of the coefficient on X estimates
mean(par.est.pnb[ , 1]) # Poisson estimates
[1] 0.4971698
mean(par.est.pnb[ , 2]) # NB estimates
[1] 0.4984487

# MSE
mean((par.est.pnb[ , 1])^2) # Poisson MSE
[1] 0.2560358
mean((par.est.pnb[ , 2])^2) # NB MSE
[1] 0.2572339

# Coverage probabilities
# Poisson SEs
coverage(par.est.pnb[ , 1], par.est.pnb[ , 3], b1,
df = n - model.p$rank)$coverage.probability
[1] 0.724
# NB SEs
coverage(par.est.pnb[ , 2], par.est.pnb[ , 4], b1,
df = n - model.nb$rank)$coverage.probability
[1] 0.946
```

The results show that both estimators produced coefficient estimates with means near the true value of 0.50. Additionally, MSE is very similar for both. However, the coverage probabilities show a big difference. The Poisson standard errors produce a coverage probability of 0.723 while the NB coverage probability is 0.946. Thus, when the data are overdispersed the Poisson model's assumptions produce estimates of coefficient variability (standard errors) that are too small.

Zero-Inflation Processes

Another possible issue with count models is having a large number of cases with the value of zero for Y. Many zeros may simply be a part of the true DGP governing all of the other counts (e.g., 1s, 2s, 3s, etc.), or the amount of zeros may be "inflated" by an additional process other than that which influences the counts that are greater than zero. In other words, the DGP may have two separate systematic processes: (1) a process influencing whether an observation produces a zero on the dependent variable or not, and (2) the actual count. One way of accounting for these two processes is with a zero-inflated count model. This type of model is actually two models in one—an equation predicting whether the observation is zero or nonzero (often with a binary model such as logit) and another equation predicting the expected count (done with a count model). Zero-inflation models work with both Poisson and NB; we will focus on the zero-inflated NB (ZINB) throughout this example.[17]

---

[17]There are also other means of handling zero inflation, such as dichotomizing the data or hurdle models (Cameron & Trivedi, 1998).

Underlying the choice between conventional count regression and zero-inflated modeling is the common tension between overfitting and successfully explaining empirical features of the data. This produces an important theoretical and empirical question: Is there a unique process that inflates the probability of a zero case? Much is at stake in the answer to this question. A "yes" amounts to more than just the addition of an explanatory variable. As mentioned above, an entire process in the form of another equation and several more parameters to be estimated is added to the model. Most important, what happens if a researcher makes the incorrect choice (i.e., choosing the standard model when the zero-inflated model should be used or incorrectly choosing the zero-inflated model)? We can answer that question with simulation.

In the following code, we simulate one dependent variable in which there is a zero-inflation component in the true DGP and a second dependent variable in which the true DGP has no zero-inflation component. We estimate both a standard NB model and ZINB model on both of these dependent variables and compare the results. To simulate the dependent variable, we create a new function called `rzinbinom()`.

```
rzinbinom <- function(n, mu, size, zprob){
ifelse(rbinom(n, 1, zprob) == 1, 0, rnbinom(n, size = size, mu = mu))
}
```

This function uses `ifelse()` to separate the zero inflation and count processes. It takes an argument `zprob` that is the probability that an observation is a 0. It uses `rbinom()` to take one draw from a Bernoulli distribution (i.e., a single coin flip) with the probability of success set to `zprob`. If this draw comes up a success, the function should return a 0. If not, the function should proceed as `rnbinom()`. With this setup, observations that have a high probability of becoming a 0 will be a 0 more often than those with low probability.

We use this function to generate the dependent variables as follows.

```
# Generate data with a zero-inflation component
Y.zi <- rzinbinom(n, mu = exp(b0 + b1*X), size = .5,
zprob = exp(b0z + b1z*Z)/(1 + exp(b0z + b1z*Z)))
# Generate data with no zero-inflation component
Y.nozi <- rzinbinom(n, mu = exp(b0 + b1*X), size = .5, zprob = 0)
```

For the dependent variable that has a zero-inflation component, we set `zprob` to the formula for the inverse logit of a linear combination of an intercept (`b0z`) and a variable `Z` multiplied by a coefficient, `b1z`. This means that we are creating a logit model just like in Section 6.3.1 in the true DGP to determine whether an observation gets a 0 or not. We also set the mean parameter of the NB to the exponentiated linear combination of an intercept, `b0c`, and a coefficient, `b1c` multiplied by an independent variable, `X`. This is the systematic portion of the count model.

For the dependent variable with no zero inflation, we set zprob to 0, which means the condition in the ifelse() statement will never be true and all of the dependent variable values will be generated with the standard rnbinom() function. In other words, the true DGP only has a count equation. Finally, we estimate both a standard NB and a ZINB with both dependent variables (four models in total). We use the zeroinfl() function from the pscl package to estimate ZINB. The complete code is listed below.

```
# Negative Binomial vs. Zero-Inflated Negative Binomial
library(pscl)
# Zero-inflated negative binomial random number generator
rzinbinom <- function(n, mu, size, zprob){
ifelse(rbinom(n, 1, zprob) == 1, 0, rnbinom(n, size = size, mu = mu))
}

set.seed(2837) # Set the seed for reproducible results

reps <- 1000 # Set the number of repetitions at the top of the script
par.est.zinb <- matrix(NA, nrow = reps, ncol = 4) # Empty matrix to store the
                                                  # estimates
b0z <- -.8 # True value for the inflation intercept
b1z <- .3 # True value for the inflation slope
b0c <- .2 # True value for the count intercept
b1c <- .5 # True value for the count slope
n <- 1000 # Sample size
X <- runif(n, -1, 1) # Create a sample of n observations on the
                     # independent variable X
Z <- rnorm(n, X, 1) # Inflation independent variable

for(i in 1:reps){
# Generate data with a zero-inflation component
Y.zi <- rzinbinom(n, mu = exp(b0c + b1c*X), size = .5,
zprob = exp(b0z + b1z*Z)/(1 + exp(b0z + b1z*Z)))

# Generate data with no zero-inflation component
Y.nozi <- rzinbinom(n, mu = exp(b0c + b1c*X), size = .5, zprob = 0)
model.nb1 <- glm.nb(Y.zi ~ X) # Standard negative binomial
model.nb2 <- glm.nb(Y.nozi ~ X)
model.zinb1 <- zeroinfl(Y.zi ~ X | Z, dist = "negbin") # Zero-inflated model
model.zinb2 <- zeroinfl(Y.nozi ~ X | Z, dist = "negbin")

# Store the estimates of the coefficient on X (count equation)
par.est.zinb[i, 1] <- model.nb1$coef[2] # Standard NB, with ZI
par.est.zinb[i, 2] <- model.nb2$coef[2] # Standard NB, no ZI
par.est.zinb[i, 3] <- as.numeric(model.zinb1$coef$count[2])  # ZI NB, with ZI
par.est.zinb[i, 4] <- as.numeric(model.zinb2$coef$count[2]) # ZI NB, no ZI
cat("Completed", i, "of", reps, "\n")
}
```

We plot the densities of the simulated estimates from the standard NB (solid lines) and ZINB (dashed lines) in Figure 6.4. Panel (a) shows the results when the true DGP includes a zero-inflation component and Panel (b) shows results without zero inflation in the true DGP. Notice that when there is a zero-inflation component (Panel a), the standard NB shows a downward bias; its estimates are being "pulled down" by the excess 0s. In contrast, the ZINB estimates are centered directly on the true parameter value of 0.50. The picture changes when we look at the DGP with no zero-inflation component (Panel b). In that case, both estimators show unbiasedness—both are centered on the true coefficient value. But notice that the standard NB is slightly more efficient. It has higher density at the peak and smaller spread (standard deviations of 0.09 [NB] and 0.093 [ZINB]).

Overall, we see from these count model simulations that different estimators perform better or worse under different DGP conditions. It is not wise to simply choose one estimator for all count data. Instead, these results show us the importance of carefully thinking about the theoretical and empirical features of the data and using that information to inform estimator selection. We will see this illustrated again in our next extended example on duration models.

6.4.3 Duration Models

Duration models, or event history models, are commonly used in social science to study the time it takes for some process to occur. Examples include how long

| Figure 6.4 | Distribution of Zero-Inflated and Standard Negative Binomial β_1 Estimates With and Without a Zero-Inflation Component in the DGP |

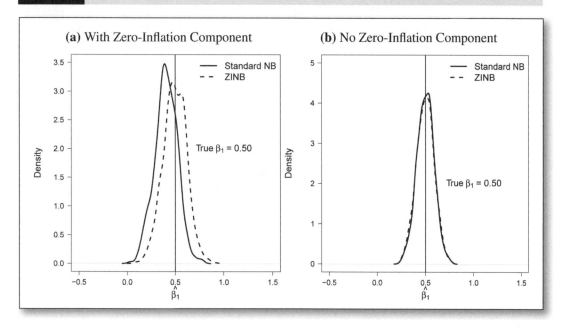

a war lasts, the length of a workers' strike, or the length of time for members of social groups to transition to adulthood. The dependent variable in these examples denotes the number of periods until the transition from one state to the other occurs (e.g., "strike" to "not strike"). There are several estimators available for duration models and many more intricacies associated with them than we can cover here, but we will give a basic introduction in this extended example.[18]

We need to define some key terms before we proceed with this section. The first is the survival function, which is defined as the probability that the transition occurs (e.g., a strike ends) later than some specified time, t.

$$S(t) = \Pr(T > t) \tag{6.14}$$

Here T is a random variable that signifies the time in which the transition occurs. The complement of the survival function is the CDF, $F(t)$, or the cumulative probability of transition.

$$F(t) = \Pr(T \leq t) = 1 - S(t) \tag{6.15}$$

The derivative of $F(t)$, denoted $f(t)$, can be used to produce the hazard rate, $h(t)$:

$$h(t) = \frac{f(t)}{S(t)} \tag{6.16}$$

The hazard rate is the risk of an observation experiencing the transition given that it has not experienced it up to the current period. The hazard rate gets the most attention in applications of duration models because it most naturally comports with research questions, such as "What is the chance a strike will end, given that it has lasted 3 months?" We can include a systematic component (i.e., independent variables) in answering this question, producing estimates of how each one influences the chances of the strike ending.

A key feature of these models is how they handle the baseline hazard rate, which is the risk of the transition occurring when the systematic component of the model is equal to zero. Thus, statements made based on the estimated coefficients of a duration model are in the language of relative risk. At any point in time, there is some chance of a strike ending. The estimators we explore here produce parameter estimates that describe the relative increase in that chance based on a change to an independent variable. Those estimates can depend on the assumed shape of the baseline hazard function. There are several parametric models available, such as the exponential and the Weibull. The former assumes a constant baseline hazard, while the latter can accommodate a baseline hazard that increases or decreases (monotonically) over time. Another possibility is the Cox (1972) Proportional Hazards Model, which has become quite popular because it

---

[18]We recommend Box-Steffensmeier and Jones (2004) as a good starting point for readers interested in learning more.

leaves the baseline hazard unspecified. We examine the Cox model in detail below.[19]

The Cox Model

The simulation we present here is based on Desmarais and Harden (2012). We seek to demonstrate how simulation can be used to address a methodological problem. Specifically, we examine two different methods for estimating the Cox model: (1) the conventional partial likelihood maximization (PLM) estimator proposed by Cox (1972) and (2) an iteratively reweighted robust (IRR) estimator that is robust to outliers (IRR, see Bednarski, 1989; Bednarski, 1993).

The Cox model is unique in that it only requires assumptions about the independent variables to identify the model. Information on the baseline hazard rate is not needed. This means, for instance, that the effect of some independent variable on the hazard rate can be estimated without considering the complicated dynamics that are common among the observations. The ubiquitous approach to estimating the parameters of the Cox model is to select the parameters that maximize the partial likelihood, a method similar to ML that we will call PLM.[20]

However, measurement error, omitted variables, and functional form misspecification all represent distinct problems for the Cox model. Bednarski (1989) shows that all of these problems result in disproportionately influential right-tail outliers or observations that last significantly longer than they are predicted to last. This produces bias in model results leading to incorrect inferences. Generally, these specification issues represent a failure of the model to reflect the real DGP. Moreover, since there is no error term or auxiliary parameter (e.g., variance term) in the Cox model, it cannot "account" for observations that, due to real-world complexity in the DGP, depart from the estimated failure ratios. This can be seen most clearly in predictions from the model that diverge markedly from the actual outcomes, such as a war that, in reality, lasted twice as long as the median war in the sample, but was predicted to be only half as long as the median.[21]

The IRR method attempts to minimize the impact of outliers (though not necessarily eliminate them completely). The method first creates a measure of "outlyingness" for each observation. Given a certain value of the hazard of event occurrence, a greater outlyingness penalty accrues with each time unit that goes by without the event occurring. For example, if the systematic component of the model predicts that a particular observation should be one of the first in the data to experience the event, but instead it was one of the last, that observation would receive a large

---

[19]We do not examine any parametric models to avoid complexity. The R package `survival` parameterizes those models with a slightly different DGP than we use for the Cox model.

[20]As Cox (1975) shows, the PLM converges, in the sample size, to the ML estimator.

[21]The emphasis on differences between reality and prediction is important. Simply observing a large value on the dependent variable is not enough to label that case as an outlier. Indeed, if that case's covariate values produce a prediction of a long duration, then it is not an outlier.

outlyingness value. IRR then adjusts each observation's influence on the model estimates based on outlyingness, with some percentage of observations having no influence on the estimation (see Bednarski, 1989; Desmarais & Harden, 2012).

The analyst must choose the level at which outliers are downweighted, which we show below amounts to a tradeoff between bias and efficiency. Downweighting outliers is appropriate if the downweighted observations depart from the DGP of the rest of the data due to measurement or specification errors. However, if all of the observations are consistent with the true DGP, this downweighting reduces the sample size with no apparent benefit. We can illustrate this with simulation using the R packages survival (for PLM) and coxrobust (for IRR).

Our strategy is to generate a model with two independent variables, X and Z, then estimate PLM and IRR only including X in the specification (i.e., an omitted variable problem). Additionally, we estimate two versions of IRR: (1) one in which we set the downweighting such that the top 5% of observations in terms of outlyingness get completely downweighted and (2) one in which the top 20% get completely downweighted. We produce the dependent variable using an exponential distribution with the systematic component of the model as the parameter λ. Again, notice that the variable Z is included in the true DGP, but not in the estimation of PLM or either IRR specification. Finally, we store the estimate of the coefficient on X (β_1) from each of the three models.

```
# Duration Models (Cox PH)
library(survival)
library(coxrobust)

set.seed(4679) # Set the seed for reproducible results

reps <- 1000 # Set the number of repetitions at the top of the script
par.est.cox <- matrix(NA, nrow = reps, ncol = 3) # Empty matrix to store the
                                                 # estimates
b1 <- .5 # True value for the slope
n <- 1000 # Sample size
X <- runif(n, -1, 1) # Create a sample of n observations on the
                     # independent variable X
Z <- runif(n, -1, 1) # Create an omitted variable

for(i in 1:reps){ # Start the loop
Y <- rexp(n, exp(b1*X + Z)) # Generate survival times
Ys <- Surv(Y, event = rep(1, n))
model.plm <- coxph(Ys ~ X, method = "breslow") # Standard PLM estimator
model.irr <- coxr(Ys ~ X, trunc = .95) # IRR, downweighting outliers (5%)
model.irr2 <- coxr(Ys ~ X, trunc = .8) # IRR, even more downweighting (20%)
par.est.cox[i, 1] <-model.plm$coef[1] # Store the estimates
par.est.cox[i, 2] <- model.irr$coef[1]
par.est.cox[i, 3] <- model.irr2$coef[1]
cat("Completed", i, "of", reps, "\n")
}
```

Figure 6.5 plots the distribution of the estimates for PLM (solid line), IRR with 5% truncation (dashed line), and IRR with 20% truncation (dotted line). Notice that all three estimators show bias, as none are centered on the true coefficient value of 0.50. However, with means of 0.397 (PLM estimates), 0.425 (IRR 5%), and 0.446 (IRR 20%), the bias gets smaller as the downweighting becomes more aggressive. Figure 6.5 also shows that the variance in the parameter estimates also differs across models; the standard deviations of the estimates are 0.050 (PLM), 0.058 (IRR 5%), and 0.071 (IRR 20%). This shows the tradeoff between bias and efficiency between the two estimators. IRR reduces bias, but is less efficient. PLM is the most biased, but also the most efficient. In this example, the IRR 20% estimator performs best according to MSE (which accounts for both bias and efficiency).[22]

| Figure 6.5 | The Effect of Omitted Variable Bias on PLM and IRR Estimates |

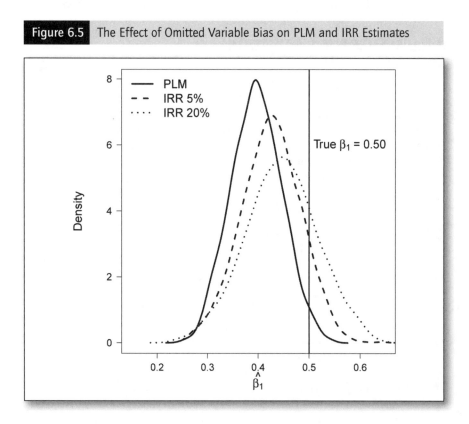

This simulation suggests that it is not wise to simply always use PLM or always use IRR. This leads to the question of how a researcher could decide between PLM and IRR in a sample of data. The relative performance of IRR to

---

[22]The MSE values are 0.013 (PLM), 0.009 (IRR 5%), and 0.008 (IRR 20%).

PLM depends on properties of the sample that are likely unknown. This presents a clear problem in applied research. Given a sample of data and a specification of the model, it is important to determine which estimator more closely characterizes the DGP of theoretical interest.

Desmarais and Harden (2012) introduce the cross-validated median fit (CVMF) test to allow researchers to determine which method provides a better fit to the majority of their data. When the PLM method provides a better fit to the majority of the observations in the sample, it is clear that a handful of outliers are not driving the results, and IRR is inferior. However, when PLM only fits a minority of the observations better than IRR, this is evidence that the benefits from the downweighting in IRR will be realized. Desmarais and Harden (2012) show in simulations similar to this one that the CVMF test, on average, selects the estimator that produces coefficient estimates closest to the true values.

6.5 COMPUTATIONAL ISSUES FOR SIMULATIONS

In running the code for these examples yourself, you may have noticed that some of them take a few minutes to run. These simulations could easily be expanded in a number of ways (e.g., more parameters or different sample sizes) that would complicate the simulation and extend (potentially dramatically) how much time it takes them to run. In Chapter 4, we briefly discussed ways of making code more efficient, but there are other ways to manage the workload of a simulation project. We close this chapter with some useful strategies for doing this. Specifically, we discuss the use of research computing and parallel processing.

6.5.1 Research Computing

The term *research computing* could refer to many different things, but what we mean is any infrastructure designed for large-scale execution of computing problems. Many universities, for example, maintain clusters of computers to which users can submit R script files as "jobs" to be executed. That means you create a script file that performs the simulation and saves the output in some form. You then submit the script file to the computing cluster. Submission procedures will vary depending on the actual computing cluster you are using, but many use Unix systems that use commands such as `bsub R CMD BATCH filename.R`. Once submitted, the cluster performs the simulation and returns the output that you can save to your own computer for analysis. This frees up your computer from doing work that may take a long time.

Using research computing means your script file must be organized to save anything you might want to use later. You will likely not be able to go back to the R session on the computing cluster to grab an object, so you should plan accordingly. One possibility is to use the `save.image()` command that we discussed in Chapter 3, which saves every object in the current R workspace. If you use this approach, this should be the last line of your code in your script file.

For instance, to save the current R workspace to the file "example.RData" you could type the following code.

```
save.image("example.RData")
```

Recall that once you have "example.RData" on your own computer, you can then access it with the load() command.

```
load("example.RData")
```

The computing cluster may operate faster than your computer, but it also may work at about the same speed. Regardless, using research computing is a good way to execute long jobs in a more convenient place, freeing your own computer for other tasks.

6.5.2 Parallel Processing

Another way to manage simulation projects so that they run faster is to use parallel processing. Parallel processing refers to the completion of multiple computing operations simultaneously—almost like making your computer "walk and chew gum at the same time." Think back to any of the simulations we have done so far. The typical approach is to iterate a `for` loop for 1,000 repetitions, generate a sample of data, and estimate one or more models each time. As it turns out, there is no real need for the `for` loop to work sequentially. It is not imperative that the sample generated in Iteration 2 exist before the sample in Iteration 543. Only the logical structure of the `for` loop makes that the case. Parallel processing speeds up the process by taking parts of the code that can be done at any time and distributes them to different computing nodes to work on. The results are then combined at the end.

This could occur in many different ways. For example, we could use a research computing cluster and divide parts of the simulation among several different computers. On a smaller scale, it is possible to divide code among the cores on a standard multicore desktop or laptop computer. These computers have the capacity to execute different "jobs" at the same time by dividing jobs among their cores. Here we will do a brief example of a simulation in which we divide the 1,000 iterations of the `for` loop among several cores. To do so, we need the following packages: `snow`, `doSNOW`, and `foreach`.

The example we will use is the simulation on standard NB and ZINB (see Section 6.4.2 of this chapter). That simulation creates two dependent variables and estimates two fairly complex models on each of them 1,000 times, which leads to a lengthy computation time. We will "parallelize" the code to see if we can shorten the completion time by dividing the work among the cores of a quad-core laptop computer.[23]

---

[23]Specifically, we did this on a Lenovo quadcore ThinkPad T520 with an Intel i5 processor and 8GB of RAM.

First, we need to alter the code slightly by making it a function. This makes it easier for R to store the results from the different cores together.[24] We copy the code from that simulation into a function called `zinb.sim()`.

```
# Simulation Function
zinb.sim <- function(n = 1000){
require(pscl)
par.est.zinb <- matrix(NA, nrow = 1, ncol = 4) # Empty matrix to store the
                                               # estimates
b0 <- .2 # True value for the intercept
b1 <- .5 # True value for the slope
X <- runif(n, -1, 1) # Create a sample of n observations on the
                     # independent variable X

# Generate data with a zero-inflation component
Y.zi <- rzinbinom(n, mu = exp(b0 + b1*X), size = .5,
zprob = exp(b0 + b1*X)/(1 + exp(b0 + b1*X)))
# Generate data with no zero-inflation component
Y.nozi <- rzinbinom(n, mu = exp(b0 + b1*X), size = .5, zprob = 0)
model.nb1 <- glm.nb(Y.zi ~ X) # Standard negative binomial
model.nb2 <- glm.nb(Y.nozi ~ X)
model.zinb1 <- zeroinfl(Y.zi ~ X | X, dist = "negbin") # Zero-inflated model
model.zinb2 <- zeroinfl(Y.nozi ~ X | X, dist = "negbin")
# Store the estimates of the coefficient on X (count equation)
par.est.zinb[ , 1] <- model.nb1$coef[2] # Standard NB, with ZI
par.est.zinb[ , 2] <- model.nb2$coef[2] # Standard NB, no ZI
par.est.zinb[ , 3] <- as.numeric(model.zinb1$coef$count[2]) # ZI NB, with ZI
par.est.zinb[ , 4] <- as.numeric(model.zinb2$coef$count[2]) # ZI NB, no ZI
return(par.est.zinb)
}
```

Notice that this function is set up to return the matrix `par.est.zinb`, which has one row and four columns. Each cell in the matrix contains an estimate of β_1 from one of the four estimators.[25] Next, we load the packages `snow`, `doSNOW`, and `foreach`. We use the `makeCluster()` and `registerDoSNOW()`

[24]There are actually many advantages to simulation with functions rather than the more "procedural" approach (i.e., creating objects then running a `for` loop) we have focused on up to this point. In particular, functions make "debugging" (finding and fixing errors) easier, can be tested more quickly, and carry more information about the environments in which they were created with them. This last benefit comes up with parallel computing because information about the environment often needs to be placed on different computing nodes. We elected to focus on the procedural approach for the majority of this book because functions and their associated capabilities can be somewhat difficult to understand for inexperienced users. We thank a manuscript reviewer for bringing this point to our attention.

[25]As in the first version of the simulation, these four are (1) the standard NB on the data that include a zero-inflation component, (2) the standard NB on the data with no zero inflation, (3) the ZINB with zero inflation, and (4) the ZINB with no zero inflation.

functions to set up the parallel processing. In this case, we use the number 4 to tell R to use four cores.

```
library(pscl)
library(snow)
library(doSNOW)
library(foreach)

cl.tmp <- makeCluster(4)
registerDoSNOW(cl.tmp)
```

Now, we are ready to run the simulation. Instead of the for() function, we will use the foreach() function. This takes slightly different syntax than we have seen before. We set the counter as i = 1:reps. Then, we set the argument .combine = rbind. This tells R to take the results from zinb.sim(), which is a vector of four coefficient estimates, and bind them together such that each iteration gets one row in a matrix of output. Finally, the code inside the % signs tells R how to execute the code. If we write %do%, R will execute the code serially, or one iteration at a time. We will do this first to get a baseline execution time. Notice that the only code we need inside the actual loop is the zinb.sim() function.

```
# Serial Processing
set.seed(2837) # Set the seed for reproducible results
reps <- 1000 # Set the number of repetitions

start.time <- Sys.time()
results <- foreach(i = 1:reps, .combine = rbind) %do% {
zinb.sim(n = 1000)
  }

end.time <- Sys.time()
end.time - start.time
```

This serial run produces the results in just under 12 minutes. The output is correct, which can be verified by checking it against the results from the original version of the simulation.[26]

```
Time difference of 11.71957 mins

head(results)
              [,1]        [,2]         [,3]        [,4]
[1,]   0.05882971 0.5623784 0.48865878 0.4683902
[2,]  -0.06915600 0.3567442 0.08945868 0.3218285
[3,]  -0.01693489 0.6521395 0.20225698 0.5924448
[4,]   0.27497556 0.5041720 0.46120764 0.5041924
[5,]   0.13497402 0.4206432 0.54417701 0.4912774
[6,]   0.13088511 0.4539706 0.33806668 0.4135637
```

[26]Using the apply() function on the results of the original simulation produces: [1] 0.2147594 0.4963802 0.4941624 0.4864211.

```
apply(results, 2, mean)
[1]  0.2150614 0.4975114 0.4810489 0.4860895
```

The next step is to run the exact same code in parallel and check the improvement in time. We already set up the "back end" of our code with the makeCluster() and registerDoSNOW() functions, so all we need to do is tell R to actually execute this code in parallel. We do that by changing %do% to %dopar%.

```
# Parallel Processing
set.seed(2837) # Set the seed for reproducible results
reps <- 1000 # Set the number of repetitions

start.time <- Sys.time()
results <- foreach(i = 1:reps, .combine = rbind) %dopar% {
zinb.sim(n = 1000)
  }

end.time <- Sys.time()
end.time - start.time
```

This produces the following results:

```
Time difference of 4.8734 mins

head(results)
              [,1]        [,2]        [,3]        [,4]
[1,]   0.15051572  0.4517511  0.5860100  0.4691888
[2,]   0.19717087  0.6604850  0.5470129  0.7190622
[3,]   0.43322114  0.4927281  0.8087086  0.4126702
[4,]   0.16557821  0.4871358  0.3542323  0.5073770
[5,]   0.46028678  0.6873374  0.7443504  0.5591115
[6,]  -0.03127193  0.4493201  0.3148359  0.4799454

apply(results, 2, mean)
[1]  0.2206657 0.4998477 0.4880605 0.4924071
```

By dividing the code across four cores, the computer took less than 5 minutes to complete the exact same code—a nearly 60% reduction in time. Notice that the results also look correct (though they are not identical). This example shows that parallel processing is quite feasible in R and can greatly reduce the time it takes to do simulations. We recommend using this procedure or a similar one for simulations that take several minutes to run in a standard for loop.

Finally, we should note again a point we made in Chapter 4: replicating results from simulations executed through parallel processing may not be accomplished in some instances simply by setting the seed. This is a complicated issue that extends beyond the scope of this book, but readers should be aware of this potential problem. Again, test your code with a limited number of iterations first to make sure it performs as expected before you launch a time-consuming simulation.

6.6 CONCLUSIONS

This chapter provided an overview of simulation with GLMs. We began with the process of simulating the DGP of a GLM, then recovering that DGP through estimation. Doing so illustrated that the basic idea of a GLM is to link the systematic component of the model to a probability distribution that produces the type of values the dependent variable can take on. We also illustrated how simulation can be used to compare competing estimators in extended examples with categorical, count, and duration models. We saw how knowing the true DGP in a simulation gives us considerable analytic leverage in assessing how estimators perform under different data conditions.

We closed this chapter with a discussion of computational issues. Many of the examples from this chapter are computationally intensive and take a relatively long time to complete. Simulations beyond those shown here could easily take hours or days to estimate on a standard computer. We addressed how research computing can make managing such computations less of a burden. We also showed a basic example of parallel processing in which we reduced run time by more than half through dividing the simulation among four cores of a computer. It is worth noting that many research computing systems available at universities consist of hundreds or even thousands of cores, making the potential time savings of parallel processing in that environment very appealing.

After two chapters of nothing but statistical simulation, it is time for a change. Social scientists use statistical methods to better understand social processes. Using simulation to illustrate and evaluate these methods is certainly a beneficial exercise. However, it is also possible to use simulation to directly evaluate substantive problems, theories, and questions. We show several examples of this in the next chapter.

Testing Theory Using Simulation

7.1 INTRODUCTION

Every use of simulation techniques to evaluate the properties or behavior of a statistical estimator also represents a potential evaluation of a theoretical proposition. As we have said, statistical estimation focuses on revealing or recovering aspects of an underlying DGP, and every DGP is at its core a theoretical statement about how some process works. Think back to the simulations from the last chapter on standard versus zero-inflated count models. By selecting a zero-inflated model, the researcher makes the statement that the process under study is theoretically composed of two distinct components: (1) one that governs whether the outcome variable is a zero or not and (2) another that influences the count of the nonzero observations. An example might be separate processes that influence whether a country decides to initiate a dispute and whether it decides to extend a dispute with another nation.

However, the analysis of statistical estimators through Monte Carlo simulation is still an indirect method of evaluating substantive theories. In this chapter, we turn our focus to using simulation techniques to directly evaluate the predictions of a theory.[1]

7.2 WHAT IS A THEORY?

A theory is a statement about how and why a process works the way it does. Theories provide answers to interesting social science questions. Why do voters vote the way that they do? Why does residential segregation emerge? Why have we seen a growth in income inequality? Theories require more than simply stating or observing a pattern, such as "Evangelical citizens in the United States are

---

[1]There are a wide range of computer simulation techniques used by researchers that fall outside the scope of this book. They are used widely in environmental science, biology, astrophysics, climatology, engineering, and a whole range of disciplines along with the social sciences. In this chapter, we focus on some simulation techniques that most closely approximate the statistical simulations that constitute the bulk of this book.

more likely to vote for candidates from the Republican Party." A theory offers an explanation for *why* a pattern exists, not just a description of a pattern.

Lave and March (1993) provide a clear discussion of the theory-building process, which they present in four steps. Here we adapt their approach to fit our purpose in this book, presenting our perspective in five steps rather than four.

Step 1: Begin by observing some events, facts, or an empirical pattern. For many researchers, this might include observing a pattern, correlation, or relationship in a data set.

Step 2: Think about those empirical observations as if they are the end result of some unknown process. In other words, treat these observations as the result of some unknown DGP.

Step 3: Offer an explanation or speculation about what that DGP looks like. What sort of process could have produced the empirical pattern you see? Why does that pattern appear and not others? This is the step in the process where you are articulating a theoretical argument because you are offering an explanation.

Step 4: Based on your theory, generate additional predictions about other patterns or events that you would expect to see if your theory is true. Many scholars would describe the first three steps we have outlined as being inductive—beginning with a set of empirical observations and deriving a theory from those observations. Step 4, however, is deductive in nature—starting with a theoretical proposition and saying, "If my theory is true, what else should I expect to observe?"

Step 5: Evaluate whether the additional predictions you made in the previous step are supported in observable data or not. Use this information to determine whether there is empirical support or not for your theory and whether or not your theory needs to be updated, changed, or discarded. If you make changes based on these new empirical observations, that is equivalent to returning to Step 3 in this process. Step 5 of this process is where theories are tested. Notice the critical need for empirical evidence in Step 5 that is independent of the empirical observations from Step 1 that you used to begin developing your theory.

This approach to theory building and testing is quite general and can be used in nearly any scientific setting. However, one of the limitations of this approach is that it does not really promote the direct consideration of alternative theories as part of Step 3. The process, as we have described it, encourages the development of one explanation followed by a round of testing that explanation. There is nothing inherently wrong with this approach, but it can lead to some confusion over whether a theory really has sufficient support based on subsequent analysis. Why? Because there might be more than one theory that would explain the original empirical pattern you observed in Step 1 as well as generate the same set of predictions that are critical to testing a theory in Step 5. In other words, if two or more DGPs are consistent with the same set of empirical findings, then those empirical findings cannot be used to help you decide which DGP is most likely to be at work in the real world.

Simulations can be used to help generate additional predictions from a given DGP, but they can also be used to help define several different DGPs that might be capable of producing the same set of predictions. In particular, simulations can be helpful in identifying whether the empirical observations used to develop or test a theory differ in a meaningful way from what we would expect to observe due to random chance. In this sense, simulations can be useful in clearly articulating a proper null hypothesis. In this chapter, we explore these issues by presenting three examples where we use simulations to evaluate substantive theories.

7.3 ZIPF'S LAW

In Chapter 17 of her book *Complexity: A Guided Tour*, Mitchell (2009) discusses how power laws appear to describe a broad range of occurrences in the social and natural world. A power law defines a mathematical relationship between two quantities where one of the quantities can be defined as the other quantity raised to some power. For example, if the frequency distribution of an event is related to some attribute of that event raised to a given power, that frequency distribution is said to follow a power law distribution. One of the examples that Mitchell presents is based on research done by Max Kleiber in the 1930s on the metabolic rates in animals. The metabolic rate of an animal measures the rate at which the animal's body converts nutrients to energy. Kleiber found that the metabolic rate in animals is proportional to that animal's body mass raised to the power of $\frac{3}{4}$.

Power laws with various exponents have been discovered to accurately describe a broad range of natural and social phenomena. One of the most interesting, and an example that we explore here in some detail, is known as Zipf's law. It is named after George Kingsley Zipf, a linguistics professor who first published his results in 1932 (Zipf, 1932). Zipf was interested in understanding the words that people choose when they communicate and how often they use particular words. He started by examining documents that contained a large number of words—a book, an entire newspaper, or a lengthy speech—and counting how often each word that appeared in those documents was used. Let's call that count the frequency count, or just the frequency, of the word. Next, he sorted the words in order from most used to least used, ranking them accordingly, with the most frequently used word ranked "1," the next most frequently used word ranked "2," and so forth. Zipf found that the frequency with which a word was used tended to be proportional to the inverse of that word's rank. To state it mathematically, Zipf found that

$$\text{Word Frequency} \approx \frac{1}{\text{Word Rank}} = \text{Word Rank}^{-1} \qquad (7.1)$$

In other words, Zipf's law proposes that word frequency follows a power law relative to word rank with an exponent of −1.

7.3.1 Testing Zipf's Law With *Frankenstein*

Our first task is to demonstrate how you might explore Zipf's law using R. Let's start by looking at Zipf's law as it applies to an actual document. We downloaded

Mary Shelley's classic tale, *Frankenstein*, from the Project Gutenberg website, http://www.gutenberg.org/(despite Shelley's warning about the overexuberant pursuit of science, we will continue on!).[2] After a bit of cleaning up that included removing the title page, stripping out punctuation and page numbers, and shuffling the text around, we produced a simple frequency count of all of the words included in the book.[3] Table 7.1 displays the 20 most frequently used words in *Frankenstein* and how many times each appeared.

Table 7.1	Top 20 Words in *Frankenstein*

Rank	Word	Frequency
1	the	4143
2	and	2885
3	of	2643
4	I	2616
5	to	2053
6	my	1545
7	a	1330
8	in	1083
9	was	968
10	that	942
11	me	803
12	with	667
13	had	663
14	which	553
15	but	519
16	his	486
17	not	483
18	as	478
19	he	459
20	by	449

---

[2]The Project Gutenberg website has a number of books available for sale as well as many books in the public domain available for free. Of particular value in this context, many of the books can be downloaded as plain text files, which makes them much easier to examine using computer tools.

[3]By no means are we presenting this example and the analysis that follows as a definitive study of this text. A much more careful cleaning of the raw text file should be conducted if one were seeking to do serious scholarly analysis. We view what we have done here as a heuristic example only, and readers should treat it as such.

Our first question is whether there is any evidence that the frequency of word usage in *Frankenstein* approaches the power law distribution with an exponent equal to −1 as suggested by Zipf's law. There are three ways we can look for such evidence. First, if Zipf's law applies, then a simple scatterplot with word rank on the *x*-axis and word frequency on the *y*-axis should decline from left to right following a convex curve. In fact, the shape of the curve should follow the shape defined by Equation 7.1.

We stored the frequency count of the 40 most frequently used words in *Frankenstein* in a comma-delimited file we named "FrankTop40.csv," read that file into R, and used the data to produce Figure 7.1. Panel (a) plots the word rank on the *x*-axis and the word frequency on the *y*-axis. The dashed line corresponds to what we would expect to see in theory if Zipf's law applied perfectly to the *Frankenstein* text. We can see from the plot that Zipf's law appears to hold pretty closely in this case. Given how widely it has been found to apply elsewhere, this comes as no surprise.

Another way to examine whether Zipf's law holds is to take natural logs of the frequency counts and the ranks associated with a set of words before producing a plot. Taking natural logs should straighten out the curve presented in Panel (a) to the point that the natural logs of the two quantities should be linearly related. We present such a plot in Panel (b) of Figure 7.1. The points depict the actual data and the line that is plotted comes from regressing the log of word frequency on the log of word rank. Again, we see evidence of what we would expect to see if Zipf's law were true.

Finally, if Zipf's law holds for a given text, then the simple regression of the natural log of the rank of words on the natural log of the frequency of words should produce an estimated slope coefficient equal to −1. In other words, the regression shown in Equation 7.2 should produce an estimate of $\beta_1 = -1$.

$$\log(\text{Rank}) = \beta_0 + \beta_1 \log(\text{Frequency}) + \varepsilon \qquad (7.2)$$

We performed this regression, the results of which are presented in Table 7.2.

We see that the estimated slope coefficient operating on the log of the word frequency is −1.039. The estimated standard error of about .031 results in a 95% confidence interval of about −0.986 to −1.102. Thus, we cannot reject the null hypothesis that the word frequencies associated with the 40 most frequently used words in *Frankenstein* adheres to Zipf's law.

The steps we have gone through are quite consistent with the process of theory development and testing we outlined at the start of this chapter. In this case, someone else recognized a pattern in a set of empirical observations that we know as Zipf's law. Zipf's law leads to three clear predictions about what we should see empirically if it applies to a new body of text. We evaluated those three predictions using new data—in this case, the full text of *Frankenstein*—and observed empirical support for all three predictions. In this way, we can say that we found empirical support for Zipf's law.

| Figure 7.1 | The Rank and Frequency of the 40 Most Frequently Used Words in *Frankenstein* |

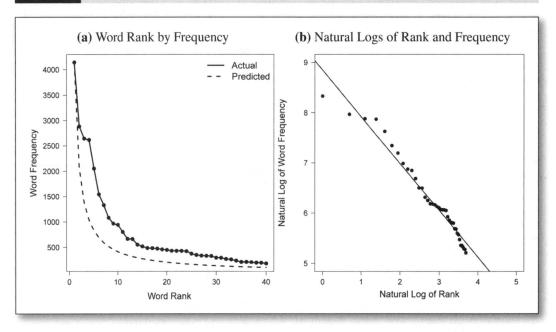

(a) Word Rank by Frequency   **(b)** Natural Logs of Rank and Frequency

| Table 7.2 | Regression of ln(Rank) on ln(Frequency) for the 40 Most Frequently Used Words in *Frankenstein* |

Variable	Coefficient	Standard Error
Intercept	9.281*	0.197
ln(Frequency)	−1.039*	0.031
N	40	
Adjusted R^2	0.966	

Note: Cell entries report OLS coefficients and standard errors. The dependent variable is the natural log of the rank order of the words used in *Frankenstein*, with rank determined by relative frequency. * $p < 0.05$ (two-tailed).

7.3.2 From Patterns to Explanations

However, one part of the theory-building and testing process that we skipped over was providing an explanation for why a body of text might follow Zipf's law. Mitchell (2009), along with Li (1992), discuss many explanations that have been provided. Zipf argued that this pattern results from people following a rule of performing an activity using the least amount of effort required.[4] The idea is that once a word is used, it takes less effort to use it again when conveying the same or similar meaning compared with coming up with another word. At the same time, writers might want to use similar but distinct words when trying to convey similar but not identical ideas. Mitchell (2009) states that Zipf demonstrated mathematically that balancing these two competing pressures could result in a power law frequency distribution of words.

Mitchell (2009) reports that others offer a theory of effective information signaling, where the question is one of balancing the amount of information conveyed in a text against the cost to both the author and the reader in terms of processing a message in order to receive the information. Still others offered a preferential treatment explanation—while all unused words have an equal probability of being used, all used words become increasingly likely to be used again as their use increases. In other words, Zipf's law is a classic case of multiple theoretical explanations leading to the same prediction of patterns we might see in the frequency distribution of word usage. We have already mentioned several of these explanations, but there is one more that is of particular interest for us here—what if it is all random?

Li (1992, p. 1) suggests that few people probably gave much notice to a comment made by George Miller in the preface to his book published in 1965 (Miller, 1965), but Miller noted that randomly generated texts also appear to conform to Zipf's law. Mitchell (2009) described this as imagining what would happen if monkeys typed randomly on a keyboard with "words" being separated from each other each time the monkey happened to hit the space bar. Whether or not random chance is responsible for Zipf's law is an important question for two reasons. First, like any other explanation, if random chance is also consistent with Zipf's law then we have yet another "theory" that is consistent with the empirical evidence.

Second, whether randomness is the explanation for some observation is a particularly powerful alternative explanation to consider. Nearly all of statistical testing involves accounting for the possibility that random chance is responsible for generating the data we observe. More generally, the notion that the DGP under study differs in a meaningful way from being random provides the basis for most applied hypothesis testing. Whenever we perform a traditional hypothesis test, the associated p value (or level of statistical significance) can be thought of as the proportion of a large number of random samples drawn from a DGP as described by the null hypothesis that would produce a value of the test statistic as large or larger than the one computed from the sample data strictly due to random chance. In this particular case, the challenge posed by Miller (1965) is whether or not Zipf's law can be taken as evidence of any of the substantive theories that have been offered as explanations or whether the observation of the pattern Zipf

---

[4]Maybe Zipf had teenage children at the time!

discovered does not meaningfully differ from what random chance would produce. In his article, Li (1992) takes up this challenge, showing mathematically and with a simulation, that Miller's comment is well founded. Let's take a closer look at such a simulation.

Li (1992) begins with a slightly different formulation of Zipf's law:

$$F(r) = \frac{C}{r^\alpha} \tag{7.3}$$

where r is the rank order of the frequency of which a word occurs, $F(r)$ is the frequency with which a word of rank r occurs, $C \approx 0.1$, and $\alpha \approx 1$. However, where Equation 7.3 captures Zipf's law in the form of $\alpha \approx 1$, Equation 7.1 captures it in the exponent on the right-hand side of the equation being -1.

The first challenge to evaluating the "randomness" hypothesis is generating truly random text. One way to think about this is a very long string of characters with a blank (or some other character) representing the space bar. This blank or special character would identify the breaks in the long string of characters that separated words from each other. So you might imagine a string of characters from the English alphabet like this:

```
vkno_iiqn_uomeoxlml_kb_sgylubl_w_iondes
```

where the "_" represents our special character separating words. In this example, the individual words are `vkno, iiqn, uomeoxlml, kb, sgylubl, w,` and `iondes`. As Li (1992) points out, the individual probability of observing the string `_w_` if the appearance of each character in the string is independent of the appearance of any other characters in the string would be $\frac{1}{27} \times \frac{1}{27} \times \frac{1}{27}$ or $\left(\frac{1}{27}\right)^3$. We use $\frac{1}{27}$ because there are 26 letters plus one space bar. Similarly, the probability of observing the string `_iiqn_` would be $\left(\frac{1}{27}\right)^6$. If every letter plus the empty space has an equal probability of appearing at any point in the sequence, then the formulas we have just presented would describe the probability of observing any specific "word" with a given length. This can be stated more generally as

$$F_i(L) = c \frac{1}{(M+1)^{L+2}} \tag{7.4}$$

where M is the number of characters in the alphabet under consideration, i is an integer ranging from 1 up to M^L, and $F_i(L)$ is the frequency of a particular word i of a given length, L, occurring. Li (1992) adds the c term, which he describes as a normalizing constant that can be determined by

$$c = \frac{(M+1)^2}{M} \tag{7.5}$$

Substituting Equation 7.5 into Equation 7.4 results in

$$F(L) = \frac{M^{L-1}}{(M+1)^L} \tag{7.6}$$

Equation 7.6 can be thought of as the null hypothesis under random word generation where every letter in an alphabet of size M has an equal probability of being selected, including the character that signifies a break between words, and all character selection is independent and identically distributed.

Let's turn our attention to the R code that can be used to generate words at random based on the DGP assumed in the discussion up to this point. We first set the seed for reproducible results. Then, we define an object N as equal to a large number, in this case 500,000. The code will be using N to indicate the total number of words we will be randomly generating. As you will see, we are going to do this with a loop that we run N times. The first time you try this yourself, you might want to set N to a much lower number.

```
# Random Word Simulation
set.seed(984646) # Set the seed for reproducible results
N <- 500000 # Number of random words to generate
RandomWords <- matrix(NA, nrow = N, ncol = 1) # Empty vector for results
WordSize <- seq(1:100) # Possible word lengths
P_WordSize <- (26^(WordSize - 1))/(26 + 1)^WordSize # Probability of observing
                                                    # a word of a given size
```

The next line of code defines an object RandomWords as a matrix full of missing values. This matrix will have the number of rows equal to the number of random words, N, we will be generating, and only one column. As we explained in Chapter 4, it is always faster when running a loop in R to define the object in which you will store your results before you start the loop.

The object WordSize is a sequence that runs from 1 through 100. This object stores the possible lengths of words that we wish to consider as we draw letters randomly from our alphabet. Allowing for words that are 100 characters long might seem silly, but rest assured that the simulation presented here produces the same basic results if we limit word length to 20.[5]

The final line of code defines an object called P_WordSize. This object is a vector that records the probability of observing any word of a given length of characters defined by WordSize based on the formula provided by Li (1992) and presented as Equation 7.6. The result is that for every value of WordSize we compute the corresponding probability of observing words of that length strictly due to random chance.

---

[5]Li (1992) presents results that are comparable even with alphabets that range from having only 2 to 6 letters and maximum word lengths limited to 2 to 6 characters.

Now that we have all of the core components of our simulation defined, we can set up the `for` loop, which runs N times.

```
for(i in 1:N){ # Start the loop
NN <- sample(WordSize, 1, prob = P_WordSize) # Draw a word size at random
L <- sample(letters, NN, replace = TRUE) # Draw NN letters at random
Word <- paste(L, collapse = "") # Combine the letters into a word
RandomWords[i] <- Word # Store the word in the empty vector
}
```

The next line of code makes use of the `sample()` function in R. Remember that the first argument in `sample()` is the object from which the sample will be drawn. The second argument is how large that sample will be and the third argument is what probabilities should be attached to each element within the object from which the sample is being drawn. Thus, this line of code defines an object NN as a random sample drawn from the vector `WordSize` of size 1, where the probability of drawing each individual element is defined by the portion of the code that reads `prob = P_WordSize`. In short, this line of code defines how long of a word we will be creating with random letters later within the loop. The `prob = P_WordSize` argument links drawing a word of length 1, of length 2, of length 3, and so on, with the corresponding probability of doing so based on Equation 7.6.

The next line of code defines an object called L, which is a collection of individual letters selected at random from the English alphabet. This line of code makes use of the `sample()` function again. Fortunately for us, R has a built in object called `letters` that is a vector of characters that are the 26 lower-case letters of the English alphabet. Thus, we are using the `sample()` function to draw a sample of size NN from the object `letters`. Because we did not define a vector of probabilities, each element of letters will have an equal chance of being drawn. Additionally, the code `replace = TRUE` tells R to sample letters with replacement.

At this point, the object L is just a collection of individual letters. We need a way to compress those individual letters into a single word, which we accomplish in the next line of code. There we define an object called `Word` as the result of applying the `paste()` function to the object L. The `paste()` function literally "pastes" together individual elements in an object into a single (or a smaller number of) element(s). There are several ways to use the `paste()` function. Here we have provided it with `collapse = ""` argument so that it will paste together the elements of L into a single object with no spaces or separators between those elements. In short, this line takes our series of random letters that constitute L and combines them into a single word in the object `Word`.

The final line of the loop writes the result of `Word` into the `RandomWords` object we defined outside the loop—specifically into row *i*. The loop then repeats by drawing a new value for NN, a new sample of NN number of letters for L,

compresses them into a new word in Word, and writes the result again to
RandomWords. The end result is the object RandomWords that is a vector of
purely randomly generated words, the lengths of which correspond to the probability that words of such length will be drawn if the drawing is done independently
and strictly by random chance. In short, we now have a vector of text with randomly generated words that we can analyze to see if Zipf's law applies.

The two lines of R code below create two objects named Count and Rank,
which record the frequency count of individual words and the rank of a word
based on its frequency. In other words, these two lines create the two measures of
our randomly generated text that we need to evaluate Zipf's law.

```
# Count, sort, and rank the results
Count <- sort(as.data.frame(table(RandomWords))$Freq, decreasing = TRUE)
Rank <- seq(1:length(Count))
```

The line that generates Count makes use of three functions embedded inside of
each other. It is easiest to understand what is happening by describing these from
the inside out. The function table() produces a frequency table of the object
RandomWords. This provides a count of the number of times a particular random
word appears in this vector. However, that frequency table is unordered by default.

The as.data.frame() function treats the frequency table that the table()
function just produced as a data frame. This results in a data frame where the
second element is labeled Freq, which records the frequency associated with
each word. This is done only so the sort() function can be used to resort the
order of the frequency table based on the values of Freq. Thus, the sort()
function is being applied to the element of the data frame named Freq as indi-
cated by specifying $Freq as the element within the data frame that should be
sorted. The argument decreasing = TRUE is given to sort() so that the
frequencies will be sorted in order from highest to lowest. Again, the result is an
object named Count that is the observed frequency of words in RandomWords
sorted in order from highest to lowest.

The final line of code takes advantage of the fact that Count is already sorted
in the proper order. Because of this, the rank ordering of frequencies within
Count is identical to the location of that frequency within Count. In other
words, the first element of Count is the highest ranking frequency, the second
element is the second highest ranking frequency, and so forth. The last line creates an object called Rank that is simply a sequence of integers starting at "1"
and continuing up to whatever the value is that is associated with the length of
the Count vector.

Testing the Randomness Explanation

Now that we have Count and Rank defined, let's repeat the three analyses we
did of the *Frankenstein* text to see if there is any evidence of Zipf's law within
our random text. Before doing so, it is important to note that there is necessarily

a stairstep quality to the data in this simulation because all words of the same length were given an equal probability of being selected (Li, 1992). Similarly, the 26 unique one-letter words as well as the rarely selected words that are very long provide some distortions to the analysis that would be smoothed out with a more plausible set of assumptions about the varying probabilities of letters, letter clusters, and rules of grammar that would apply to the behavior of an actual language. Thus, the analysis presented here focuses on just a subset of the data.

The first step is to see if plots of word rankings (or logged rankings) on the *x*-axis and word frequencies (or logged frequencies) on the *y*-axis produce the convex curve (or line) predicted by Zipf's law that we saw in Figure 7.1. We plot both of these graphs in Figure 7.2, limiting the analysis to the 400 most frequently occurring words except for the one-letter words.

Panel (a) of Figure 7.2 shows the stairstep feature noted above, but also clearly shows the same basic shape as predicted by Zipf's law. The predicted line corresponding to an exponent of −1 (e.g., the dashed line in Panel (a) of Figure 7.1) again follows a similar pattern to the actual results, but we omit it here because it is difficult to see without including one-letter words. Panel (b) of Figure 7.2 presents the plot of the natural logs of word rank and frequency, and as before, we see essentially a linear relationship between the two.

Last, we regressed the natural log of word rank on the natural log of word frequency for the 400 most frequently occurring words in our randomly generated text. The results, given in Table 7.3, show an estimated slope coefficient of −0.986. With an estimated standard error of 0.037 and a 95% confidence interval of [−0.914, −1.058], these results fail to reject the null hypothesis of a slope coefficient equal to −1.

In sum, Figure 7.2 and Table 7.3 provide evidence that randomly generated words—monkeys typing at the keyboard—produces text compatible with Zipf's law. Just as Miller (1965) suggested and Li (1992) demonstrated, we used a simulation study to show that evidence of the frequency of words in a text following a power law with a −1 exponent—in other words, following Zipf's law—cannot be taken as evidence that differs meaningfully from what random chance would produce. This discovery represents a direct challenge to all other substantive theories offered as explanations for why large texts seem to follow this distribution. This is not to say that any of the processes regarding the use of language described by Zipf or others as possible explanations for observing this power law distribution are wrong. Our simulation (and really the work of scholars like Miller, 1965, and Li, 1992) just suggests that observing that a body of text follows such a power law distribution should probably not be taken as evidence of any of these processes because this evidence alone is not enough to reject a null hypothesis of randomness.[6]

---

[6]This example barely scratches the surface of the tools available in R for the analysis of text. Interested readers should explore some of the add-on packages in R that can be used for text analysis, including `RTextTools`, `tm`, `topicmodels`, and `lda`. There is also a package devoted to the analysis of Twitter feeds called `twitteR` and one for the kinds of analysis we simulated here called `zipfR`.

Figure 7.2 The Rank and Frequency of the 400 Most Frequently Used Words in the Random Words Simulation

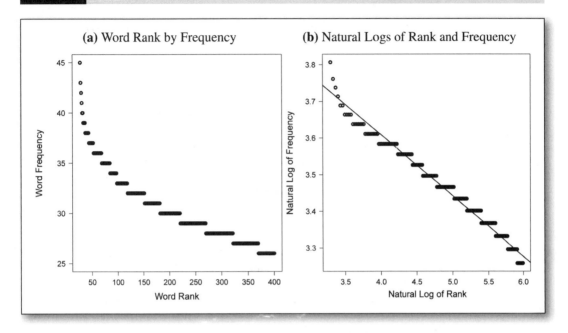

(a) Word Rank by Frequency   **(b)** Natural Logs of Rank and Frequency

7.4 PUNCTUATED EQUILIBRIUM AND POLICY RESPONSIVENESS

Punctuated equilibrium is a theory developed in evolutionary biology to describe how changes occur in species over time. The argument is that there is little or no change in a species most of the time—its development holds steady at its current equilibrium status. However, evolutionary change can and does occur, and when it does, it tends to be relatively substantial in magnitude and abrupt in terms of timing.[7] Of course, what counts as "abrupt" in evolutionary time is still quite gradual—occurring over many hundreds or even thousands of years. Still, the general notion is one of relatively long periods of little or no change and relatively shorter periods of more substantial change. This theory stands in contrast to a view of evolution as occurring at a roughly steady, gradual rate. Following our process of theory building, the development of punctuated equilibrium emerged from the observation of long periods of stasis in the fossil record coupled with relatively shorter periods that suggested more rapid change. Thus, an empirical pattern was noticed and an explanation called punctuated equilibrium was derived. It is not our

---

[7]Interested readers should begin with Mayr (1954) and then the foundational paper by Eldredge and Gould (1972) for more details.

| Table 7.3 | Regression of ln(Rank) on ln(Frequency) for the 400 Most Frequently Appearing Randomly Generated Words | |

Variable	Coefficient	Standard Error
Intercept	8.570[*]	0.136
ln(Frequency)	−0.986[*]	0.037
N	400	
Adjusted R^2	0.645	

Note: Cell entries report OLS coefficients and standard errors. The dependent variable is the natural log of the rank order of randomly generated words using the R code presented in this section, with rank determined by relative frequency. [*]$p < 0.05$ (two-tailed).

objective to debate the subsequent scientific debate regarding punctuated equilibrium in evolutionary biology. Rather, we provide this background in order to understand how the theory might relate to social processes.

Indeed, the notion of punctuated equilibrium has been applied to a wide range of social processes. The idea is that many social processes continue uninterrupted in a steady state of equilibrium for relatively long periods of time. Then, when changes do occur, they tend to be relatively dramatic and occur over relatively short periods of time. Applications include the study of how groups of individuals, organizations, and scientific fields develop, the study of organizational theory, and the study of technological change.

One particular application of punctuated equilibrium theory to social processes involves the study of policy change in representative governments. This area of research has its roots in Baumgartner and Jones (1993), but has been adopted by a broad range of scholars studying U.S. national and state policy as well as policy in other countries. The impact on the study of policy representation has been substantial, though not without some controversy (Prindle, 2012).[8] While our example will focus on one aspect of the punctuated equilibrium argument applied to the study of policy change, this literature is much broader and richer than we have space to consider here. It would also be a mistake to view this as the only area in social science where the idea of punctuated equilibrium has had a significant impact. Going one step further, this is just one of a broad range of biological and other natural science theories that have been imported as theories, or at least as metaphors, by social scientists.

---

[8]Interested readers can learn more about recent developments in the work sparked by Baumgartner and Jones (1993) at the Policy Agendas Project website (http://www.poli cyagendas.org/).

The dominant view of how changes took place within species in evolutionary biology prior to the work of Eldredge and Gould (1972) was one of gradualism. Similarly, the dominant view of how policy change took place prior to the work of Baumgartner and Jones (1993) was one of incrementalism. Policies changed, but gradually over time as forces like inertia, stickiness, institutional obstacles, and adherence to standard operating procedures limited prospects for major changes. At the same time, stasis was viewed as unlikely because public opinion, party control of government, and external events that create pressures for policy change were in a constant state of flux.

In contrast, the punctuated equilibrium perspective argues that policy change is characterized by relatively long periods of little or no change, but also short periods of fairly dramatic change. Several arguments have been offered for exactly why this is the case. Some arguments focus on the idea that both policy-makers and citizens demanding policy representation face cognitive limitations that simply prevent them from devoting their attention to every area of policy that would be needed for all policy to respond efficiently to every change in demand or circumstances. A few areas dominate the agenda and receive all of the attention. The vast majority of policy areas are largely left alone, and a simple "keep doing what we are doing" decision rule dominates those areas. If a policy area gets far enough afield from citizen preferences, or if some exogenous shock happens to raise the salience of the policy area, it (a) moves onto the agenda and (b) likely changes in a more dramatic way than incrementalism would predict. The notion is that the reason the policy area became salient is precisely that circumstances now highlight that it is out of step and needs to be changed.

Other explanations focus on the slow, multistep decision-making process that dominates policy making and strongly favors the status quo. Just the core steps of how a bill becomes a law in the United States, for example, requires legislative actions in subcommittees, committees, full chambers, conference committees, and the signature of the executive—and that ignores all of the bureaucratic obstacles to implementation along with judicial branch barriers. For a new proposal to change an existing policy, it has to win at every stage of this process. For the status quo to remain, the new proposal only has to be defeated once at any one of these stages. The result is a set of institutional reasons for why most policies do not change much at all, but that dramatic change is possible once enough pressure builds to force policymakers away from the status quo.

We could continue, but the picture is clear—there are several reasons why change in policy might look more like it follows a punctuated equilibrium process rather than an incremental process. In other words, there are competing theories that all predict punctuated equilibrium. The important question for us is what scholars point to as evidence of punctuated equilibrium behavior.

7.4.1 Testing Punctuated Equilibrium Theory

One principal piece of evidence offered in support of punctuated equilibrium is the repeated finding that changes in spending for overall budgets as well as within individual policy areas are not distributed normally. Instead, changes in spending tend to exhibit leptokurtosis. Figure 7.3 shows three probability distributions. The solid line is a standard normal distribution. The dashed line represents the logistic distribution scaled to have an equal variance to the normal. The dotted line represents a Student's *t* distribution with *df* = 5.

Your eye will quickly notice that the highpoint of the scaled logistic distribution reaches above the normal distribution but that the highpoint of the *t* distribution does not. Kurtosis is generally described as a measure of peakedness, and so you might be inclined to think that the scaled logistic distribution shows high (or excess) kurtosis, and that the *t* distribution shows lower kurtosis than does the normal. However, that is actually not the case. Kurtosis is indeed a measure of peakedness, but it is not just informed by the height of the peak. It can also be thought of as a measure of the "fatness" or "heaviness" of the tails of a distribution. As Figure 7.3 shows, the scaled logistic distribution and especially the *t* distribution show tails that are heavier, or fatter, than are the tails of the normal distribution. In the limit, the normal distribution has a kurtosis of 3, the logistic has a kurtosis of 4.2, and the expected value of kurtosis for the *t* distribution equals $\dfrac{6}{df-4}$, which with *df* = 5 should result in a kurtosis equal to 6.[9]

Figure 7.3	Illustration of a Normal Probability Distribution and Two Distributions With Relatively High Kurtosis

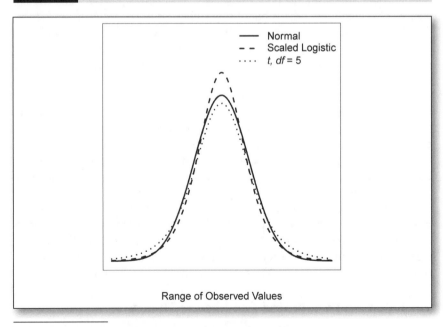

Range of Observed Values

---

[9]This formula applies for degrees of freedom greater than 2. The kurtosis of a Student's *t* is infinity for degrees of freedom $(1 < df \leq 2)$ and is undefined otherwise.

Numerous studies show that policy change appears to be distributed with higher than normal kurtosis. Figure 7.4, for example, which is taken from Baumgartner, Foucault, and Francois (2006), shows the annual percentage change in 10 French ministerial budgets from 1868 through 2002.[10] As evidenced by the heavy tails, this graph shows clear signs of high kurtosis. As we noted, graphs like this are very common in the punctuated equilibrium literature—there are lots of examples of policy changes demonstrating higher than normal kurtosis.

7.4.2 From Patterns to Explanations

Why would changes in policy spending follow a leptokurtic (higher than normal kurtosis) distribution if the process is driven by punctuated equilibrium? The argument goes back to the central limit theorem. Among other things, the central limit theorem states that the sum of a large number of random variables will follow a normal distribution. By extension, changes in a normally distributed random variable will also be normally distributed. If all of the pressures on the policy-making process were aggregated—summed—into a single variable that we might call "policy demand," authors in this field argue that it should be normally distributed. Similarly, changes in demand should also be normally distributed. If the policy-making process efficiently translates policy demand into

Figure 7.4   Distribution of Changes in Spending in 10 French Ministerial Budgets, 1986–2002. Reproduced from Baumgartner et al. (2006)

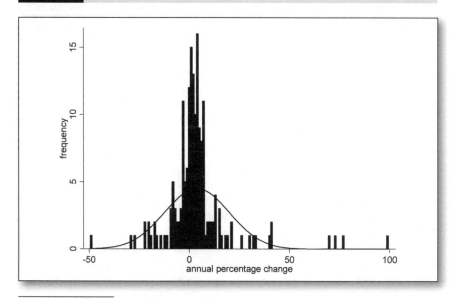

---

[10]All changes over 150% were collapsed by the authors to equal 150% to make presentation of the graph easier.

policy outputs, then the argument is that changes in policy outputs should also be normally distributed. In contrast, if the policy-making process does not respond to changes in demand efficiently, the distribution of policy changes will not be normally distributed. Specifically, if policy making is characterized by long periods of little or no change coupled with occasional periods of large change, then policy changes will bunch up more tightly around a mean of zero change, resulting in the more peaked distribution. While large changes will be limited in number, we would expect to observe more large changes than we would otherwise because pressure systematically builds up to produce large changes, resulting in the fatter tails, which represent a greater likelihood of relatively extreme values. That pressure would not build up if policy making responded efficiently to normal changes in demand.

As we noted, scholars have provided a number of explanations for the relatively high kurtosis that characterizes the distribution of changes in government spending. However, similar to our example regarding Zipf's law, one explanation that has not been explored is whether simple random chance might also produce higher kurtosis in the distribution of spending changes. Carsey and Desmarais (2013) conduct an extensive analysis of this question. We focus on one of their simulations here to illustrate how simulations can be used to evaluate the prediction of punctuated equilibrium.

Carsey and Desmarais (2013) begin with the same starting point assumed by scholars of punctuated equilibrium—that change in aggregate demand for policy can be represented on a single dimension, and that it follows a normal distribution. However, one of the questions they raise is whether policy responsiveness should also be assumed to fall on a single dimension. In other words, does looking at changes in government spending in various policy areas completely capture how the policy-making process responds to changes in demand? They suggest that even if demand for policy change follows a univariate normal distribution, that policy responsiveness might be best represented as multidimensional.

For example, suppose there is an increase in demand for environmental protection policy. The policy-making process might attempt to meet this demand through a comparable increase in spending on environmental protection. However, policymakers might also respond by passing stiffer regulations, tightening the enforcement of penalties on violations, or making it harder for industry polluters to get permits for expansion. None of these responses would necessarily require more money to enact, but they still constitute responses to increased demand. The question is, if policy responsiveness is multidimensional, what would the distribution of changes on any one of those dimensions such as spending look like?

Carsey and Desmarais (2013) conduct a simulation where changes in demand for policy follow a univariate normal distribution, but policymakers have two (and only two) policy tools that they can use to respond—(1) spending and (2) regulation. The R code we used to conduct this simulation is given below. We first load the moments package because it includes a function to calculate the kurtosis of a data vector. We also set the seed.

```
# Kurtosis Simulation
library(moments)
set.seed(364849) # Set the seed for reproducible results
```

Next, we create several objects for our simulation. We first define N to be a large number. In this simulation, N is best thought of as the number of observations of policy demand and policy. In a real empirical example, having 100,000 observations would be unlikely. As is typical for simulations, we use a large number to smooth out our results. We create an object called Demand, which is meant to capture demand for policy at any point in time. Demand is drawn from a univariate normal distribution. In this case, we draw a sample of N with a mean of zero and a standard deviation of 1.[11] This comports with the simple assumption about demand for policy that anchors the punctuated equilibrium argument.

```
N <- 100000 # A large sample of policy demand and policy
Demand <- rnorm(N, 0, 1) # Demand for policy
```

The next line defines an object named Split as a draw from a random uniform distribution bounded by 0 and 1. The two lines of code after that use Split to randomly divide how policy responds to demand into the two tools of spending and regulation. We first define an object called Spend, which is some proportional response to demand (captured by Split*Demand). Similarly, the object Reg is the remaining proportion of demand (captured by (1-Split)*Demand). Finally, we create our total policy response by defining the object Policy as the sum of spending and regulation.

```
Split <- runif(N, 0, 1) # Used to divide response into spending and regulation
Spend <- Split*Demand
Reg <- (1 - Split)*Demand
Policy <- Spend + Reg # Total policy response
```

The next four lines of code compute measures of change in demand, spending, regulation, and policy because the punctuated equilibrium theory is focused on the distribution of changes. In each line of code, we use the square bracket indexing functionality in R to take each element in one of the vectors and subtract from it the next element in the sequence. Doing so treats each vector as measuring its respective concept over consecutive periods in time. Then, we define an object called Kurts as the kurtosis measures for the four vectors of difference scores. Finally, we print the results of Kurts to the screen.

```
# Measures of change in demand, spending, regulation, and policy
DiffDemand <- diff (Demand)
DiffSpend <- diff (Spend)
```

---

[11]The choice of mean and standard deviation is made for convenience and has no bearing on the results of the simulation.

```
DiffReg <- diff (Reg)
DiffPolicy <- diff (Policy)

# Compute the kurtosis of the change measures
Kurts <- c(kurtosis(DiffDemand), kurtosis(DiffPolicy),
kurtosis(DiffSpend), kurtosis(DiffReg))

Kurts
[1] 2.992689 2.992689 4.145126 4.126110
```

We summarize the results in Figure 7.5. Panel (a) plots the distribution of simulated changes in policy demand (the dashed line) along with a comparable normal distribution. This simply confirms that our simulation is based on normally distributed changes in policy demand. Within our simulation, the measure of kurtosis for changes in demand is 2.993, which is quite near the theoretical expected value of 3.

Our simulation assumes a complete and perfect policy response to changes in demand, but that the response is divided between changes in spending and changes in regulation. Thus, some proportion of the response comes from changes in spending, while 1 minus that proportion comes from changes in regulation. Panel (b) of Figure 7.5 shows that our simulation captures the complete and efficient total policy response to changes in demand. Importantly, that distribution also shows no evidence of leptokurtosis. In fact, Panels (a) and (b) are identical to each other, which means changes in total policy also evidence a kurtosis measure equal to 2.993. In short, there is no evidence of high kurtosis in demand or in total policy response in this simulation by construction—our hypothetical government is responding efficiently and accurately to changes in demand.

However, Figure 7.6 shows that, when we look at each of the two dimensions of policy responsiveness in isolation, we see clear evidence of high kurtosis. Panel (a) plots the distribution of change in spending while Panel (b) plots change in regulation. In each case, we see a greater bunching of relatively small changes in the center of the distribution while also seeing somewhat fatter tails. This indicates that outliers occur somewhat more often than would be expected under a normal distribution. In our simulation, both changes in spending and changes in regulation produced kurtosis measures of about 4.1. Panels (a) and (b) look very similar to each other because our simulation gives each policy tool an equal likelihood of being used to respond to changes in demand at any point in time.[12]

As Carsey and Desmarais (2013) explain, the key feature of this simulation is not really the division of policy responsiveness into two different policy tools (or dimensions). The key feature is that it is done with varying probabilities.

---

[12]As we discuss more below, this simulation—which is meant only as an illustration here—is based on an extremely simplified view of the policy-making process. There is nothing in this simulation that incorporates the cognitive limitations of policymakers or the institutional advantages enjoyed by the status quo.

| Figure 7.5 | Simulated Changes in Policy Demand and Total Policy |

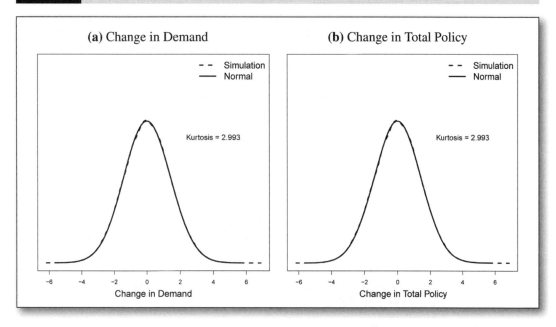

Sometimes the majority of the response to policy demand happens in the form of spending, but sometimes the majority of the response happens in the form of regulation. Repeating the simulation with a permanent constant split of demand into the two policy tools would produce distributions of change in spending and change in regulation that were both normal (and identical to changes in demand in this particular case). It is the variability in policy responsiveness across the two dimensions that matters. In fact, Carsey and Desmarais (2013) argue that anything that introduces nonconstant variance into the policy responsiveness process will produce evidence of higher than normal kurtosis in any one dimension of policy responsiveness.[13]

It would be a mistake to conclude from this simulation that none of the processes that might slow down, delay, or limit the policy responsiveness of government described by adherents of punctuated equilibrium theory are not present, nor do Carsey and Desmarais (2013) make that claim. All of these features likely do play important roles in how policy is made. This simulation is much more focused than that. It merely suggests that observing a pattern of relatively high kurtosis in changes in government spending could result even if changes in

---

[13]In fact, Carsey and Desmarais (2013) show that even if (a) policy responsiveness could be captured in a single dimension, (b) changes in policy demand are distributed normally, and (c) policy responsiveness is efficient, if the variance in changes in policy demand is not constant, changes in policy responsiveness will evidence high kurtosis.

demand are normally distributed *and* policy responsiveness is perfectly efficient. Thus, simply observing high kurtosis in one dimension of policy responsiveness may not be compelling evidence for any of these processes, or for punctuated equilibrium more generally. Similar to our example for Zipf's law, this simulation shows that data generated by a very simple and purely random DGP can produce results that could be misinterpreted as strong evidence in favor of a more complex theory. In other words, simulations using very basic assumptions can be used to examine the claims made by more complicated theories.

7.5 DYNAMIC LEARNING

How individuals (or animals for that matter) learn in response to rewards and punishments has been a central question in behavioral psychology for decades. If you have ever taken an introductory psychology class, you have likely heard about Pavlov's dogs and B. F. Skinner's pigeons, and the various experiments they and others conducted. A great deal has been learned through work like this. In this section, we show how you can use computer simulations as experiments to mimic the conduct of actual laboratory experiments to study theories of learning over time. We motivate this section by focusing on a specific type of dynamic learning: superstition.

| Figure 7.6 | Simulated Changes in Policy Responsiveness |

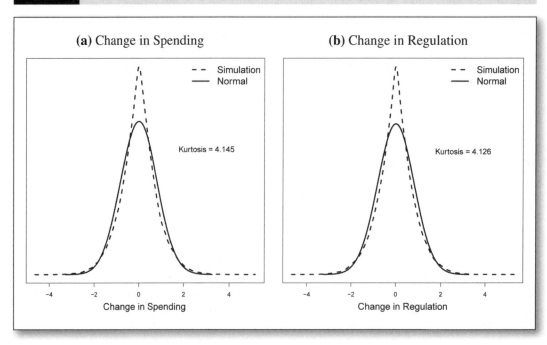

The idea of a superstition often conjures in the minds of people images of magic or supernatural forces at work in the universe. While such forces might be part of a superstition, we have in mind a less dramatic definition. We will define superstition as a belief about a causal process that lacks evidence to support that belief or when events or outcomes are falsely viewed as evidence to support a causal process. In other words, a superstitious belief is a mistaken belief that X causes Y. Lave and March (1993) present some examples of superstitious learning in their chapter on adaptive behavior, some of which we discuss here.

We begin with a simple situation where an individual can make one of two choices and is faced with one of two outcomes. The choices might be to go out or stay home, vote for the Democrat or for the Republican, or turn left or turn right. The outcomes, however, are always going to be either being rewarded for a particular choice or not being rewarded for a particular choice—(e.g., the person can receive a positive reward or a negative reward).[14] This leaves us with a total of four possible sequences of events: (1) take option 1, get positive reward; (2) take option 1, get negative reward; (3) take option 2, get positive reward; and (4) take option 2, get negative reward.

A basic model of learning represents how the actual event that a person experiences shapes their behavior the next time they are faced with making the same choice. How much the experience of a single event affects the next decision a person makes can be thought of as the rate at which experiences are incorporated into a person's views about what choices to make, or more simply, their learning rate. Generally speaking, if a person receives a positive reward for a choice, we would expect them to be more likely to make that same choice again the next time they are faced with it. However, if they get a negative reward, we could assume that they would be less likely to make that choice again the next time around. Receiving a positive or negative reward might produce different rates of learning, so we will allow those rates to differ. With these simple rules, we can write down formulas that describe the four possible events, much the way Lave and March (1993) do.

$$\text{Event 1: Choice 1 and positive reward} \rightarrow P1_{t+1} = P1_t + a(1 - P1_t) \quad (7.7)$$

$$\text{Event 2: Choice 1 and negative reward} \rightarrow P1_{t+1} = P1_t - b(P1_t) \quad (7.8)$$

$$\text{Event 3: Choice 2 and positive reward} \rightarrow P2_{t+1} = P2_t + a(1 - P2_t) \quad (7.9)$$

$$\text{Event 4: Choice 2 and negative reward} \rightarrow P2_{t+1} = P2_t - b(P2_t) \quad (7.10)$$

Here $P1$ is the probability of selecting Choice 1, $P2$ is the probability of selecting Choice 2, a is the learning rate associated with receiving a positive reward, and b is the learning rate associated with receiving a negative reward. As rate parameters, they will be bounded between 0 and 1. They can be thought of as the

---

[14]You could create more categories, such as positive reward, negative reward, and no reward, but there is no need to do so for any of the ideas we are presenting. Thus, we opt to keep it simple.

proportion by which the probability of the event they are multiplied by is changed. The subscripts t and $t + 1$ refer to points in time. So to read the equation associated with Event 1, we would say that the probability of choosing Option 1 at the next point in time is equal to the probability of having selected that choice at the current point in time plus a learning rate multiplied by 1 minus the probability of having selected Choice 1 at the current point in time.[15]

In order to use this set of equations to simulate a model of learning, we will need to set some values for $P1$, $P2$, a, and b. Most important, we will also need to determine which of these equations to employ in a given analysis. We illustrate this with a simple example. Suppose a person is going to the movies, and there are only two kinds of movies: (1) comedies and (2) dramas. These two types of movies constitute Choice 1 and Choice 2. Let's say that our hypothetical person starts with an equal probability of choosing one over the other—the person might even literally toss a coin. In other words, we start with $P1 = 0.5$ and $P2 = 0.5$. Now, suppose the comedy is a good movie such that the person is rewarded for seeing it, but the drama is bad, resulting in a negative "reward" for seeing it. Let's further suppose that our person learns faster from positive rewards compared with negative rewards. Thus, we would define a equal to some larger value and b to some smaller value. Let's set $a = .35$ and $b = .2$.

Now, let's suppose our person chose to go see the comedy. The learning question is "How does that choice, and the resulting reward, affect the probability that our person will go see a comedy instead of a drama the next time she goes to the movies?" This situation is described by Equation 7.7 above—a person who selected Choice 1 and was rewarded. By plugging in the values we defined into the equation, we find that the probability of our person going to a comedy the next time she goes to the movies is

$$P1_{t+1} = 0.5 + .35(0.5) = 0.5 + 0.175 = 0.675$$

In other words, the positive experience from seeing the comedy the first time at the movies has increased the probability that she would select a comedy over a drama the next time she goes to the movies. Because these are the only two movie options, then $P2_{t+1} = 1 - P1_{t+1} = 0.325$.

What if our moviegoer had chosen the drama at time t? This would correspond to Equation 7.10 above associated with Event 4: selecting Choice 2 and getting a negative reward. Again, we can use our starting values to evaluate the probability of selecting a drama (or comedy) at the next time she attends the movies:

$$P2_{t+1} = 0.5 - .2(0.5) = 0.5 - 0.1 = 0.4$$

The negative reward from going to a drama the first time results in a lower probability of going to a drama the next time (and a corresponding higher probability equal to 0.6 of going to a comedy the next time instead).

---

[15]Note that if Choice 1 and Choice 2 are mutually exclusive and exhaustive, then $1 - P1_t = P2_t$ and $1 - P2_t = P1_t$.

Of course, we are really not interested in predicting the behavior of just one person for just one point in time. We are interested in extrapolating from the model to make more general predictions. For example, we might want to know if our movie goer has the same basic experiences each time she goes to the movies, after going many times, will her behavior evidence a predictable pattern? Remember, whether she chose a comedy or a drama the first time was essentially a coin flip. Similarly, what if we wanted to study 100 moviegoers (or a thousand, or 10 million)—how many of them would we expect to end up going to comedies versus dramas? Some simple mathematical models like these can be solved analytically, but we are going to show you how to use simulation to study them.

Let's explore three examples of 100 people attending the movies. In every example, we will keep the same starting values for $P1$, $P2$, a, and b that we used before. In each example, we will plot the expected probability of making Choice 1 (i.e., going to the comedy instead of the drama) over 30 time periods for each of our 100 persons as a line.

7.5.1 Reward and Punishment

This example builds directly on our first illustration where individuals who select Choice 1 are positively rewarded and those who select Choice 2 are negatively rewarded. The first thing to realize is that this means that Equations 7.7 and 7.10 characterize this learning environment. Because a is larger than b, we can say that learning takes place at a faster rate in response to positive rewards than it does for negative rewards. However, both possible events should push individuals toward selecting Choice 1 in the future. The following R code captures this example.

```
# Reward and Punishment
set.seed(16568)
Sim <- 100 # Number of people
N <- 30 # Number of time periods
Time <- seq(1:N) # Time sequence
StartP1 <- .5 # Model parameters
a <- .35
b <- .2
```

The first line sets the seed as usual. Then, we define an object called `Sim` to be equal to the number of individuals we want to simulate. The object `N` is set to the number of time periods we are going to simulate. Next, we define `Time` as a sequence from 1 up through the value we pick for `N`. The object `StartP1` defines the initial probability of selecting Choice 1, which in this case is equal to 0.5. We then define a and b to the same values as before.

```
P1 <- matrix(NA, nrow = N, ncol = Sim) # Empty matrix to store the results
P1[1, ] <- StartP1 # Starting probability of making choice 1
```

The results of our simulation will be stored in an object called `P1`. We again create this as a matrix full of missing values. This matrix will have `N` rows to correspond to each time period and a total of `Sim` columns. In other words, each column of the matrix `P1` will contain the probability of a single individual selecting Choice 1 at 30 consecutive points in time. The line `P1[1,] <- StartP1` establishes the same initial probability of selecting Choice 1.

```
for(i in 1:Sim){ # i loop over people
for(j in 2:N){ # j loop over time periods
Options <- c(1, 2) # The two choices available
Probs <- c(P1[j - 1, i], (1 - P1[j - 1, i])) # Compute probabilities of each
                                              # choice for person i at time j
```

The core of the simulation requires the use of two `for` loops. The outer loop, indexed by `i in 1:Sim`, repeats the simulation for as many people as we want, defined by the value of `Sim`. The inner loop indexed by `j in 2:N` simulates the series of choices each individual will make over time. Notice that this indexing starts at 2 rather than 1. That is because the initial probability of selecting Choice 1 is defined outside the loop as equal to 0.5 for each individual. This loop will start computing the probability of making Choice 1 for the next 29 time periods.

Within the inner loop, we first define an object called `Options` as containing two elements, the numbers 1 and 2. These represent the two choices that a person can make. Next, we define an object called `Probs` that includes the corresponding probabilities of selecting Choice 1 and Choice 2. The first probability is indexed to the value in matrix `P1` as element `j - 1, i`. We use `j - 1` because the loop initializes `j` as running from 2 through N, but we need to step back to the first row in `P1`. Note that we defined the probability of selecting Choice 2 as 1 minus the probability of selecting Choice 1.

```
Choice <- sample(Options, 1, prob = Probs) # Make a choice based on Probs
if(Choice == 1){ # If Choice 1 is selected,
                 # compute probability for next choice...
P1[j, i] <- P1[j - 1, i] + a*(1 - P1[j - 1, i]) # ...using Equation 7.7
}
if(Choice == 2){ # If Choice 2 is selected,
                 # compute probability for next choice...
P1[j, i] <- 1 - ((1 - P1[j - 1, i]) - b*(1 - P1[j - 1, i])) # ...using
                                                            # Equation 7.10
}
} # End the j loop
} # End the i loop
```

Next, we define an object called `Choice` that represents the choice a person makes. They make this choice probabilistically—selecting one choice from the elements included in `Options` with associated probabilities defined in the object `Probs`. We then use two `if` statements to evaluate whether Choice 1 or

Choice 2 was selected. This tells us which equation to use to update the value of the probability of selecting Choice 1 at the next time point. The inner loop then repeats up to `i = N`, and the outer loop then repeats up to `j = Sim`.

Figure 7.7 presents the results of this simulation. The graph shows that all 100 individuals learn pretty quickly to always select Choice 1 because it provides a positive reward and to never select Choice 2 because it provides a negative reward. The lines are separated from each other between time periods 2 and about 10 because those individuals who selected Choice 2 sometime early in the process learned at a slower rate than those who selected Choice 1 more frequently early in the process.

The results in this example are not too surprising. If people always benefit from making one choice and always lose from making the opposite choice, they should learn to always make the positive choice. Our next two examples change the conditions of the experiment by changing the possible events that can occur.

7.5.2 Damned If You Do, Damned If You Don't

What if we change the environment such that regardless of the choice a person makes, they will only receive a negative reward? In other words, what if we limit

| Figure 7.7 | Simulation of Dynamic Learning Under Reward and Punishment |

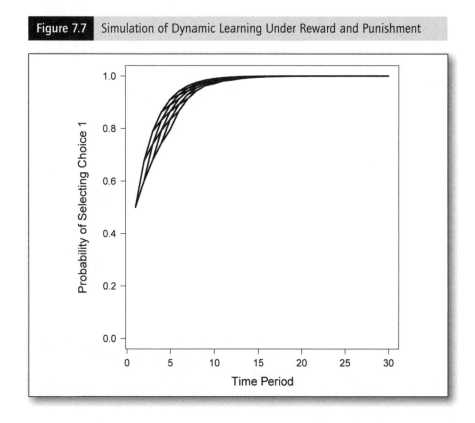

ourselves to Equations 7.8 and 7.10? Citizens in a dictatorship might face either complying with the dictator and losing their freedom or rebelling against the dictator and going to prison. A candidate may be faced with adhering to an unpopular viewpoint or being accused of flip-flopping if they change their position. A student might be faced with working on a homework assignment that generates frustration or not working on it and getting a bad grade. In every case, a person faces a negative reward whether they select Choice 1 or Choice 2. Assuming that they have to make a choice, what does our learning model predict?

The R code necessary to run this simulation is a modification of the last example. The only difference in this code compared with the previous example is that the `if` command associated with selecting Choice 1 is altered to use Equation 7.8, the negative reward now associated with that choice.

```
# Damned if you Do, Damned if you Don't
set.seed(97656)
Sim <- 100 # Number of people
N <- 30 # Number of time periods
Time <- seq(1:N) # Time sequence
StartP1 <- .5 # Model parameters
a <- .35
b <- .2


P1 <- matrix(NA, nrow = N, ncol = Sim) # Empty matrix to store the results
P1[1, ] <- StartP1 # Starting probability of making choice 1
for(i in 1:Sim){ # i loop over people
for(j in 2:N){ # j loop over time periods
Options <- c(1, 2) # The two choices available
Probs <- c(P1[j - 1, i], (1 - P1[j - 1, i])) # Compute probabilities of each
                                              # choice for person i at time j
Choice <- sample(Options, 1, prob = Probs) # Make a choice based on Probs
if(Choice == 1){ # If Choice 1 is selected,
                 # compute probability for next choice...
P1[j, i] <- P1[j - 1, i] - b*P1[j - 1, i] # ...using Equation 7.8
}
if(Choice == 2){ # If Choice 2 is selected,
                 # compute probability for next choice...
P1[j, i] <- 1 - ((1 - P1[j - 1, i]) - b*(1 - P1[j - 1, i])) # ...using
                                                            # Equation 7.10
  }
} # End the j loop
} # End the i loop
```

Figure 7.8 presents the results. The graph shows that all 100 people evidence a probability of selecting Choice 1 that oscillates between about 0.2 and 0.8, with most of the probabilities being between 0.3 and 0.7. In other words, all of the people we simulate here continue to waffle back and forth between making

Choice 1 and Choice 2, never settling on one of them. This is because the model consistently pushes them away from the choice they just made regardless of which choice that was.

More generally, this model suggests that individuals placed in situations where they view all of their choices as negative may behave in unpredictable ways. People are "learning" after each period, but there is no consistency in their choices over several time periods because both available choices lead to negative outcomes.

7.5.3 The Midas Touch

Now, let's suppose a world in which whatever choice a person makes he or she receives a positive reward—everything they touch turns to gold. This might characterize a candidate who wins an election whether she runs a positive or a negative campaign, a person who becomes wealthy whether she went to college or not, or a person who enjoys the movie whether it was a comedy or a drama. Lave and March (1993) offer as an example an infant who gets picked up and cuddled whether it coos or cries. In short, imagine a world in which any choice a person makes results in receiving a positive reward.

Figure 7.8	Simulation of Dynamic Learning When Both Choices Produce Negative Rewards

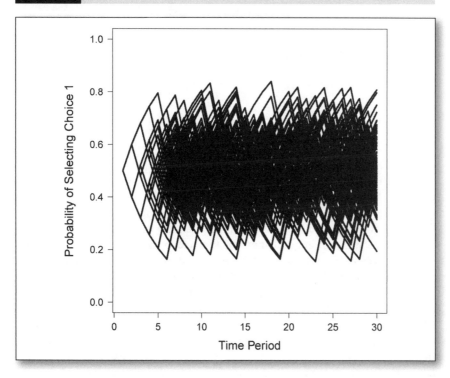

From our baseline learning model, this situation means that Equations 7.7 and 7.9 describe the set of possible outcomes. In the R code, the only change we make is to insert these equations into the appropriate if statements.

```
# The Midas Touch
# N = 30
7.5. DYNAMIC LEARNING 173
set.seed(884616)
Sim <- 100 # Number of people
N <- 30 # Number of time periods
Time <- seq(1:N) # Time sequence
StartP1 <- .5 # Model parameters
a <- .35
b <- .2

P1 <- matrix(NA, nrow = N, ncol = Sim) # Empty matrix to store the results
P1[1, ] <- StartP1 # Starting probability of making choice 1
for(i in 1:Sim){ # i loop over people
for(j in 2:N){ # j loop over time periods
Options <- c(1, 2) # The two choices available
Probs <- c(P1[j - 1, i], (1 - P1[j - 1, i])) # Compute probabilities of each
                                             # choice for person i at time j
Choice <- sample(Options, 1, prob = Probs) # Make a choice based on Probs
if(Choice == 1){ # If Choice 1 is selected,
                 # compute probability for next choice...
P1[j, i] <- P1[j - 1, i] + a*(1 - P1[j - 1, i]) # ...using Equation 7.7
}
if(Choice == 2){ # If Choice 2 is selected,
                 # compute probability for next choice...
P1[j, i] <- 1 - ((1 - P1[j - 1, i]) + (a*P1[j - 1, i])) # ...using
                                                        # Equation 7.9

}
} # End the j loop
} # End the i loop
```

In our first example, the rewards pointed to a consistent behavior in favor of Choice 1. In our second example, when any choice that was made resulted in a negative reward, we saw individuals switching back and forth between the two choices they were offered. In this example, when making either choice results in a positive reward, your intuition might be to also expect either switching behavior or maybe even random behavior. However, the results present a different pattern. We graph the output from the code above in Panel (a) of Figure 7.9.

What Panel (a) shows is some initial oscillation by most of our 100 individuals, but that most of them fairly quickly converge toward either always selecting Choice 1 or never selecting Choice 1 (i.e., always selecting Choice 2). A handful of individuals oscillate for a longer period of time, but if we ran the simulation for enough time periods, all of them will eventually converge to one choice or the other. This is more clear in Panel (b) of Figure 7.9, in which we repeated the simulation with N, the number of time periods, set to 100. In short, individuals who are faced with receiving a positive reward regardless of the choice they make will eventually "learn" to always make the same choice.

Lave and March (1993) define this as superstitious learning—a situation where individuals make choices with the belief that they produce a desired effect, but where the choice is actually irrelevant to their enjoyment of a positive reward. Baseball players who refuse to change their socks during a hitting streak, candidates who mimic the campaigns of last year's winners (whether the campaign choices of last year's winners actually mattered or not), or people who copy the management style of a successful entrepreneur when that success resulted from the product rather than management style may all be engaged in superstitious learning. People are simply making choices based on what appears to them to have worked before without considering that their choices may have nothing to do with their success or that other choices might also lead to a similar positive outcome. In other words, superstitious learning is an example of a classic case of treating correlation as causation.

The important lesson from this final simulation as compared with the first example is that simply observing a pattern of consistent behavior is not enough to determine the nature of the learning environment in which people are immersed. In our final example, we can predict that the proportion of individuals who end up selecting Choice 1 consistently depends on the initial probability of selecting Choice 1. Similarly, the behavior of any one individual is best predicted by the first choice they make, which in our example was randomly made with

---

Figure 7.9   Simulation of Dynamic Learning When Both Choices Produce Positive Rewards

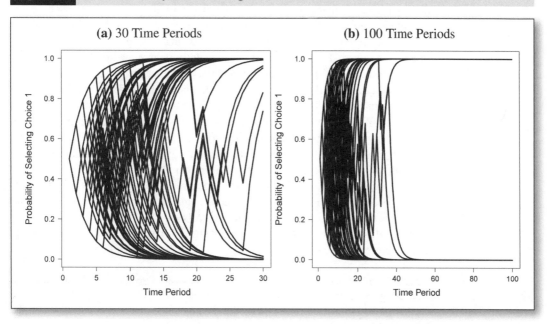

equal probability. It was this sort of learning model that B. F. Skinner explored with pigeons many years ago (Skinner, 1948). Similarly, the lesson from our second simulation is that behavior that might initially appear as random or erratic may in fact be responding in a very systematic way to a set of decision rules.

A great deal of work has been done with a basic learning model (sometimes called an adaptation model) characterized by Equations 7.7 to 7.10 above. Researchers have explored different levels of a and b. They have also studied situations in which rewards occur after every event, or after some events but in a predictable pattern, or that happen randomly. You could extend the number of choices, make rewards and nonrewards based on more than just the most recent choice, or even make choices or rewards dependent on the behavior of others. We would encourage you to explore these sorts of modifications to the basic learning model by altering the sample code we have provided.

7.6 CONCLUSIONS

In this chapter, we turned our focus away from simulations based on the properties of statistical estimators and toward simulating propositions directly derived from substantive theories. We cannot cover all of the types of simulations like this that are possible, but we hope that we have provided a useful introduction to doing such research.[16] Just like any other Monte Carlo simulation, every simulation we explored here required us to define a DGP and use that to produce simulated data. In each case, we compared a theoretical prediction about the patterns we would see in that data with the patterns our DGP actually produced. A common theme across all three examples in this chapter is to consider what sort of patterns would emerge in data drawn from a simple DGP based on random choices to see how those patterns compare with what a given theory might predict. In every case, we saw evidence that predictions from a given theory might be hard to distinguish from a null hypothesis of random behavior or that a single pattern of behavior might be associated with two or more very plausible explanations.

Like mathematical models and game theory, simulations require the researcher to be very clear and specific about the model they believe describes the situation they are studying. What simulations permit is the exploration of the emergent properties of such a model over time and under a wide range of conditions even if there is no formal mathematical solution available. Again, like any Monte Carlo simulation, the researcher controls the theoretically defined DGP and then evaluates patterns that emerge in data drawn from that DGP.

In the next chapter, we shift our attention to resampling methods. The key difference between resampling methods and the simulations we have been exploring thus far is that the researcher no longer controls the DGP when using resampling methods. Instead, the researcher works from an existing sample of observable data, using resampling methods to assist in describing the unknown DGP.

---

[16]One class of simulations interested readers might wish to explore further fall under the head of agent-based models. Such models generally include multiple actors who make decisions based in part on rules that govern their own behavior and in part based on the behavior of other actors.

8

Resampling Methods

Resampling methods are a natural extension of simulation.[1] The analyst uses a computer to generate a large number of simulated samples, then analyzes and summarizes patterns in those samples. The key difference is that the analyst begins with the observed data instead of a theoretical probability distribution. Thus, in resampling methods, the researcher does not know or control the DGP. However, the goal of learning about the DGP remains.

Resampling methods begin with the assumption that there is some population DGP that remains unobserved, but that this DGP produced the one sample of observed data that a researcher has. The analyst then mimics the "in repeated samples" process that drives simulations by producing new "samples" of data that consist of different mixes of the cases in the original sample. That process is repeated many times to produce several new simulated "samples." The fundamental assumption is that all information about the DGP contained in the original sample of data is also contained in the distribution of these simulated samples. If so, then resampling from the one observed sample is equivalent to generating completely new random samples from the population DGP.[2]

Resampling methods can be parametric or nonparametric. In either type, but especially in the nonparametric case, they are useful because they allow the analyst to relax one or more assumptions associated with a statistical estimator. The standard errors of regression models, for example, typically rely on the central limit theorem or the asymptotic normality of ML estimates. What if there is good reason to suspect these assumptions are not valid? As Mooney and Duval (1993), point out, it is sometimes "better to draw conclusions about the characteristics of

---

[1]For book-length treatments of resampling methods, see Chernick and LaBudde (2011), Efron and Tibshirani (1993), Good (2005), or Mooney and Duval (1993).

[2]Another way to think about this is that if the sample of data you have in your hands is a reasonable representation of the population, then the distribution of parameter estimates produced from running a model on a series of resampled data sets will provide a good approximation of the distribution of that statistic in the population.

a population strictly from the sample at hand, rather than by making perhaps unrealistic assumptions about that population" (p. 1).

Within this context, the key question is how we can actually produce new simulated samples of data from the observed data that effectively mimic the "in repeated samples" framework. We discuss three common methods here: (1) permutation tests, in which the analyst "reshuffles" the observed data, (2) jackknifing, which involves iteratively dropping an observation and reestimating, and (3) bootstrapping, which uses repeated draws with replacement from the observed sample to create the simulated samples. Of these three, bootstrapping is the most versatile and widely used.

8.2 PERMUTATION AND RANDOMIZATION TESTS

Permutation tests are the oldest form of resampling methods, dating back to Ronald A. Fisher's work in the 1930s (e.g., Fisher, 1935; Pitman, 1937). They are typically used to test the null hypothesis that the effect of a treatment is zero. Rather than assuming a particular form for the null distribution, the analyst uses the observed data to create one. This is done by randomly shuffling the sample many times, creating new samples that "break" the relationship in the observed sample each time. Then, the statistic of interest is computed in each reshuffled sample. Finally, the estimate from the original sample is compared with the distribution of estimates from the reshuffled samples to evaluate how different the observed estimate is from random reshuffling. If every single reshuffling combination is computed, the procedure is called a permutation (or exact) test. Another option is to perform a "large" number of reshuffles, in which case it is called a randomization test. We briefly introduce these methods here. For more complete accounts, see Rosenbaum (2002), Good (2004), or Manly (2006).

Suppose you had a sample of individuals. One subset of them received a treatment while the remaining individuals did not. The actual sample of data records measures for every individual on a dependent variable of interest, Y, and whether that person received the treatment. Suppose you were interested in recording whether the means of Y differ for the two groups. A permutation test would reshuffle the data by keeping every individual's observed value of Y unchanged, but randomly assigning which individuals to record as having received the treatment and which to record as having not received the treatment. The difference in the means of Y between these two "groups" would be computed and saved. This process of reshuffling who was recorded as receiving the treatment or not would be done many times, with the difference in the means of Y being recorded each time. The actual observed difference in the means of Y for the original sample would then be compared with the distribution of these simulated differences in means that emerged from randomness. The objective is to evaluate whether the observed difference in means in the actual sample differs enough from the distribution of randomly generated ones for the researcher to conclude that the treatment has an impact on Y.

Permutation and randomization tests assume exchangeability, which means that the observed outcomes across individuals come from the same distribution regardless of the value(s) of the independent variable(s) (Kennedy, 1995). This is a weaker assumption than the iid assumption, which also includes the notion of independence. As we discuss later, resampling methods can be easily adapted to nonindependence between observations. Before getting to that point, we illustrate permutation and randomization tests with two basic examples.

8.2.1 A Basic Permutation Test

To develop an intuition for the logic of permutation tests, we start with a simple experiment using six observations. We create a true DGP in which there is a treatment effect: Cases in the treatment group (observed.treatment = 1) have larger values of the dependent variable (observed.y) than do those in the control group (observed.treatment = 0).

```
# Basic Permutation Test
library(combinat)
set.seed(98382)

case.labels <- letters[1:6] # ID labels for each case
observed.treatment <- c(1, 1, 1, 0, 0, 0) # Treatment assignment
# The dependent variable
observed.y <- rnorm(6, mean = observed.treatment*5, sd = 1)
# Put the data together
observed.data <- data.frame(case.labels, observed.treatment, observed.y)
observed.data

  case.labels observed.treatment observed.y
1           a                  1   5.2889932
2           b                  1   5.5227244
3           c                  1   5.7360698
4           d                  0  -0.6683198
5           e                  0   1.9418637
6           f                  0   0.9191380
```

The mean of the treatment group in this case is 5.52 compared with 0.73 for the control group (a difference of 4.79). We can conduct a difference-in-means test to arrive at the p value associated with observing this difference due to chance, which produces $t = 6.21$ and $p = 0.02$. However, this requires that we assume the difference we compute can be assumed to follow a t distribution. With a sample this small, it turns out that we can also compute the exact probability of observing this outcome with a permutation test.

The following function p.test() performs the permutation test. It takes the dependent variable (y), treatment variable (treatment), and case label variable (labels) as inputs. Then, it creates all of the possible combinations of treatment assignment for those cases. In the observed data, treatment is assigned to cases a through f as $1, 1, 1, 0, 0, 0$, which means a, b, and c get the treatment and d, e, and f are in the control group. However, there could be many other possible assignments that could have happened, such as $0, 1, 1, 0, 1, 0$ or $1, 0, 1, 0, 0, 1$. In fact, there are exactly $\binom{6}{3} = 20$ possible combinations of three treatment and three control cases with a sample size of 6. The formula $\binom{N}{K}$ can be read as having a set of size N from which you choose K, or more simply as "N choose K." It is equal to $\dfrac{N!}{K! \times (N-K)!}$. In R, you could compute this by typing `choose(6,3)`.[3]

The code that follows creates a function that will generate all 20 of these possible combinations. Note that it uses the `combinat` package.

```
p.test <- function(y, treatment, labels){ # Inputs: data, case labels
require(combinat) # Requires the combinat package

# This lists all possible combinations of treatment assignment
combinations <- unique(permn(treatment))
reshuffle.treatment <- matrix(unlist(combinations),
nrow = length(combinations), ncol = length(treatment), byrow = TRUE)

# Compute the difference-in-means for each combination
reshuffle.dm <- numeric(nrow(reshuffle.treatment))
for(i in 1:nrow(reshuffle.treatment)){
reshuffle.dm[i] <- mean(y[reshuffle.treatment[i, ] == 1]) -
mean(y[reshuffle.treatment[i, ] == 0])
}

# Return the difference-in-means for each combination
result <- cbind(reshuffle.treatment, reshuffle.dm)
colnames(result) <- c(as.character(labels), "DM")
return(result)
}
```

After listing each of these 20 combinations in the object `reshuffle.treatment`, the function computes the difference-in-means between the two groups for each combination. For example, for the combination $0, 1, 1, 0, 1, 0$, it computes the difference-in-means between observations b, c, and e ("treatment") and observations a, d, and f ("control").

The result from applying this function to these data is shown below. Each row is a different combination of treatment assignment (note the first row is the assignment found in the observed data). The first six columns indicate whether

---

[3]Factorials can be computed with the `factorial()` command, though this command may produce incorrect answers due to rounding error that R encounters with very large integers. You can solve this problem by installing the `gmp` package and using its `factorialZ()` function.

each observation is in treatment (1) or control (0). The last column provides the difference-in-means of the dependent variable under that combination. The distribution of these means constitutes the null distribution of no difference between the treatment and control groups, which you can confirm by noting that the mean of this column is zero—the average difference between "treatment" and "control" groups when treatment is assigned randomly is zero.

```
        a b c d e f           DM
 [1,]   1 1 1 0 0 0      4.7850352
 [2,]   1 1 0 1 0 0      0.5154421
 [3,]   1 0 1 1 0 0      0.6576724
 [4,]   0 1 1 1 0 0      0.8134931
 [5,]   1 1 0 0 1 0      2.2555645
 [6,]   1 0 1 0 1 0      2.3977947
 [7,]   0 1 1 0 1 0      2.5536155
 [8,]   0 1 0 1 1 0     -1.7159776
 [9,]   1 0 0 1 1 0     -1.8717983
[10,]   0 0 1 1 1 0     -1.5737473
[11,]   0 0 1 1 0 1     -2.2555645
[12,]   0 1 0 1 0 1     -2.3977947
[13,]   0 1 1 0 0 1      1.8717983
[14,]   1 0 1 0 0 1      1.7159776
[15,]   1 0 0 1 0 1     -2.5536155
[16,]   1 1 0 0 0 1      1.5737473
[17,]   1 0 0 0 1 1     -0.8134931
[18,]   0 1 0 0 1 1     -0.6576724
[19,]   0 0 1 0 1 1     -0.5154421
[20,]   0 0 0 1 1 1     -4.7850352
```

Notice that the observed difference, 4.79, is the largest of the 20 values. If the null hypothesis were true, we would expect to see this value in one out of every 20 samples, which corresponds to an exact p value of 0.05. Figure 8.1 shows a histogram of the results to reinforce this point. The observed difference-in-means (solid line) falls in the tail of the distribution—an indication that it is unlikely to appear due to random chance under the null hypothesis.

Finally, note that doing this procedure for larger data sets can become extremely complex. This small example with six observations produces 20 possible combinations of treatment assignment. However, a data set of 50 observations with 25 in the treatment group would produce $\binom{50}{25} = 126,410,606,437,752$ combinations! Clearly, this is more than we want to actually construct, which is why researchers move from permutation testing to randomization testing when the number of possible permutations becomes unwieldy.

8.2.2 Randomization Tests

A randomization test is a permutation test in which a large number of the possible permutations are assembled and analyzed instead of every one of them. We

Figure 8.1	Distribution of Differences-in-Means From All Permutations of the Null Distribution

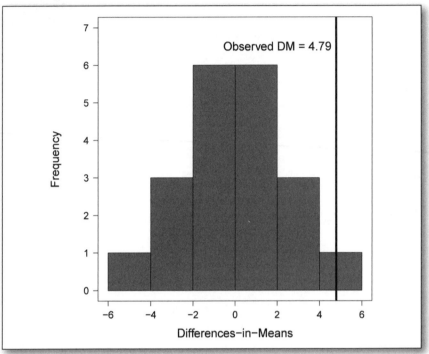

illustrate how a randomization test works using data from the 1970s on the effect of the National Supported Work (NSW) job training programs on income (LaLonde, 1986). These data have been analyzed in several different ways and are part of a larger discussion of causal inference and experimental and observational studies in the social sciences (e.g., Dehejia & Wahba, 1999). We only use these data as an example; we do not make any causal claims from the results.

Our dependent variable in this example is the change in earnings between 1974 and 1978, which represent pre- and post-treatment measurement. Participants in the treatment group ($n = 185$) received job training during that period while those in the control group ($n = 429$) did not.[4] We evaluate whether the change in earnings was larger, on average, for those in the treatment group compared with those in the control group. The difference-in-means is $2,888.64, meaning that earnings for those in the program increased by nearly $3,000 more than earnings increased for those not in the program. Using a conventional t test, this estimate is statistically significantly different from zero ($p = 0.0001398$).

---

[4]The control group was constructed from survey data in the CPS.

We can also do the analysis with a randomization test.[5] The following function r.test() is very similar to p.test() from above. The difference is that while p.test() listed each combination of 1s and 0s to compute each permutation of treatment and control, r.test() computes 1,000 permutations by randomly drawing 1s and 0s with the sample() command. In other words, it takes a large random sample of all the possible permutations. This number can be set with the reps argument (the default is 1,000). As the number of randomly selected permutations gets larger, the randomization test gets closer and closer to an exact test.

```
# RT Function
r.test <- function(y, reps = 1000){ # Inputs: data, number of repetitions

# The sample command randomly draws a 1 or 0 for each observation
# The replicate command tells R to do this 'reps' times
# The result is a matrix in which each column is a new reshuffling
reshuffle.treatment <- replicate(reps, sample(0:1, length(y), replace = TRUE))

# Compute the difference-in-means for each reshuffling
reshuffle.dm <- numeric(reps)
for(i in 1:reps){
reshuffle.dm[i] <- diff(t.test(y ~ reshuffle.treatment[ , i])$estimate)
}
return(reshuffle.dm)
}
```

Figure 8.2 plots results from the function on the LaLonde (1986) data. The histogram shows the distribution of the average difference between the two groups when the treatment and control group labels were randomly shuffled. It is centered at zero with most of its values falling between −$1,000 and $1,000. The solid line at $2,888.64 shows the result from the observed sample. This observed difference is a very extreme value compared with the null distribution; in fact, none of the estimates computed in the randomization test are larger than the observed estimate.[6] Thus, it appears very unlikely that the observed difference between the two groups' change in earnings arose due to random chance, though, as we stated before, we do not wish to make any causal claims because there are issues with these data that we do not address here.[7]

---

[5]Note that if we wanted to do a permutation test, the total number of combinations is an integer that starts with 5 and is followed by 161 additional digits—clearly too many to manage.

[6]We performed the randomization test again with reps set to 100,000. Even that many repetitions yielded no reshuffles that produced a larger difference than the observed value.

[7]Specifically, a more complete analysis would focus on whether the treatment and control groups are comparable to one another (see Dehejia & Wahba, 1999).

Figure 8.2	Distribution of Differences-in-Means From 1,000 Permutations of the Null Distribution in the LaLonde (1986) Job Training Data

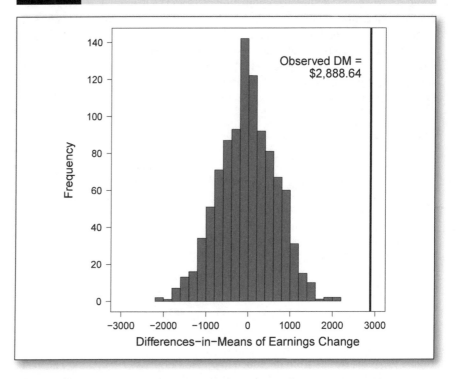

8.2.3 Permutation/Randomization and Multiple Regression Models

These examples only show permutation and randomization testing in an experimental setting, which, in our view, is where they are best suited (see Keele, McConnaughy, & White, 2012). However, randomization experiments can also be extended to the regression framework. A key issue in using a randomization test with observational data and/or multiple regression models is the procedure for reshuffling. Kennedy (1995) reviews several possibilities, ultimately concluding that simply reshuffling the values of the independent variable of interest is sufficient (see also, Kennedy & Cade, 1996).[8] However, it is also recommended that when conducting inference, the analyst should store the t values in each reshuffle rather than the coefficient estimate on the variable of interest (Erikson, Pinto, & Rader, 2010). The reason for this is that while the DGP can naturally produce collinearity between independent variables, the reshuffling in a randomization test

---

[8]Other possibilities include reshuffling the values of the dependent variable or reshuffling the residuals across observations.

breaks that collinearity, which reduces the variability of the coefficient estimates that are computed on the permutation samples (recall the simulation from Chapter 5 on multicollinearity).

We advise caution when using randomization testing in a multiple regression model. The method was designed primarily to get a p value for a statistic of interest. This is different from estimation of the covariance matrix of a set of parameter estimates (and thus, their resulting standard errors). While we tend to focus on the standard errors of coefficients the most in social science applications, the estimates of covariance between two coefficients are often just as important. Parameter estimates will covary in statistical models—certainly in all of the models we described in Chapters 5 and 6—to the degree that any of the independent variables in those models are correlated with each other. To see this, we encourage you to return to the simulation on multicollinearity we presented in Chapter 5 and to plot the simulated estimates of the two slope coefficients operating on X_1 and X_2 for different levels of correlation between these two variables. You should see that as X_1 and X_2 become increasingly positively correlated, the estimates of their respective coefficients become increasingly negatively correlated. The covariance between model parameters is, thus, an important component of understanding a statistical model's uncertainty.

Fortunately, the full covariance matrix of a model's parameter estimates is a complete representation of model uncertainty, which can be used to compute a p value or a confidence interval. The problem is that randomization testing in a multiple regression setting—at least when the independent variables are reshuffled—does not allow for computing the covariance between coefficients. This is problematic because a covariance estimate is often needed for analysis of model results.[9] For instance, conducting joint F tests, calculating confidence intervals for the marginal effects of variables in interaction models, and simulating quantities of interest (which we will learn in Chapter 9) all *require* an estimate of covariance between coefficients of interest. This does not make randomization testing incorrect, but we feel it has limited applicability outside of the experimental setting or when simply comparing two groups, and readers should be aware of these limitations.

8.3 JACKKNIFING

The jackknife is another relatively old resampling method, dating back to the 1950s (e.g., Tukey, 1958). The goal is to create resampled data by iteratively deleting one observation from the data, computing the statistic of interest using the remaining data, then putting the observation back in and deleting another case.[10] This is done until each observation has been removed once. Thus, the

---

[9]This is less of a concern if the dependent variable or residual is reshuffled because doing so leaves the independent variable covariances intact. However, those approaches are less common in practice (see Erikson et al., 2010; Kennedy, 1995; Kennedy & Cade, 1996).

[10]This review draws primarily from Rizzo (2008).

number of resamples is equal to the size of the original sample. Formally, following Rizzo's (2008, p. 191) notation, if x is the observed random sample, the ith jackknife sample, $x_{(i)}$, is the subset of the sample that leaves out observation x_i: $x_{(i)} = (x_1, ..., x_{i-1}, x_{i+1}, ..., x_n)$. In most applications, jackknifing is used to estimate uncertainty. For a sample size n, the standard error of a statistic $\hat{\theta}$ is defined as

$$\sqrt{\frac{n-1}{n} \sum_{i=1}^{n} \left(\hat{\theta}_{(i)} - \bar{\hat{\theta}}_{(.)} \right)^2} \tag{8.1}$$

where $\bar{\hat{\theta}}_{(.)} = \frac{1}{n}\sum_{i=1}^{n}\hat{\theta}_{(i)}$, which is the mean of the estimates from each of the resamples (Rizzo, 2008, pp. 190–191).

Jackknifing can be accomplished in R by using the bracket notation. Recall from Chapter 3 that the minus sign can be used to specify all elements in a vector or matrix except a certain element. For example, the code [-3] would call all elements in a vector except for the third element. This can be used with the counter in a for loop to remove one observation at a time, as shown below.

```
v <- 1:5
for(i in 1:length(v)){
print(v[-i])
}
[1] 2 3 4 5
[1] 1 3 4 5
[1] 1 2 4 5
[1] 1 2 3 5
[1] 1 2 3 4
```

Imagine that the numbers printed out above are observation labels. In the first line, we could estimate the statistic of interest on all observations except #1; in the second line, we estimate it on all observations except #2, and so on.

8.3.1 An Example

We illustrate jackknifing with data on macroeconomic indicators for 14 countries during the period 1966–1990 that is available in the Zelig package (Imai et al., 2012). We specify an OLS model of the unemployment rate (unem) as a function of three independent variables: (1) GDP (gdp), (2) capital mobility (capmob), (3) trade (trade), and indicator variables for all countries except Austria (i.e., country fixed effects). An easy way to include indicator variables in R is to use the factor() function.

```
library(Zelig)
data(macro)

ols.macro <- lm(unem ~ gdp + capmob + trade + factor(country), data = macro)
summary(ols.macro)
```

```
Call:
lm(formula = unem ~ gdp + capmob + trade + factor(country), data = macro)

Residuals:
    Min      1Q  Median      3Q     Max
-3.9811 -1.2594 -0.2674  0.9630  4.9581

Coefficients:

                              Estimate  Std. Error  t value  Pr(>|t|)
(Intercept)                   -5.84319     0.99674   -5.862  1.10e-08 ***
gdp                           -0.11016     0.04510   -2.443    0.0151 *
capmob                         0.81468     0.19156    4.253  2.75e-05 ***
trade                          0.14420     0.01138   12.669   < 2e-16 ***
factor(country)Belgium        -1.59865     0.66631   -2.399    0.0170 *
factor(country)Canada          6.75941     0.63342   10.671   < 2e-16 ***
factor(country)Denmark         4.31070     0.50798    8.486  7.14e-16 ***
factor(country)Finland         4.80987     0.56277    8.547  4.63e-16 ***
factor(country)France          6.90479     0.62070   11.124   < 2e-16 ***
factor(country)Italy           9.28969     0.60618   15.325   < 2e-16 ***
factor(country)Japan           5.45862     0.71636    7.620  2.66e-13 ***
factor(country)Netherlands    -1.45929     0.60332   -2.419    0.0161 *
factor(country)Norway         -2.75371     0.54409   -5.061  6.91e-07 ***
factor(country)Sweden          0.92533     0.52102    1.776    0.0766 .
factor(country)United Kingdom  5.60078     0.57706    9.706   < 2e-16 ***
factor(country)United States  10.06622     0.87617   11.489   < 2e-16 ***
factor(country)West Germany    3.36355     0.61641    5.457  9.49e-08 ***
---
Signif. codes: 0 *** 0.001 ** 0.01 * 0.05 . 0.1   1

Residual standard error: 1.775 on 333 degrees of freedom
Multiple R-squared: 0.7137,   Adjusted R-squared: 0.6999
F-statistic: 51.88 on 16 and 333 DF, p-value: < 2.2e-16
```

This produces the conventional standard errors from the formula for OLS (OLS-SE). Let's compute jackknife standard errors (JSE) as a comparison using the following function, jackknife(), that we create. The function takes the names of the model and data objects as inputs. Then, it iterates through the data, removing one observation at a time, estimating the model again, and storing the results.[11] Once estimates have been computed with each observation removed, it applies the formula from Equation 8.1 to each coefficient.

```
jackknife <- function(model, data){ # Inputs: Model and data
n <- nrow(data) # Computes the sample size
```

---

[11]Notice the use of formula() to insert the model formula inside the function without needing to type it out.

```
# This creates an empty matrix to store the jackknife estimates
# Each row is one iteration and each column is a coefficient
jk.est <- matrix(NA, nrow = n, ncol = length(model$coef))

# The next step is to loop through the observations, removing
# one each time, estimating the model, then storing the results
for (i in 1:n){
jk.est[i, ] <- lm(formula(model), data = data[-i, ])$coef
}

# Empty vector for the SEs
jk.se <- numeric(ncol(jk.est))

# Loop through the coefficients, computing the SE for each one with
# the formula for JSE
for (i in 1:ncol(jk.est)){
jk.se[i] <- sqrt(n/(n-1)*sum((jk.est[ , i] - mean(jk.est[ , i]))^2))
}
return(jk.se)
}
```

We can now use this function to compute JSE. We also bind the coefficients, OLS-SE, and JSE together, round them to three digits, and print the results.

```
jk.macro <- jackknife(ols.macro, macro)
round(data.frame("Coefficients" = ols.macro$coef,
"OLS.SE" = sqrt(diag(vcov(ols.macro)))), "JSE" = jk.macro), digits = 3)
```

	Coefficients	OLS.SE	JSE
(Intercept)	-5.843	0.997	1.089
gdp	-0.110	0.045	0.045
capmob	0.815	0.192	0.201
trade	0.144	0.011	0.013
factor(country)Belgium	-1.599	0.666	0.659
factor(country)Canada	6.759	0.633	0.615
factor(country)Denmark	4.311	0.508	0.459
factor(country)Finland	4.810	0.563	0.511
factor(country)France	6.905	0.621	0.721
factor(country)Italy	9.290	0.606	0.660
factor(country)Japan	5.459	0.716	0.699
factor(country)Netherlands	-1.459	0.603	0.567
factor(country)Norway	-2.754	0.544	0.490
factor(country)Sweden	0.925	0.521	0.475
factor(country)United Kingdom	5.601	0.577	0.673
factor(country)United States	10.066	0.876	0.898
factor(country)West Germany	3.364	0.616	0.626

In some cases, the OLS-SE and JSE are equal (to three digits) while in others they are not. Sometimes the OLS-SEs are larger and sometimes the JSEs are larger. It does not appear that using JSE produces a substantial difference in statistical inference in this case. This leads to the question of when JSE might be beneficial to use over the conventional standard errors of a model. We examine such an example below.

8.3.2 An Application: Simulating Heteroskedasticity

Having shown the basic operation of the jackknife, our next task is to demonstrate when it might be useful. In this example, we take the simulation on heteroskedasticity from Chapter 5 and add the estimation of jackknifed standard errors to it. We compare this JSE with the conventional standard errors produced by OLS. Because jackknifing is an empirical, nonparametric means of estimating uncertainty that does not assume constant variance, we expect that the JSE will perform better than OLS-SE.

We described this simulation in more detail in Chapter 5. The most important points are that we generate the variance of the error term as a function of the independent variable, X. This produces larger error variance at higher values of X and smaller error variance at smaller values of X (see Figure 5.4). In this case, we set the sample size to 200 rather than 1,000 because the jackknife slows down the simulation by a considerable amount.[12]

The code for the simulation is given below. We use the same `jackknife()` function from the example above. Inside the `for` loop we generate the data, estimate the model, then store the estimate of β_1 (the coefficient on the independent variable) and its estimated OLS-SE and JSE.

```
# Heteroskedasticity
# CP Function
coverage <- function(b, se, true, level = .95, df = Inf){ # Estimate,
                                              # standard error,
                                              # true parameter,
                                              # confidence level,
                                              # and df
qtile <- level + (1 - level)/2 # Compute the proper quantile
lower.bound <- b - qt(qtile, df = df)*se # Lower bound
upper.bound <- b + qt(qtile, df = df)*se # Upper bound
# Is the true parameter in the confidence interval? (yes = 1)
true.in.ci <- ifelse(true >= lower.bound & true <= upper.bound, 1, 0)
cp <- mean(true.in.ci) # The coverage probability
mc.lower.bound <- cp - 1.96*sqrt((cp*(1 - cp))/length(b)) # Monte Carlo error
mc.upper.bound <- cp + 1.96*sqrt((cp*(1 - cp))/length(b))
return(list(coverage.probability = cp, # Return results
           true.in.ci = true.in.ci,
           ci = cbind(lower.bound, upper.bound),
           mc.eb = c(mc.lower.bound, mc.upper.bound)))
}
```

---

[12]This is because in each iteration of the simulation, the jackknife has to estimate the model n times.

```
set.seed(38586) # Set the seed for reproducible results

reps <- 1000 # Set the number of repetitions at the top of the script
par.est.jack <- matrix(NA, nrow = reps, ncol = 3) # Empty matrix to store the
                                                  # estimates
b0 <- .2 # True value for the intercept
b1 <- .5 # True value for the slope
n <- 200 # Sample size
X <- runif(n, -1, 1) # Create a sample of n observations on the
                     # independent variable X
gamma <- 1.5 # Heteroskedasticity parameter

for(i in 1:reps){ # Start the loop
Y <- b0 + b1*X + rnorm(n, 0, exp(X*gamma)) # Now the error variance is a
                                           # function of X plus random noise

model <- lm(Y ~ X) # Estimate OLS model
vcv <- vcov(model) # Variance-covariance matrix
par.est.jack[i, 1] <- model$coef[2] # Store the results
par.est.jack[i, 2] <- sqrt(diag(vcv)[2])
par.est.jack[i, 3] <- jackknife(model, data.frame(Y, X))[2]
cat("Just completed iteration", i, "\n")
} # End the loop
```

We then use the `coverage()` function from Chapter 5 to compare OLS-SE and JSE.

```
# OLS-SE
coverage(par.est.jack[ , 1], par.est.jack[ , 2], b1,
df = n - model$rank)$coverage.probability
[1] 0.883

# JSE
coverage(par.est.jack[ , 1], par.est.jack[ , 3], b1,
 df = n - model$rank)$coverage.probability
[1] 0.946
```

As we saw in Chapter 5, the OLS-SEs are too small in the presence of heteroske-dasticity, on average, with a 95% confidence interval coverage probability of 0.88 in this example. In contrast, the JSEs are the correct size; the coverage probability is 0.946 with simulation error bounds that include 0.95: [0.932, 0.960]. Thus, we conclude that jackknifing is a better method for computing standard errors in the presence of heteroskedasticity than is the conventional method. Using the sample data to produce an estimate of uncertainty outperforms the OLS-SE, which assume constant variance.

8.3.3 Pros and Cons of Jackknifing

The jackknife certainly has advantages, such as its nonparametric nature that makes it robust to some assumption violations. Like other resampling methods, it can also be adapted to many different data structures, such as clustered data, in which entire groups of observations (rather than just one observation) are dropped in each iteration. It is also good for detecting outliers and/or influential cases in the data. Indeed, its leave-one-out procedure is similar to Cook's D, which is often used to detect outliers in linear regression models (Cook, 1977).

However, there are also limitations to jackknifing. It does not perform as well if the statistic of interest does not change "smoothly" across repetitions. For example, jackknifing will underestimate the standard error of the median in many cases because the median is not a smooth statistic (see Rizzo, 2008, p. 194). In such cases, it is necessary to leave more than one observation out at a time (Efron & Tibshirani, 1993). Additionally, the jackknife can be problematic in small samples because the sample size dictates the number of repetitions/resamplings that are possible.[13] A key theme throughout this book has been that adding more repetitions increases the precision of an estimate, but the number of repetitions is capped at N for the jackknife. Fortunately, this limitation is not faced by the most versatile and perhaps most common resampling method: bootstrapping.

8.4 BOOTSTRAPPING

Bootstrapping was formally introduced by Efron (1979). It gets its name from the phrase "to pull oneself up by the bootstraps," which typically refers to a person improving her situation in life through her own efforts. Bootstrapping reflects this quality by getting the most information you can about a population DGP from the one sample of data you have. While there are several varieties of bootstrapping, at their core is a common process of simulating draws from the DGP using only the sample data.[14]

The bootstrap process usually unfolds according to the following steps. Denote a sample $S = \{x_1, x_2, x_3, \ldots, x_n\}$ of size n drawn from a population P. A statistic of interest, θ, that describes P can be estimated by calculating $\hat{\theta}$ from S. The sampling variability of $\hat{\theta}$ can then be calculated via the bootstrap in the following way:

1. Draw a sample of size n from S *with replacement* such that each element is selected with probability $\dfrac{1}{n}$. Denote this "bootstrap sample," S_{boot1}.

2. Calculate a new estimate of θ from S_{boot1}. Denote this bootstrap estimate $\hat{\theta}_1^*$.

3. Repeat Steps 1 and 2 J times, storing each $\hat{\theta}_j^*$ to create V, a vector of bootstrap estimates of the parameter of interest, θ.

---

[13]To see this illustrated, try computing JSE for a model from the Ehrlich (1973) crime data set used in Chapter 3, which has only 47 observations. The JSE differ considerably from the OLS-SE in that case.

[14]There are numerous treatments of bootstrapping that go into much greater detail than we can in this section. Interested readers should examine Efron and Tibshirani (1993), Good (2005), Mooney and Duval (1993), and chapter 7 of Rizzo (2008).

For a sufficiently large J, the vector V from Step 3 can be used to estimate a standard error and/or confidence interval for θ through several different methods.[15]

There are several key features of this process. First, the draws must be *independent*—each observation in S must have an equal chance of being selected. Additionally, the bootstrap sample drawn in Step 1 should be size n to take full advantage of the information in the sample (although some bootstrap methods draw smaller samples). Finally, resampling must be done *with replacement*. This means that in any given bootstrap sample, some individual observations might get selected more than once while others might not get selected at all. If replacement did not occur, every bootstrap sample of size n would be identical to each other and to the original sample.

To see this illustrated, consider the following sample of 10 countries. First, we sample without replacement. Notice that doing so produces the exact same sample of 10 countries (though in a different order). Computing any statistic of interest would be identical each time when sampling is done without replacement.

```
countries <- c("United States", "Canada", "Mexico", "England", "France",
"Spain", "Germany", "Italy", "China", "Japan")

sample(countries, replace = FALSE)
 [1] "France"  "Italy"  "China"  "Spain"  "United States"
 [6] "England" "Japan"  "Canada" "Mexico" "Germany"
```

Now, we sample with replacement three times. Notice that sometimes one or more countries do not make it into a particular sample and other times a particular country is repeated in a given sample. This produces the variation needed to compute measures of uncertainty in the statistic of interest.

```
sample(countries, replace = TRUE)
 [1] "United States" "Italy"      "Italy"   "China"   "Germany"
 [6] "Italy"         "England"    "Japan"   "Italy"   "Canada"

sample(countries, replace = TRUE)
 [1] "England"       "United States" "Germany" "Mexico"        "Canada"
 [6] "England"       "United States" "England" "United States" "Spain"

sample(countries, replace = TRUE)
 [1] "Canada" "Italy" "Spain" "Canada" "Italy" "China" "China"
 [8] "Japan"  "Spain" "Germany"
```

Below we go through several different types of bootstrapping. The most important point to keep in mind is that bootstrapping is a lot like simulation. The difference is that instead of drawing multiple random samples from a theoretical

---

[15]We use a single parameter, θ, to illustrate how bootstrapping works, but θ could just as easily represent a set of parameters of a statistical model (e.g., the βs in a regression model).

DGP (as we do with simulation), we are drawing multiple random samples from the observed data.

8.4.1 Bootstrapping Basics

We start with a basic example of bootstrapping to compute the standard error of a mean, μ, and compare it with simulation. We first draw a sample from a normal distribution using `rnorm()`. Then, we compute the mean and standard error for that sample using the formula for the standard error of a mean: $\dfrac{\hat{\sigma}}{\sqrt{n}}$.

```
# Bootstrap a Mean
set.seed(34738)
n <- 500 # Sample size
n.boot <- 1000 # Number of bootstrap samples

b <- rnorm(n, 4, 5) # The sample, from a DGP of mean = 4, SD = 5
mean.b <- mean(b) # Sample mean
se.b <- sd(b)/sqrt(n) # SE of the mean
se.b
[1] 0.2065029
```

We can bootstrap the standard error of μ by resampling from the data many times (n.boot = 1,000 here) and computing the mean of each of those bootstrapped samples. We do this in a `for` loop with the code below. The object `ind` is the key component. That object is a sample of observation numbers drawn with replacement. We insert that object into the brackets in the next line—`b[ind]`— to reference those observation numbers in the sample.

```
boot.b <- numeric(n.boot) # Vector for the bootstrap samples
for(i in 1:n.boot){ # Start the loop
# Observation indicators for the bootstrap sample
ind <- sample(1:n, replace = TRUE)
boot.b[i] <- mean(b[ind]) # Compute the mean of the bootstrap sample
} # End the loop
```

We can also draw 1,000 samples from the true DGP to compare with the bootstrap estimates. Remember that this is what bootstrapping is trying to mimic, so the two procedures should look very similar.

```
# Random draws from the DGP
dgp.b <- numeric(n.boot)
for(i in 1:n.boot){
dgp.b[i] <- mean(rnorm(n, 4, 5))
}
```

We show the results in Figure 8.3. Panel (a) plots a histogram of the 1,000 boot-strapped means, generated by resampling the observed data. Panel (b) plots a histogram of 1,000 means from repeatedly using `rnorm()` to draw from the true DGP. Notice that the two distributions look very similar; both are centered near the true mean of 4 and show about the same spread. In short, we can see that bootstrapping does mimic the process of drawing repeated samples from the sta-tistic's sampling distribution, which in this case is the true DGP.[16]

To arrive at the bootstrap standard error of the mean, we can simply compute the standard deviation of the 1,000 bootstrap estimates of the mean. Notice that this produces an estimate that is very close to the standard error we computed using the formula above.

```
# Bootstrap estimate of the SE of the mean
boot.se <- sd(boot.b)
boot.se
[1] 0.2111522

se.b
[1] 0.2065029
```

Figure 8.3	Histograms of 1,000 Bootstrap Sample Means and Simulated Means

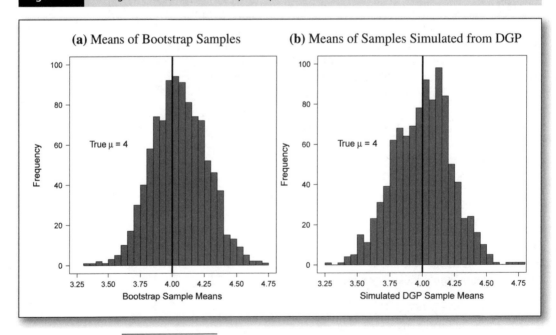

---

[16]This is due to the fact that the sample mean is an unbiased estimator of the population mean. If the estimator were biased, its sampling distribution would be different from the true DGP.

We can then compute a 95% confidence interval with the standard error as $\hat{\mu} \pm 1.96 \times \text{SE}_{\text{boot}}$.

```
# 95% confidence interval (parametric)
mean.b - 1.96*boot.se # Lower bound
[1] 3.648022

mean.b + 1.96*boot.se # Upper bound
[1] 4.475739
```

This is a parametric confidence interval because it uses properties of the normal distribution (i.e., the critical value of 1.96 multiplied by the standard error). For this to be appropriate, it must be reasonable to assume that the statistic of interest follows a normal distribution. For sample means, the central limit theorem makes this plausible, but this will not always be the case.

More generally, it strikes us as a bit odd to use a nonparametric resampling method to generate a simulated distribution of a parameter of interest, but then to use a parametric method to summarize the distribution of those parameter estimates. A completely distribution-free 95% confidence interval can be computed using the 2.5th and 97.5th quantiles of the bootstrap estimates.

```
# 95% confidence interval (nonparametric)
quantile(boot.b, .025) # Lower bound
    2.5%
3.656705

quantile(boot.b, .975) # Upper bound
   97.5%
4.47584
```

In this case, the two are very similar because the true DGP is a normal distribution. If the true DGP were not normal, these two methods would produce different results. Similarly, if the true DGP were not symmetric, the quantile method would capture that with a 95% confidence interval with bounds that were not equidistant from the mean. Thus, the quantile method (sometimes called the percentile method) is more flexible and better suited to recover a wider range of possible DGPs.

There are limits to the percentile method, however. First, the method requires you to have a fairly large sample of data so that you can be confident that the tails of the underlying population probability distribution are adequately represented in the sample data (Mooney & Duval, 1993). In other words, observations that are unlikely to appear given the true DGP may be completely unrepresented in a small sample of data rather than appearing rarely as they should. The percentile method can also be biased and inefficient (see Good, 2005). Still, if your original sample size is large, the percentile method is attractive because it does not impose any parametric assumptions.

We have discussed the two most common methods of generating confidence intervals via the bootstrap, but there are many others. Another problem with the percentile method is that you must assume that the distribution of the bootstrapped parameters of interest is an unbiased estimate of the true distribution of those parameters in the population. This is less restrictive than assuming the distribution must be normal, but still an assumption. In response, scholars have introduced a bias-corrected bootstrap confidence interval.[17]

Another approach to getting a proper confidence interval is to use a double-bootstrapping method to produce an estimate of the standard error of a statistic.[18] For this method, you still draw your large number of resamples to generate estimates of the parameter of interest. However, for each of those replicated samples, you perform another bootstrap on that replicated sample to generate an estimate of the standard error of that statistic. Rizzo (2008) offers a step-by-step discussion of how this procedure unfolds (section 7.4.4 starting on page 201). The main obstacle to this procedure is the computational time involved. If you draw 1,000 resamples to compute your parameters of interest, but also perform a bootstrap of 1,000 draws on each of those initial draws, you end up taking 1,000 × 1,000, or a total of 1,000,000 resampled draws from your data. If the statistical model you are estimating is even slightly computationally intensive, running it 1 million times will be very time-consuming.

The various methods described here for generating bootstrap confidence intervals (and a few others) are available to researchers in several R packages. These include the `boot` package, the `bootstrap` package, and the `bootcov()` function that is part of the `rms` package. We encourage interested readers to explore these packages and the publications we have cited if they are interested in learning more.

8.4.2 Bootstrapping With Multiple Regression Models

Bootstrapping is probably most useful to applied social scientists in the context of computing standard errors for multiple regression models. In the example below, we compute bootstrapped standard errors for the following model from the Ehrlich (1973) crime data used in Chapter 3.

```
set.seed(8873)
library(foreign)
crime <- read.dta("crime.dta")
```

---

[17]See Efron and Tibshirani (1993), Good (2005), Mooney and Duval (1993), or Rizzo (2008) for more discussion of this approach

[18]Good (2005) and Rizzo (2008) refer to this method as the bootstrap *t* interval, but Mooney and Duval (1993) call it the percentile *t* method.

```
# OLS model from the crime data
crime.1 <- lm(crime1960 ~ imprisonment + education + wealth +
+ inequality + population1960, data = crime)
summary(crime.1)

Call:
lm(formula = crime1960 ~ imprisonment + education + wealth +
    inequality + population1960, data = crime)

Residuals:
    Min      1Q  Median      3Q     Max
-525.23 -178.94  -25.09  145.62  771.65

Coefficients:
                 Estimate  Std. Error  t value  Pr(>|t|)
(Intercept)    -4213.3894   1241.3856   -3.394  0.001538 **
imprisonment   -3537.8468   2379.4467   -1.487  0.144709
education         113.6824     65.2770    1.742  0.089088 .
wealth              0.3938      0.1151    3.422  0.001420 **
inequality        101.9513     25.9314    3.932  0.000318 ***
population1960      1.0250      1.3726    0.747  0.459458
---
Signif. codes: 0 *** 0.001 ** 0.01 * 0.05 . 0.1   1

Residual standard error: 297 on 41 degrees of freedom
Multiple R-squared: 0.4744,   Adjusted R-squared: 0.4103
F-statistic: 7.4 on 5 and 41 DF, p-value: 5.054e-05
```

There are several packages available to do bootstrapping in R, but we will start by writing our own because it helps develop intuition. The function we create takes two arguments: (1) the name of the model and (2) the number of bootstrap samples desired, which is set to a default of 1,000.[19] The first object created inside the function, boot.est, is an empty matrix to store the coefficient estimates from the bootstrap samples. It has a row for every bootstrap sample and a column for every coefficient estimate to be stored.[20] Next, the function starts a bootstrap loop that creates a new bootstrap sample each time.

```
# Inputs: the model name and the number of bootstrap samples
bootstrap <- function(model, n.boot){
# This creates an empty matrix for the bootstrap estimates
boot.est <- matrix(NA, nrow = n.boot, ncol = model$rank)
for(i in 1:n.boot){ # Start bootstrap loop
```

---

[19]Efron and Tibshirani (1993) contend that this number need not be large (e.g., 50–200). We recommend a large number such as 1,000 to improve precision (see also Rizzo, 2008).

[20]The object rank in a model object gives the number of coefficients estimated in that model.

Inside the bootstrap loop, the first step is to draw a sample of data from the observed data. As before, we use `sample()` to draw *n* observation numbers with replacement. Next, we create an empty matrix called `datai` that will be the data matrix of the bootstrap sample. We fill this matrix row by row in a second `for` loop. To do this, we use the `model` object that can be called from any estimation object in R (such as `lm()`). This object stores the entire data matrix used in estimation. We index the row numbers from `model` using the numbers sampled with replacement. At the end of this loop, `datai` is a matrix with *n* rows and a column for each variable in the model. Some observations from the original data may be repeated in multiple rows, and some observations may not appear at all. The final lines coerce this matrix into a data frame and assign the variables names.

```
# Select observations to go in bootstrap sample
boot.sample <- sample(1:nrow(model$model), replace = TRUE)
# Initiate bootstrap sample data
datai <- matrix(NA, nrow = length(boot.sample), ncol = model$rank)
for(j in 1:length(boot.sample)){ # Start data loop
datai[j, ] <- as.numeric(model$model[boot.sample[j], ]) # Coefficients from
                                                        # bootstrap sample
                                                        # j go into row
                                                        # j of datai

} # End bootstrap sample data
datai <- data.frame(datai)
colnames(datai) <- colnames(model$model)
```

The final task is to estimate the model on this bootstrapped sample and store the results. We use the `formula()` function to paste the model's formula and set the data to the object `datai`. We fill each row of `boot.est` with the coefficients. Once that is complete, the bootstrap loop is complete. The last step is to return the results. We include two objects in the `return()` function: (1) the actual bootstrap coefficient estimates in a matrix and (2) the variance–covariance matrix of those estimates, which we obtain with the `cov()` function.[21]

```
# Run the model on the bootstrap sample,
# then collect coefficients in boot.est matrix
boot.est[i, ] <- coef(lm(formula(model), data = datai))
cat("Completed", i, "of", n.boot, "bootstrap samples", "\n")
} # End bootstrap loop

# Return the matrix of coefficient estimates and the
# bootstrapped variance-covariance matrix
return(list(boot.est = as.matrix(boot.est), boot.vcv = cov(boot.est)))
} # End function
```

---

[21]Note that this is a parametric means of estimating uncertainty. We could also compute confidence intervals for each coefficient with the quantiles of each set of bootstrap estimates.

We can then use the function on the crime data model and compare the results with the OLS standard errors. The `bootstrap()` function takes about 15 seconds to complete the process. In this case, the bootstrapped standard errors are the larger of the two for all of the coefficient estimates.

```
system.time( # Check how long it takes
crime.boot <- bootstrap(crime.1)
)
   user system elapsed
  14.71   0.03   14.78
```

```
crime.se <- cbind(coef(crime.1), sqrt(diag(vcov(crime.1))),
sqrt(diag(crime.boot$boot.vcv)))
colnames(crime.se) <- c("Coefficients", "Conventional SE", "Bootstrapped SE")
crime.se
```

	Coefficients	Conventional SE	Bootstrapped SE
(Intercept)	-4213.3894135	1241.3856333	1549.2743323
imprisonment	-3537.8467727	2379.4467146	3093.9600328
education	113.6824207	65.2769966	81.4374504
wealth	0.3937634	0.1150612	0.1516832
inequality	101.9513371	25.9314385	28.7289504
population1960	1.0250156	1.3725803	1.7785137

Increasing Computation Speed

Although our `bootstrap()` function works, it is somewhat slow because it relies on a `for` loop. A faster option is the `bootcov()` function in the `rms` package, which uses vectorized operations. To use the function, we first need to use the package's `ols()` function instead of `lm()` to estimate the model.[22]

```
library(rms)

crime.2 <- ols(crime1960 ~ imprisonment + education + wealth +
inequality + population1960, x = TRUE, y = TRUE, data = crime)
```

Then, we insert the model name into `bootcov()` and set the argument B to the number of bootstrap samples.

```
system.time( # Check how long it takes
crime.boot2 <- bootcov(crime.2, B = n.boot)
)
```

---

[22]The `rms` package also has several other GLM functions that work with `bootcov()`. The arguments x = TRUE, y = TRUE tell R to save the independent variables and dependent variable in a matrix, which the bootstrapping function requires.

```
         user system elapsed
         0.17   0.00    0.17

crime.boot2
Linear Regression Model

ols(formula = crime1960 ~ imprisonment + education + wealth +
    inequality + population1960, data = crime, x = TRUE, y = TRUE)

     n Model  L.R.       d.f.          R2    Sigma
    47      30.23          5      0.4744      297

Residuals:
    Min      1Q Median      3Q     Max
-525.23 -178.94 -25.09 145.62 771.65

Coefficients:
                        Value   Std. Error         t     Pr(>|t|)
Intercept          -4213.3894    1565.4927   -2.6914    0.0102514
imprisonment       -3537.8468    3114.1249   -1.1361    0.2625267
education            113.6824      80.1067    1.4191    0.1634172
wealth                 0.3938       0.1518    2.5940    0.0130963
inequality           101.9513      28.2689    3.6065    0.0008343
population1960         1.0250       1.6787    0.6106    0.5448257

Residual standard error: 297 on 41 degrees of freedom
Adjusted R-Squared: 0.4103
```

Notice that `bootcov()` took less than 1 second to complete the operation—a substantial improvement over `bootstrap()`. Additionally, the standard errors produced by `bootcov()` look similar to those from `bootstrap()`, but they are not exactly the same. This highlights an important feature of bootstrapping. Because a different set of bootstrap samples could be drawn in each successive run of the code, the standard errors will be different each time. However, the analyst controls the number of repetitions, and adding more repetitions reduces the variation between calculations. Additionally, setting the seed beforehand will produce the same estimates each time.

Alternative Versions

We have focused primarily on bootstrapping by resampling complete observations, which is the most common approach. However, there are several alternatives that may also be useful. For example, one option is to resample residuals and assign them to observations. This comports better with the assumptions that the independent variables are fixed in repeated samples and that the error is what is random. Another possibility is an approach called the wild bootstrap, in which residuals are resampled and multiplied randomly by some number, such as 1 or − 1 or a random draw from a standard normal distribution. Wu (1986) shows that this can improve bootstrap performance in the presence of heteroskedasticity. There are also several modifications to correct for bias if the distribution of bootstrap estimates is skewed (e.g., bias-corrected bootstrap or accelerated bootstrap, see Chernick & LaBudde, 2011; Efron, 1987; Good, 2005; Rizzo, 2008).

8.4.3 Adding Complexity: Clustered Bootstrapping

As we briefly mentioned above, the resampling methods we examine here can be adapted to several features of the data. For instance, the block bootstrap is designed to be used with time-series data (Künsch, 1989). Similarly, it is possible to resample groups of observations instead of individual observations if there is nonindependence due to clustering in the data. For example, recall the model on macroeconomic indicators in 14 countries from 1966 to 1990 from above. Each country appears in the data set multiple times. Because observations from each country likely share something in common that is not captured in the systematic component of the model, the residuals among observations clustered within each specific country are likely to be correlated with each other. We saw in Chapter 5 that this produces a downward bias in the standard error estimates we calculated. As an alternative, we can bootstrap the standard errors, resampling clusters of observations by country rather than individual observations. To do so, we make a small change to the code in the `bootcov()` function. First, here is the model with the conventional OLS standard errors (notice we removed the country indicator variables).

```
ols.macro2 <- ols(unem ~ gdp + capmob + trade
+ , x = TRUE, y = TRUE, data = macro)

ols.macro2
Linear Regression Model

ols(formula = unem ~ gdp + capmob + trade, data = macro, x = TRUE,
    y = TRUE)

   n Model    L.R.     d.f.        R2   Sigma
 350          118.8       3    0.2878   2.746

Residuals:
    Min     1Q  Median      3Q     Max
-5.3008 -2.0768 -0.3187 1.9789 7.7715

Coefficients:
            Value Std.     Error        t   Pr(>|t|)
Intercept     6.18129  0.450572   13.719   0.000e+00
gdp          -0.32360  0.062820   -5.151   4.355e-07
capmob        1.42194  0.166443    8.543   4.441e-16
trade         0.01985  0.005606    3.542   4.517e-04

Residual standard error: 2.746 on 346 degrees of freedom
Adjusted R-Squared: 0.2817
```

To bootstrap the standard errors by country, we use the `cluster` argument in the `bootcov()` function. This tells the function to resample countries instead of individual observations. In other words, if a country is drawn, all of its observations in the data enter the bootstrap sample rather than just one observation. If a country is resampled more than once, then all of its observations enter the sample more than once.

```
macro.boot <- bootcov(ols.macro2, B = n.boot, cluster = macro$country)


macro.boot
Linear Regression Model

ols(formula = unem ~ gdp + capmob + trade, data = macro, x = TRUE,
    y = TRUE)

      n Model  L.R.     d.f.        R2      Sigma
    350        118.8       3    0.2878      2.746

Residuals:
     Min     1Q   Median      3Q      Max
 -5.3008 -2.0768 -0.3187  1.9789   7.7715

Coefficients:
                 Value   Std. Error        t      Pr(>|t|)
Intercept      6.18129      1.35613    4.558     7.171e-06
gdp           -0.32360      0.09519   -3.399     7.541e-04
capmob         1.42194      0.54369    2.615     9.303e-03
trade          0.01985      0.01874    1.059     2.902e-01

Residual standard error: 2.746 on 346 degrees of freedom
Adjusted R-Squared: 0.2817
```

Notice that the bootstrapped standard errors (1.36, 0.10, 0.54, and 0.02) are considerably larger than the conventional OLS standard errors (0.45, 0.06, 0.17, and 0.01). This leads to the question of which standard error method is better. We can use simulation to produce an answer. Recall that in Chapter 5 we simulated clustered data and compared several different estimators for coefficient estimates and standard errors. We conduct a version of that simulation below and compare the OLS standard errors (OLS-SEs), robust cluster standard errors (RCSEs), and bootstrap cluster standard errors (BCSEs).[23]

The code for this simulation is a modification of the code from Chapter 5. We set the sample size to 200, the number of clusters to 25, and we set the independent variable, X, to vary at the cluster level. We estimate an OLS model, then compute the OLS-SE, RCSE, and BCSE.

---

[23]This is a short version of simulations done in Harden (2011).

```
# Simulation with BCSE
library(mvtnorm)
library(rms)
# Function to compute robust cluster standard errors (Arai 2011)
rcse <- function(model, cluster){
require(sandwich)
M <- length(unique(cluster))
N <- length(cluster)
K <- model$rank
dfc <- (M/(M - 1)) * ((N - 1)/(N - K))
uj <- apply(estfun(model), 2, function(x) tapply(x, cluster, sum))
rcse.cov <- dfc * sandwich(model, meat = crossprod(uj)/N)
return(rcse.cov)
}


set.seed(934656) # Set the seed for reproducible results


reps <- 1000 # Set the number of repetitions at the top of the script
par.est.cluster <- matrix(NA, nrow = reps, ncol = 4) # Empty matrix to store
                                                     # the estimates
b0 <- .2 # True value for the intercept
b1 <- .5 # True value for the slope
n <- 200 # Sample size
p <- 0.5 # Rho
nc <- 25 # Number of clusters
c.label <- rep(1:nc, each = n/nc) # Cluster label


for(i in 1:reps){ # Start the loop
i.sigma <- matrix(c(1, 0, 0, 1 - p), ncol = 2) # Level 1 effects
i.values <- rmvnorm(n = n, sigma = i.sigma)
effect1 <- i.values[ , 1]
effect2 <- i.values[ , 2]


c.sigma <- matrix(c(1, 0, 0, p), ncol = 2) # Level 2 effects
c.values <- rmvnorm(n = nc, sigma = c.sigma)
effect3 <- rep(c.values[ , 1], each = n/nc)
effect4 <- rep(c.values[ , 2], each = n/nc)


X <- effect3 # X values unique to level 2 observations
error <- effect2 + effect4


Y <- b0 + b1*X + error # True model


model.ols <- lm(Y ~ X) # Model estimation


vcv.ols <- vcov(model.ols) # Variance-covariance matrices
vcv.rcse <- rcse(model.ols, c.label)
vcv.bcse <- bootcov(ols(Y ~ X, x = TRUE, y = TRUE),
B = n.boot, cluster = c.label)
```

```
par.est.cluster[i, 1] <- model.ols$coef[2] # Coefficients
par.est.cluster[i, 2] <- sqrt(diag(vcv.ols)[2])
par.est.cluster[i, 3] <- sqrt(diag(vcv.rcse)[2])
par.est.cluster[i, 4] <- sqrt(diag(vcv.bcse$var)[2])
cat("Just completed iteration", i, "\n")
} # End the loop
```

Next, we compute the coverage probabilities of each standard error method.

```
ols.cp <- coverage(par.est.cluster[ , 1], par.est.cluster[ , 2], b1,
 df = n - model.ols$rank)
ols.cp$coverage.probability
[1] 0.641

rcse.cp <- coverage(par.est.cluster[ , 1], par.est.cluster[ , 3], b1,
 df = n - model.ols$rank)
rcse.cp$coverage.probability
[1] 0.909

bcse.cp <- coverage(par.est.cluster[ , 1], par.est.cluster[ , 4], b1,
 df = n - model.ols$rank)
bcse.cp$coverage.probability
[1] 0.923
```

As we saw in Chapter 5, the OLS-SE is severely biased downward, with a coverage probability of 0.641. Additionally, while RCSE is better, it still shows evidence of being too small, with a coverage probability of 0.909 and simulation error bounds of [0.891, 0.927]. Finally, bootstrapping by cluster performs the best of the three, though it is still biased slightly downward. The BCSE coverage probability is 0.923 with error bounds [0.906, 0.940]. Overall, among these alternatives, bootstrapping by cluster provides the best method of estimating standard errors in the presence of clustered data (for more details, see Harden, 2011).[24] This example shows both the benefits of bootstrapping as a method of estimating standard errors and the use of a simulation to evaluate competing methods.

8.5 CONCLUSIONS

Resampling methods are similar to simulation in that they use an iterative process to summarize the data. The main difference is that they rely on the observed sample of data rather than a theoretical DGP. This empirical basis typically gives resampling methods robustness to assumption violations, as shown by the jackknife estimate of standard errors in the presence of heteroskedasticity, the BCSE

---

[24]The BCSE method can also be extended to multilevel model standard errors (Harden, 2012a).

performance with clustered data, and the quantile method of computing bootstrap confidence intervals. Data from the real world are rarely perfectly well behaved, so we recommend that researchers consider using resampling methods in their own work.

Within the various methods, there are cases where each one may be most appropriate. Permutation and randomization testing are typically best for experimental data where there is a clear treatment variable and null hypothesis of no effect. Randomization testing has been extended to the multiple regression framework (e.g., Erikson et al., 2010), but we do not recommend it because it does not allow for estimation of the full variance–covariance matrix of the coefficient estimates. Jackknifing is a good option when the analyst is concerned about the undue influence of particular data points. However, it performs poorly in small samples and when the statistic of interest is not smooth.

We recommend bootstrapping for most cases because it is flexible and robust to many different types of data. It also allows for estimation of the full covariance matrix in a multiple regression model while also generally performing well in small samples (Efron & Tibshirani, 1993). Moreover, its strong connection to the conceptualization of simulating repeated samples makes the method intuitively appealing. In short, while not a panacea, bootstrapping is a very useful tool for applied social scientists.

Having completed chapters on simulation and on resampling methods, we bring the two together in the next chapter. First, we look at a method for simulating from the observed data as a means of generating quantities of interest from model results. Then, we discuss cross-validation as a "resampling-like" tool for evaluating the fit of statistical models.

9

Other Simulation-Based Methods

In the preceding chapters, we have covered simulation of statistical models, simulation of substantive theoretical processes, and resampling methods. These topics are certainly useful for researchers, but there are many other simulation-based methods employed by social scientists, including methods for better understanding statistical models, evaluating models, and even estimating model parameters.[1] While detailing all of these would take us well beyond the scope of this book, in this chapter we highlight two methods that are particularly useful for social scientists: (1) simulating quantities of interest from model results and (2) cross-validation. Both of these methods combine elements of the material we have already covered, but are unique in their objectives.

Simulation can be used as a method for generating substantively meaningful "quantities of interest" (QI) from the results of a statistical model (see King et al., 2000, for an excellent overview). Instead of simply reporting the coefficients of a regression model, researchers can simulate quantities such as expected values of the dependent variable, expected probabilities associated with various outcomes on the dependent variable, or first differences, as well as measures of uncertainty, to give readers a clearer sense of the model results. In other words, a researcher can make a statement such as "the expected probability of voting increases by between 25 and 33 percentage points for strong partisans compared to independents." This is more informative than simply reporting the coefficient from a logistic regression model and its statistical significance.

Cross-validation is a general method of evaluating the fit of statistical models. It can be done in many forms, but the general idea is to evaluate a model by separating the data used to fit, or estimate, the model from the data used to test the model. The reason for this is that evaluating a model on the same data used to fit it will always produce a positive bias in the fit. Every sample of data has odd quirks that are unique to that sample, such as the random noise we add to the

---

[1]Examples include Markov Chain Monte Carlo (MCMC) and simulated ML (see Gamerman & Lopes, 2006; Gill, 2007; Lee, 1995).

data in each iteration of a simulation. Estimating and evaluating the model on the same data risks allowing some of the random oddities of the data you have to be attributed to the systematic component of the model.

9.2 QI SIMULATION

Simulating QI from model output has become increasingly popular in the social sciences with the introduction of software that makes it easy to do, such as Clarify in Stata and the `arm` and `Zelig` packages in R (Gelman et al., 2012; Imai et al., 2012; King et al., 2000). This popularity stems from the fact that QI are more useful in reporting empirical results than are model coefficients.[2] It is more effective to communicate in terms of expected probabilities than logit coefficients or changes in the hazard rate than Cox model coefficients.

Of course, we can compute an expected probability with just the model's coefficients, so why do we need simulation? The answer is that simulation provides a straightforward way to include confidence intervals around that expected probability. Remember that the coefficients in any statistical model are estimated with uncertainty. We have only one sample of data, but we want to make a general statement about the population from which that sample came. If we had happened to collect a different sample, our estimates for those coefficients would be different. Because there is uncertainty in the coefficient estimates, anything computed from those coefficients are also estimates with uncertainty. Simulation helps us quantify that uncertainty. Below we go through the method of QI simulation in detail with examples of how to simulate QI in R without any software packages. Then, we will show how `Zelig` makes simulating QI easy to do in R.

9.2.1 Statistical Overview

In the simulation and resampling methods we have explored so far, a key step was creating many sets of data to be used for analysis. With QI simulation, the main idea is to create many sets of coefficients by simulating from the sampling distribution of the model estimates, and then to compute the QI with each of those sets of coefficients.[3] This produces a distribution of the QI that can be summarized by computing the mean, median, and/or quantiles. Simulating multiple sets of coefficient estimates from the sampling distribution of the model is typically done by sampling from a multivariate normal distribution, though bootstrapping is also a possibility (Imai et al., 2012).

---

[2]It should be emphasized that QI are simply a more useful and intuitive way of *presenting* results. Reporting QI does not relax any model assumptions or solve problems uncovered by model diagnostics.

[3]This summary draws primarily from King et al. (2000).

Recall that through the central limit theorem we assume that the coefficient estimates from regression models are normally distributed.[4] Our uncertainty about the estimates we have from our data, often called estimation uncertainty, comes from the fact that the sample of data is finite and any other sample may produce an estimate of β_1 that is a little bit larger or smaller. As we have already seen, we can mimic the process of "in repeated samples" by making random draws from a distribution. The difference here is that instead of drawing data from a distribution with a known true DGP (i.e., the simulations from earlier chapters), we use simulation to draw parameter estimates from the sampling distribution of those parameters.

The sampling distribution from which we will draw simulated sets of the parameter estimates is defined by combining our estimated parameters, the estimated variance–covariance matrix of the parameters, and the assumption that the parameters follow a multivariate normal distribution. Specifically, the simulation unfolds as follows (King et al., 2000, p. 350):

1. Estimate the model and store the coefficient estimates and variance–covariance matrix.

2. Make a random draw from a multivariate normal distribution in which the mean and variance–covariance matrix are set to the coefficient estimates and variance–covariance matrix of the coefficient estimates from Step 1, respectively.

3. Repeat Step 2 a large number of times (e.g., 1,000) and store the random draws each time.

The result of this is a large number of "plausible" estimates for the coefficients. Because the full variance–covariance matrix is used in the simulation, the random draws will properly reflect the variability of each coefficient *and* any covariance between the coefficients. For any given draw, some of these estimates will be larger and some will be smaller than the estimates based on the real data. This reflects the estimation uncertainty from the model. If there is a lot of uncertainty (i.e., large standard errors), some estimates will be much larger or smaller whereas if there is little uncertainty the variation between estimates will be small.

The next step is to do something with all of these estimates. We could summarize the distribution of the random draws, but that would not tell us much more than simply looking at the estimates from the model and their standard errors. We know by construction that the means of each vector of simulated parameter estimates will be centered on the mean of the original estimates, and we know they will follow a normal distribution, because our simulation constructs them this way. A more informative option would be to compute a substantively meaningful quantity from those estimates. This quantity will differ depending on the model and the goal of the analysis, but can be broadly categorized as an expected or predicted value of the dependent variable. These two types of quantities have a

---

[4]A similar assumption of normality of the coefficients exists for ML models (King, 1998).

subtle but important difference that relates to the kind of uncertainty that is inherent in each one.

Expected Versus Predicted Values

Statistical models contain two types of uncertainty: (1) estimation uncertainty and (2) fundamental uncertainty. Estimation uncertainty stems from the fact that we only have a sample of data and so we are uncertain about the true values of the model's parameters. Fundamental uncertainty is "variability arising from sheer randomness in the world" (King et al., 2000, p. 350). An expected value is a QI computed from the model that averages over the model's fundamental uncertainty. It is computed only from the systematic component of the model. For example, we could generate expected values of how much a candidate for Congress will spend on an election campaign with an OLS model. We would estimate the model, then set the independent variables to some values and multiply them by their respective coefficient estimates to produce an expected value. If we did this many times with the set of simulated coefficients, we would get a distribution of expected values that we could summarize by computing the mean and quantiles. If the mean of this distribution was $10,000 and the 2.5th and 97.5th quantiles were $5,000 and $15,000, respectively, we could make a very clear substantive statement: Given the values of the independent variables we chose, we expect a candidate to spend $10,000, on average, give or take about $5,000. Notice that the only variability in the simulated expected values from one analysis to the next comes from using a new set of simulated parameter estimates each time.

In contrast, a predicted value includes both types of uncertainty; it gets generated by combining the systematic and stochastic components of the model. To compute a predicted value, we compute the expected value as before, but take the additional step of plugging it into the formula for the assumed DGP. For example, we could insert the expected value from the campaign spending example into rnorm() and draw one value with σ set to $\hat{\sigma}$ (the estimate of the residual standard deviation from the regression). Notice that this procedure allows for the stochastic element to play a role; the coefficients and independent variable values combine to set the mean of the distribution from which we draw, but $\hat{\sigma}$ will ensure that there is some additional variance in the process that simulates the unpredictable (or at least unmodeled) nature of the election campaign. Most important, we could do this for all of the 1,000 sets of simulated coefficients to produce 1,000 predicted values, then summarize the distribution of predicted values.

Both predicted and expected values are reasonable quantities to report. The decision about which one to use depends on exactly what the analyst wants to communicate to readers. The difference lies in whether the main point is to show only uncertainty about the estimated model or to make a prediction, which is subject to the model's uncertainty and uncertainty in the world. We show examples of both below.

9.2.2 Examples

This process is best understood with real examples, of which we go through two here: one from the OLS model in Ehrlich's (1973) crime data and one from the logit model of voter turnout. In both cases, we do "manual" coding of the simulations rather than using functions designed to do them. We will then show how Zelig can make this type of simulation easy and efficient.

Crime Data

We have used the crime data set throughout this book as an example of an OLS model. Here we will generate expected and predicted values of the dependent variable—the number of offenses per 100,000 people in each state in 1960—based on certain values of the independent variables. The model can be estimated in R with the following code.

```
library(foreign)
crime <- read.dta("crime.dta")

# OLS model from the crime data
crime.1 <- lm(crime1960 ~ imprisonment + education + wealth +
inequality + population1960, data = crime)
summary(crime.1)

Call:
lm(formula = crime1960 ~ imprisonment + education + wealth +
    inequality + population1960, data = crime)

Residuals:
    Min      1Q  Median      3Q     Max
-525.23 -178.94  -25.09  145.62  771.65

Coefficients:
                 Estimate  Std. Error  t value  Pr(>|t|)
(Intercept)    -4213.3894   1241.3856   -3.394  0.001538 **
imprisonment   -3537.8468   2379.4467   -1.487  0.144709
education        113.6824     65.2770    1.742  0.089088 .
wealth             0.3938      0.1151    3.422  0.001420 **
inequality       101.9513     25.9314    3.932  0.000318 ***
population1960     1.0250      1.3726    0.747  0.459458
---
Signif. codes: 0 *** 0.001 ** 0.01 * 0.05 . 0.1   1

Residual standard error: 297 on 41 degrees of freedom
Multiple R-squared: 0.4744,  Adjusted R-squared: 0.4103
F-statistic: 7.4 on 5 and 41 DF, p-value: 5.054e-05
```

Expected Values

The first step to generate expected values is to simulate many plausible values of the coefficients of the model. Recall that we do this by making draws from a multivariate normal distribution due to the central limit theorem. This procedure uses random numbers, so we set the seed first for reproducible results. The function we use is the familiar `rmvnorm()` function from the `mvtnorm` package. The arguments it takes are the number of draws to be made from the distribution (`n.draws`), the mean of the distribution from which the draws are to be made (which we set to the model's coefficients), and the variance–covariance matrix of the distribution from which the draws are to be made (which we also take from the model).

```
# Expected Value Example
# Draw simulated coefficients from a multivariate normal
library(mvtnorm)
set.seed(139742)

n.draws <- 1000 # Number of simulated sets of coefficients
crime.sim <- rmvnorm(n.draws, crime.1$coef, vcov(crime.1))
```

Below we print out the first few rows of the result and compute the mean of each row to check that it worked.

```
head(crime.sim)
       (Intercept)  imprisonment  education    wealth   inequality  population1960
[1,]    -5117.900    -5767.6322   125.1408   0.4836934  121.30463    0.4999360
[2,]    -6041.387      958.8372   122.2575   0.6089795  121.98862    0.3774749
[3,]    -3975.439    -3127.8922    76.9253   0.4211162  101.21474    2.0959224
[4,]    -4523.379    -3458.5296   107.6257   0.4480932  110.83247   -1.3675068
[5,]    -6368.000      352.3883   162.4849   0.5684617  129.88450    1.1675662
[6,]    -3685.106    -4750.4992   119.9829   0.3319707   90.62398    1.7744874

apply(crime.sim, 2, mean)
   (Intercept)    imprisonment      education       wealth     inequality
 -4216.1293840   -3493.8848720    111.6725241    0.3973089   102.0888091
 population1960
    1.0356389
```

The results show that the simulated coefficients average out to be very close to the actual estimated coefficients. Furthermore, remember that we could increase this precision simply by making the object `n.draws` a larger number.

The next step is to compute a meaningful QI with these sets of simulated coefficients. We can create a distribution of expected values by setting the independent variables at some values, then multiplying those values by the coefficients. First, we can set the independent variable values using the `data.frame()` command. In this case, we set all of them to their means.

```
# Set hypothetical values for the independent variables
crime.x <- data.frame(intercept = 1, imprisonment = mean(crime$imprisonment),
education = mean(crime$education), wealth = mean(crime$wealth),
inequality = mean(crime$inequality),
population1960 = mean(crime$population1960))
```

Next, in a `for` loop, we iterate through all of the simulated sets of coefficients, multiplying them by the data frame `crime.x` each time. We store the result in the vector `crime.expected`. Recall that the code `%*%` tells R to perform matrix multiplication.

```
# Matrix multiply crime.x and each set of simulated coefficients
crime.expected <- numeric(n.draws)
for(i in 1:n.draws){
crime.expected[i] <- as.matrix(crime.x) %*% crime.sim[i, ]
}
```

Each set of simulated coefficients produced a slightly different expected value. For example, the expected value from simulated Coefficient Set 12 is 865.89 while the expected value from Coefficient Set 784 is 941.96. Importantly, the mean of all of these expected values is 904.87, which is very close to the expected value produced by the actual coefficients (905.08). Figure 9.1 plots a histogram of the expected values. The 2.5th and 97.5th quantiles are [826.56, 994.17]. Thus, the substantive claim we can make from this is that with all of the independent variables set to their means, we expect a state to have between 827 and 994 offenses per 100,000 people, with an average of 905.

Although this is better than simply reporting coefficients and standard errors, it still does not tell us much about the impact of the independent variables. For that, we can change the code above to create a comparison. We set the independent variables to some values, compute the expected value of the dependent variable, then change the value of one independent variable and repeat the process. This produces two distributions of expected values that we can compare. In this case, we will perform the operation at the minimum and maximum of the `inequality` variable, which is measured as the percentage of families in each state earning below half the median income. It ranges from 12.6 to 27.6.

Our first step is to create the two sets of independent variable values, which we again do with the `data.frame()` function. Notice that we use the `c()` function for the inequality variable to create two values for that variable. Everything else is set to its mean.

```
crime.x2 <- data.frame(intercept = 1, imprisonment = mean(crime$imprisonment),
education = mean(crime$education), wealth = mean(crime$wealth),
inequality = c(min(crime$inequality), max(crime$inequality)),
population1960 = mean(crime$population1960))
```

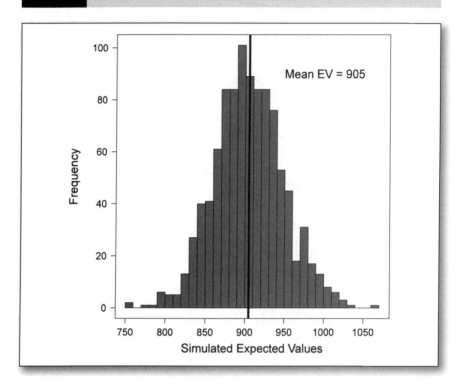

| Figure 9.1 | Simulated Expected Values From the Ehrlich (1973) Crime Data Model With All Variables at Their Means |

Next, we create an empty matrix called `crime.expected2` in which to store the expected values. We then matrix multiply the two sets of independent variable values by the simulated coefficients and store the results.

```
# Matrix multiply both sets of hypothetical values
# and each set of simulated coefficients
crime.expected2 <- matrix(NA, nrow = n.draws, ncol = 2)
for(i in 1:n.draws){
crime.expected2[i, 1] <- as.matrix(crime.x2[1, ]) %*% crime.sim[i, ]
crime.expected2[i, 2] <- as.matrix(crime.x2[2, ]) %*% crime.sim[i, ]
}
```

The result is 1,000 expected values of the dependent variable generated when setting `inequality` to its lowest level and 1,000 expected values of the dependent variable generated when `inequality` was set at its highest level. Panel (a) of Figure 9.2 shows two histograms of these values. Notice that the low `inequality` distribution (light gray) has smaller expected values than does the high `inequality` distribution (dark gray), with means of 211 and 1,742, respectively. In fact, these two distributions do not overlap with each other at all, further supporting the claim that different levels of `inequality` are associated with different levels of crime. This comports with the positive and statistically significant coefficient on `inequality` in the OLS model; holding the rest of the model constant, as `inequality` increases, the number of criminal offenses per 100,000 people also increases.

Panel (b) of Figure 9.2 shows a different QI called a first difference, which we compute by subtracting the low `inequality` expected values from the high `inequality` expected values. This is often useful because it reduces the data from two QI (a mean for low `inequality` and a mean for high `inequality`) down to one QI (the difference between those means). The mean difference is 1,531, with a 95% confidence interval of 736 to 2,279. Thus, we can conclude that holding the rest of the model constant at its mean and moving from the minimum to the maximum value of `inequality` corresponds with an average expected difference of between 736 and 2,279 offenses per 100,000 people.

Predicted Values

As we noted above, we can generate predicted values of the dependent variable by computing expected values, then adding random draws from the appropriate distribution. In the case of OLS, we assume a normal distribution for the dependent variable, with the independent variables influencing the parameter μ. To generate a predicted value, we substitute our expected values for μ and make draws from the distribution.

Figure 9.2	Simulated Expected Values and First Differences From the Ehrlich (1973) Crime Data Model With `inequality` at Its Observed Minimum and Maximum

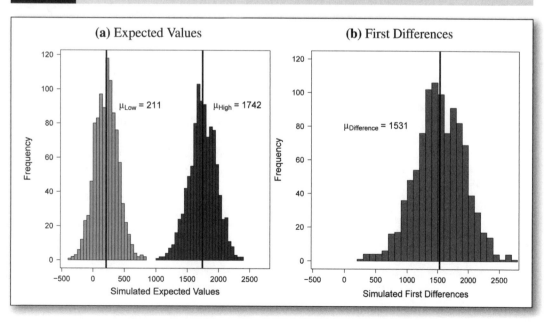

However, before we can do this, we need to account for the normal distribution's other parameter, σ. There are several different formulas for estimating this parameter from the data. The R command lm() uses the following formula, where Y is the dependent variable, X is a matrix of independent variables, $\hat{\beta}$ is a vector of coefficients estimates, n is the sample size, and p is the number of estimated coefficients.

$$\hat{\sigma} = \sqrt{\frac{\sum_{i=1}^{n}(Y_i - X_i\hat{\beta})^2}{n-p}} \tag{9.1}$$

The numerator is the residual sum of squares (RSS) while the denominator scales the estimate by the degrees of freedom.

We cannot simply use the value of $\hat{\sigma}$ from the model for predicted values of the dependent variable because, like the coefficients, that value is also an estimate. Thus, to generate predicted values we need the simulated estimates of the coefficients (the object crime.sims) *and* a set of simulated estimates of $\hat{\sigma}$. We can simulate $\hat{\sigma}$ by computing Equation 9.1 with each set of simulated coefficients.

```
crime.df <- crime.1$df.residual # Model residual df
crime.sim.sigma <- numeric(n.draws) # Empty vector

for(i in 1:n.draws){ # Loop through the sets of simulated coefficients
# Create the matrix of independent variables
x <- as.matrix(cbind(1, crime.1$model[ , -1]))
# Compute the RSS for each set of simulated coefficients
rss <- sum((crime$crime1960 - (x %*% crime.sim[i, ]))^2)
# Estimate sigma
crime.sim.sigma[i] <- sqrt(rss/crime.1$df.residual)
}
```

Now, we can generate a single predicted value by inserting the following two quantities into rnorm(): (1) the expected value computed from the simulated coefficients, $\hat{\beta}$, (mean) and (2) the simulated $\hat{\sigma}$(sd). Doing this for each set of simulated coefficients and $\hat{\sigma}$ value incorporates both estimation uncertainty and fundamental uncertainty into our predicted values. The code below shows this for the example in which all of the independent variables are set to their means.

```
# Matrix multiply crime.x and each set of simulated coefficients to create mu,
# then take a random draw from the normal distribution with mean equal to mu
# and sd equal to sigma
crime.predicted <- numeric(n.draws)
for(i in 1:n.draws){
mu <- as.matrix(crime.x) %*% crime.sim[i, ]
sigma <- crime.sim.sigma[i]
crime.predicted[i] <- rnorm(1, mu, sigma)
}
```

We can also generate predicted values at the two different values for `inequality`.

```
# Matrix multiply both sets of hypothetical values to create mu1 and mu 2,
# then take random draws from the normal distribution with means equal to mu1
# and mu2 and sd equal to sigma
crime.predicted2 <- matrix(NA, nrow = n.draws, ncol = 2)
for(i in 1:n.draws){
mu1 <- as.matrix(crime.x2[1, ]) %*% crime.sim[i, ]
mu2 <- as.matrix(crime.x2[2, ]) %*% crime.sim[i, ]
sigma <- crime.sim.sigma[i]
crime.predicted2[i, 1] <- rnorm(1, mu1, sigma)
crime.predicted2[i, 2] <- rnorm(1, mu2, sigma)
}
```

Figure 9.3 reproduces the expected value plots with these predicted values. Panel (a) shows histograms of the predicted values (light gray) and expected values from Figure 9.1 (white). Notice that both distributions are centered very close to one another (with similar means), but the predicted values show considerably more dispersion than do the expected values. Panel (b) shows two graphs, which reproduce Figure 9.2 with the predicted values. The same pattern still emerges. In the top graph, the predicted values when inequality is low (light gray) are generally smaller than the values when inequality is high (dark gray). In the bottom graph, the first differences average out to just over 1,500 offenses. However, both graphs show more dispersion in the predicted values than the expected values, which are plotted in white histograms.

These graphs show that accounting for fundamental uncertainty, which is necessary to make predictions, produces more noise. This makes sense because any type of prediction is subject to some level of randomness.[5] Both expected and predicted values are useful QI to compute and report. Applied researchers must choose which is most useful for the message they wish to convey, or they can also report both and let their readers decide.

Voter Turnout Data

Our next example uses the 2000 CPS voter turnout data from Chapter 3 that is included in the `Zelig` package. Recall that the logit model we estimated is as follows.

```
library(Zelig)
data(voteincome) # Use 2000 CPS data

vote.1 <- glm(vote ~ income + education + age + female,
family = binomial (link = logit), data = voteincome)
summary(vote.1)
```

[5]Notice that we estimated, then simulated, that level of randomness through the simulation of $\hat{\sigma}$.

```
Call:
glm(formula = vote ~ income + education + age + female,
family = binomial(link = logit),
    data = voteincome)

Deviance Residuals:
    Min       1Q    Median       3Q       Max
-2.4247   0.3936    0.4869   0.5913    1.0284

Coefficients:
             Estimate Std. Error z value Pr(>|z|)
(Intercept)-0.877591   0.375796   -2.335 0.019529 *
income      0.094331   0.021666    4.354 1.34e-05 ***
education   0.224927   0.090063    2.497 0.012510 *
age         0.016464   0.004328    3.804 0.000142 ***
female      0.309880   0.151031    2.052 0.040193 *
---
Signif. codes:  0 *** 0.001 ** 0.01 * 0.05 . 0.1   1

(Dispersion parameter for binomial family taken to be 1)

    Null deviance: 1240.0 on 1499 degrees of freedom
Residual deviance: 1185.6 on 1495 degrees of freedom
AIC: 1195.6

Number of Fisher Scoring iterations: 5
```

| Figure 9.3 | Simulated Expected and Predicted Values and First Differences From the OLS Crime Data Model |

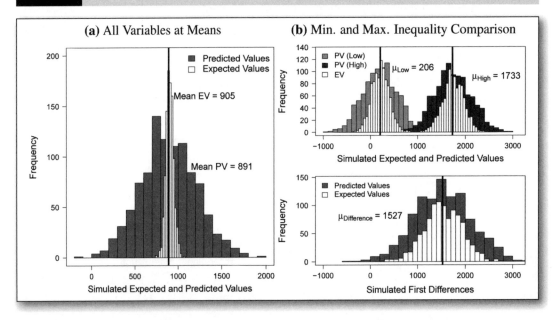

Logit coefficients are relatively unintuitive because they report the rate of change in the log odds of the dependent variable for a one-unit change in an independent variable. To make a more intuitive statement about the model, we could compute the expected probability of voting. This is equivalent to the expected value from above. Furthermore, to show the effect of a particular variable on the expected probability of voting, we could set all of the independent variables except one we wish to examine to certain values, then vary that one variable across its observed range. We show this with the income variable below.

First, we have to generate our simulated coefficients as we did in the OLS model. We set the seed, then use `rmvnorm()` as before.[6]

```
set.seed(22374)
vote.sim <- rmvnorm(n.draws, vote.1$coef, vcov(vote.1))

head(vote.sim)
     (Intercept)     income education        age       female
[1,]  -1.3281902 0.13716731 0.1563643 0.02406525 -0.01073198
[2,]  -0.6986615 0.07991900 0.1332169 0.01701637  0.65924932
[3,]  -0.8249512 0.09446016 0.1753189 0.02128742  0.10399616
[4,]  -1.3091259 0.10506045 0.2058838 0.02138801  0.33157549
[5,]  -1.4049381 0.11072998 0.3152566 0.01953482  0.23449633
[6,]  -1.4323554 0.09049466 0.3500474 0.02236034  0.40504236

apply(vote.sim, 2, mean)
(Intercept)      income   education         age      female
-0.96753651  0.09279441  0.25963467  0.01751938  0.26467956
```

Next, we create a sequence that spans the entire range of the independent variable we want to manipulate. In this case, `income` is coded as several different categories, with an observed range of 4–17.[7] The object `inc.range` is a sequence from 4 to 17, counting by 1s. After creating this object, we set the independent variables in a data frame. We set `income` to its range while the other variables are set to their means or modes. This produces 14 independent variable profiles in which the value of `income` is different each time, but the values of the other variables stay the same.

```
# Make the sequence going across the range of income
inc.range <- min(voteincome$income):max(voteincome$income)
# Set the values of the independent variables. Income is set to inc.range and
# everything else is set to its mean or mode
vote.x <- data.frame(intercept = 1, income = inc.range,
education = mean(voteincome$education), age = mean(voteincome$age),
female = 0)
```

---

[6]Remember that we are using the multivariate normal distribution even though this is a logit model because we are sampling parameters from the probability distribution that the parameter estimates follow and *not* from the sampling data from the probability distribution that *Y* follows.

[7]The categories are income brackets, ranging from "less than \$5,000" to "\$150,000 or more". See `http://www.census.gov/cps/files/questionnaire/Labor%20 Force.pdf`.

```
vote.x
   intercept income education       age female
1          1       4 2.651333 49.26133       0
2          1       5 2.651333 49.26133       0
3          1       6 2.651333 49.26133       0
4          1       7 2.651333 49.26133       0
5          1       8 2.651333 49.26133       0
6          1       9 2.651333 49.26133       0
7          1      10 2.651333 49.26133       0
8          1      11 2.651333 49.26133       0
9          1      12 2.651333 49.26133       0
10         1      13 2.651333 49.26133       0
11         1      14 2.651333 49.26133       0
12         1      15 2.651333 49.26133       0
13         1      16 2.651333 49.26133       0
14         1      17 2.651333 49.26133       0
```

The next step is to create a `for` loop that will iterate through all of the independent variable profiles in `vote.x`. In each iteration, we will compute the expected value of the model on the logit scale and its lower and upper 95% confidence bounds.[8] To do this, we first create empty vectors to store these QI and define our inverse logit function. Then, we begin the `for` loop.

```
# Empty vectors to store the point estimates and confidence intervals
pe <- numeric(length(inc.range))
lo <- numeric(length(inc.range))
hi <- numeric(length(inc.range))

# Inverse Logit Function
inv.logit <- function(p){
return(exp(p)/(1 + exp(p)))
}

for(i in 1:length(inc.range)){ # First for loop goes across inc.range values
```

Once inside the `for` loop, the objective is to compute the expected value on the logit scale a large number of times (i.e., 1,000 times), to produce a distribution of expected values just like in our OLS example. We do this by creating a second loop. First, we create the object pp to store the expected values. Then, inside the loop we multiply the current independent variable profile by each of the 1,000 simulated sets of coefficients.

```
# Empty vector to store the calculations
pp <- numeric(n.draws)
# Now loop through all the simulated coefficients and each time calculate the
# probability with income set to the current value on inc.range and everything
# else at its mean
```

---

[8]We will convert these expected values into probabilities in the next step.

```
for(j in 1:n.draws){
pp[j] <- as.matrix(vote.x[i, ]) %*% vote.sim[j, ]
} # End calculation loop
```

The last step is to summarize the distribution of the 1,000 simulated values as expected probabilities—the real QI. We do this by computing the mean and quantiles of the *inverse logit* of those expected values. This yields a point estimate for the expected probability and 95% confidence bounds. Finally, we end the first for loop that iterates through the values of inc.range.

```
# Compute the point estimate on the probability scale for a given value of
# inc.range
pe[i] <- mean(inv.logit(pp))
lo[i] <- quantile(inv.logit(pp), .025) # CIs on the probability scale
hi[i] <- quantile(inv.logit(pp), .975)
} # End inc.range loop
```

To summarize, this code loops through the observed income values in the object inc.range. At each iteration of inc.range, it simulates 1,000 probabilities of voting using the 1,000 simulated coefficients in vote.sim. Then, it summarizes those estimates by computing the mean and quantiles. Then, the code goes to the next value in inc.range and repeats the process.

We plot the result in Figure 9.4. The *x*-axis gives the observed range of income (i.e., inc.range). The *y*-axis is the probability of voting. The solid line indicates the mean expected probability of voting at each level of income and dashed lines indicate the 95% confidence intervals around those expected probabilities. This graph allows us to communicate results from the model much more easily. It shows that the expected probability of voting increases by nearly 20 percentage points from the smallest to largest observed values of income in the sample (holding the other variables constant at their means or modes). Furthermore, the confidence interval allows us to assess the amount of estimation uncertainty inherent in those computations.[9]

9.2.3 Simulating QI With Zelig

The examples above go through the process of QI simulation step by step. We did so to give readers a sense of what is happening "under the hood." However, the process can be done more quickly using functions available in the Zelig package. We show examples of this below. We encourage readers to make sure that they understand the process of QI simulation in the examples above first before going through these applications. Additionally, this is only a brief

---

[9]Also notice the series of tick marks at the bottom of the graph, which is often called a "rug plot." A rug plot, which can be added to a plot with the rug() function, shows where the observed values of income—one for each tick—are actually located in the sample of data. This is helpful in assessing what ranges of the income variable are common or uncommon.

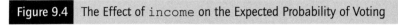

Figure 9.4   The Effect of `income` on the Expected Probability of Voting

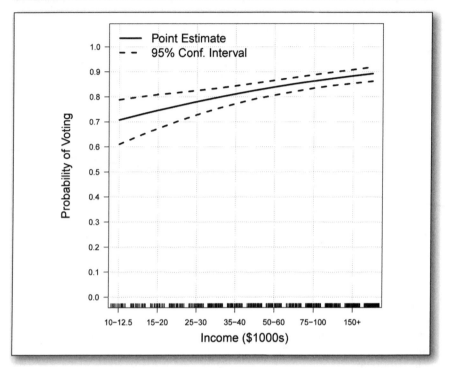

introduction to simulating QI in `Zelig`. See the documentation for more details (Imai et al., 2012).

Crime Data

In our first example, we repeat the crime data simulation from above with `Zelig`. First, we estimate the model using the `zelig()` function.

```
library(Zelig)
crime.2 <- zelig(crime1960 ~ imprisonment + education + wealth +
inequality + population1960, model = "ls", data = crime, cite = FALSE)
```

Next, we define our desired values for the independent variables with the `setx()` command. The first argument is the name of the model, and the rest of the arguments are names of variables and the values we specify for each one. In this case, we create an object for the minimum of `inequality` and another object for its maximum.

```
crime.x2.lo <- setx(crime.2, imprisonment = mean(crime$imprisonment),
education = mean(crime$education), wealth = mean(crime$wealth),
inequality = min(crime$inequality),
population1960 = mean(crime$population1960))
```

```
crime.x2.hi <- setx(crime.2, imprisonment = mean(crime$imprisonment),
education = mean(crime$education), wealth = mean(crime$wealth),
inequality = max(crime$inequality),
population1960 = mean(crime$population1960))
```

Finally, we create the simulation object with `sim()`. The first argument is again the name of the model. The argument x is the object with our desired independent variable values. The optional argument x1 can be used for a second set of independent variable values in case we want to compute first differences. With these inputs, the command simulates a set of 1,000 model parameters as we did above and computes QI.

```
set.seed(26422)
crime.sim2 <- sim(crime.2, x = crime.x2.lo, x1 = crime.x2.hi)
```

The default is to simulate the coefficients from a multivariate normal distribution as we have done to this point. However, it is also straightforward to draw coefficient values via bootstrapping with the `bootstrap = TRUE` option in `sim()`. This takes slightly longer to execute, but is useful if the analyst does not wish to assume the sampling distribution of the coefficients is multivariate normal. Note that the default is 100 bootstrap replications, but this can be changed with the `num` argument.

```
set.seed(32457)
crime.sim.boot <- sim(crime.2, x = crime.x2.lo,
   x1 = crime.x2.hi, bootstrap = TRUE, num = 1000)
```

To extract the QI from a simulation object, type `$qi`. For example, to see the expected values, type `crime.sim2$qi$ev`. First differences are listed under `crime.sim2$qi$fd`. Figure 9.5 plots the first difference distribution from the crime data model with `inequality` set to its minimum and maximum. Panel (a) gives the results using the multivariate normal, and Panel (b) gives the bootstrapped results. Notice that the two graphs look almost identical, although there is a little more variance in the estimated first differences generated from bootstrapping (standard deviation of 453 in Panel b compared with 394 in Panel a).

Survival Data

The contents of `$qi` change based on the model. For instance, we could estimate a Cox model and simulate the ratio of the hazard function at two values of an independent variable (X and X_1). From Box-Steffensmeier and Jones (2004, p. 48), the hazard ratio is defined as

$$\frac{h(t \mid x_1)}{h(t \mid x)} = \exp[(X_1 - X)\beta] = \frac{\exp(X_1\beta)}{\exp(X\beta)} \qquad (9.2)$$

Figure 9.5 Simulated and Bootstrapped First Differences From the Ehrlich (1973) Crime Data Model With `Zelig`

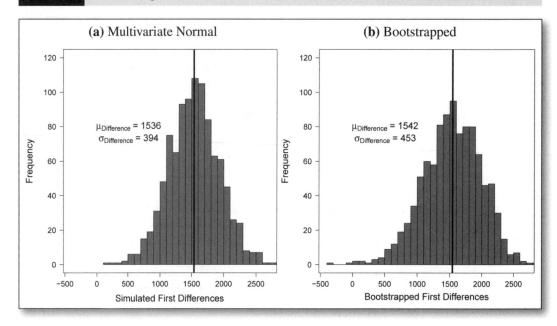

The data for this example come from the lung cancer data of the North Central Cancer Treatment Group (Loprinzi et al., 1994). We model the survival of patients as a function of several independent variables including a measure of health called an ECOG (Eastern Co-operative Oncology Group) score (Oken et al., 1982), which runs from 0 (fully active) to 3 (> 50% of time in bed) to 5 (death). Here we will examine the difference in the hazard of dying for hypothetical patients with different values of the ECOG score.[10]

We first load the data from the `survival` package and estimate the model.

```
library(survival) # Load the data
data(cancer)
cancer$female <- ifelse(cancer$sex == 2, 1, 0)
set.seed(12448)
# Estimate the model
cancer.1 <- zelig(Surv(time, status) ~ age + female + meal.cal + wt.loss +
ph.ecog + ph.karno, model = "coxph", data = cancer, cite = FALSE)
```

---

[10]We are not experts in this field or experts on this data set, but the observant among you may be wondering whether it seems silly to estimate the "hazard" of dying for someone who already has an ECOG score of 5. We are bemused as well, but we will continue on for illustrative purposes.

Next, we set our low and high values of the ECOG score to 0 and 3 and set our two independent variable profiles.

```
# Set the independent variable values
lo.ecog <- 0
hi.ecog <- 3

cancer.x <- setx(cancer.1, age = mean(cancer$age), female = 1,
meal.cal = mean(na.omit(cancer$meal.cal)),
wt.loss = mean(na.omit(cancer$wt.loss)),
ph.ecog = lo.ecog, ph.karno = mean(na.omit(cancer$ph.karno)))

cancer.x1 <- setx(cancer.1, age = mean(cancer$age), female = 0,
meal.cal = mean(na.omit(cancer$meal.cal)),
wt.loss = mean(na.omit(cancer$wt.loss)),
ph.ecog = hi.ecog, ph.karno = mean(na.omit(cancer$ph.karno)))
```

Finally, we use `sim()` to simulate the QI. We can extract the hazard ratio with `$qi$hr`. In this case, the ratio of ECOG = 3 to ECOG = 0 is about 25, indicating that, given survival to the current period, the chance of death for a patient with ECOG = 3 is about 25 times greater than it is for a patient with ECOG = 0. The 95% confidence interval indicates a plausible range for this QI of about 5 to 76.

```
# Simulate QI
cancer.sim <- sim(cancer.1, x = cancer.x, x1 = cancer.x1)

# Report the mean and 95% confidence intervals
hr <- data.frame(mean = mean(cancer.sim$qi$hr),
lo = as.numeric(quantile(cancer.sim$qi$hr, .025)),
hi = as.numeric(quantile(cancer.sim$qi$hr, .975)))

hr
       mean        lo      hi
1 24.83245  5.078747  76.315
```

9.2.4 Average Case Versus Observed Values

To this point, all of the QI simulation we have shown has focused on manipulating one independent variable of interest, such as moving across its observed range or between two theoretically interesting values, and computing the QI at each of those values (or a first difference). We have been content to simply set the other variables in the model to some "reasonable" values, such as their means or modes. In other words, we have constructed a hypothetical observation that is near the center of the data on the control variables and changed just the variable of interest. Hanmer and Kalkan (2013) refer to this as analyzing an "average case." They discuss several problems with this approach in the context of nonlinear models such as binary or count dependent variable models.[11] For instance, it is rare that social science theories are focused so specifically on an average case (or any one case for that matter). Additionally, an observation with all of those average values may not actually appear in the data. Finally, often in practice, researchers choose what some would argue are nonsensical values for their control variables, such as the mean of a binary variable (for more details, see Hanmer & Kalkan, 2013).

In response, Hanmer and Kalkan (2013) advocate for the "observed value" method as a solution. In this approach, instead of setting the other variables to their means or modes and computing the QI, we set the values for all of the independent variables to their observed values of each observation in the data, compute the QI for each one of those sets of values (i.e., once for each observation), and take the mean of the QI over all those observations. This produces an analysis that is based on the sample as a whole rather than one arbitrary and hypothetical "observation" that may not even exist in the data. Hanmer and Kalkan (2013) argue that the observed value method "better serves the goal of theory-driven empirical research—making inferences about the population of interest from the sample" (p. 7).

We can demonstrate this approach with data on votes to confirm U.S. Supreme Court nominees (Epstein, Lindstädt, Segal, & Westerland, 2006). The unit of analysis is a senator vote, and the dependent variable is a binary indicator of whether the senator voted in favor of confirming the nominee. An important independent variable is the ideological distance (`eucldist`) between a senator and the nominee. Epstein et al. (2006) expect that as that distance increases, the probability of voting "yea" to confirm the nominee decreases. In addition, the model includes control variables for the nominees' qualifications (`lackqual`, a continuous variable), an indicator for a "strong president" (`strongpres`, see Epstein et al., 2006), and an indicator for whether the nominee and senator are in the same party (`sameprty`).

```
# Average Case vs. Observed Value
library(foreign)
library(Zelig)
library(mvtnorm)

nominees <- read.dta("nominees.dta")

# Estimate the Model
logit.nominees <- glm(vote ~ lackqual + eucldist + strongpres +
sameprty, family = binomial (link = logit), data = nominees)

summary(logit.nominees)
```

---

[11]The average case method is less of a concern with linear models because the marginal effect of an independent variable is constant across all values of the other independent variables.

```
Call:
glm(formula = vote ~ lackqual + eucldist + strongpres + sameprty,
    family = binomial(link = logit), data = nominees)

Deviance Residuals:
    Min     1Q Median     3Q    Max
-3.2420 0.0871 0.1982 0.3983 2.1454

Coefficients:
            Estimate  Std.Error  z value  Pr(>|z|)
(Intercept)   3.2755     0.1629   20.106   <2e-16 ***
lackqual     -4.3460     0.2339  -18.579   <2e-16 ***
eucldist     -4.1067     0.2826  -14.531   <2e-16 ***
strongpres    1.4624     0.1365   10.711   <2e-16 ***
sameprty      1.3952     0.1519    9.182   <2e-16 ***
---
Signif. codes:  0 '***' 0.001 '**' 0.01 '*' 0.05 '.' 0.1 ' ' 1

(Dispersion parameter for binomial family taken to be 1)

    Null deviance: 2717.5 on 3708 degrees of freedom
Residual deviance: 1684.4 on 3704 degrees of freedom
AIC: 1694.4

Number of Fisher Scoring iterations: 6
```

After estimating the model, the next step is to compute the expected probability across the range of `eucldist` using both methods. We create a vector called `distance` that is composed of 10 values spanning the range of `eucldist`. For the average case method, we set `lackqual` to its mean and `sameprty` and `strongpres` to their modes (1 in each case). Our hypothetical "average senator" is voting on a nominee with average qualifications, is voting during a time with a strong president, and is in the same party as the nominee. Importantly, such a case does not occur in the entire data set of 3,709 observations, though some are close. For instance, Edwin C. Johnson (D-Colorado) voted to confirm fellow Democrat Fred Vinson—the nominee with a value of `lackqual` closest to its mean—in 1946, which was a time of a strong president (Truman). Thus, what seems at first to be a general estimate of the effect of ideological distance is actually a very specific scenario.

```
# Inverse Logit Function
inv.logit <- function(p){
return(exp(p)/(1 + exp(p)))
}

# Seed and number of repetitions
set.seed(12484)
n.draws <- 1000
```

```
# Simulate Coefficients
nominees.sim <- rmvnorm(n.draws, logit.nominees$coef, vcov(logit.nominees))

# Average Case Expected Probabilities

# A sequence of numbers spanning the range of ideological distance
distance <- seq(min(nominees$eucldist), max(nominees$eucldist), length = 10)

# Create the average case (a hypothetical independent variable profile)
x.nominees <- data.frame(intercept = 1, lackqual = mean(nominees$lackqual),
  eucldist = distance, strongpres = 1, sameprty = 1)

# Compute the expected probabilities and
# confidence intervals using the simulated coefficients
pp.sim <- matrix(NA, nrow = n.draws, ncol = length(distance))

for(i in 1:n.draws){
pp.sim[i, ] <- inv.logit(as.matrix(x.nominees) %*% nominees.sim[i, ])
}

pe.ac <- apply(pp.sim, 2, mean)
lo.ac <- apply(pp.sim, 2, quantile, prob = .025)
hi.ac <- apply(pp.sim, 2, quantile, prob = .975)
```

We then compute the same expected probability using the observed value method. In that case we allow `lackqual`, `strongpres`, and `sameprty` to vary naturally over all the observations, then average the resulting quantities. Note that this code requires three `for` loops. The first (`j`) loops over the `distance` range (10 values). The second loop (`k`) goes over the 1,000 sets of simulated coefficients. Finally, the third loop goes through each observation in the data, computing the probability at the current value of the `distance` range (i.e., the current place in the `j` loop) and current set of simulated coefficients (the current place in the `k` loop).[12]

```
# Empty vectors to store the point estimates and confidence intervals
pe.ov <- numeric(length(distance))
lo.ov <- numeric(length(distance))
hi.ov <- numeric(length(distance))

for(j in 1:length(distance)){ # First for loop goes across distance values

# Set the other independent variables to all of their observed values
nominees.x <- data.frame(intercept = 1, lackqual = nominees$lackqual,
  eucldist = distance[j], strongpres = nominees$strongpres,
  sameprty = nominees$sameprty)
```

---

[12]Not surprisingly, this takes a long time to run. This is exactly the kind of situation in which placing the code on a research computing cluster or parallelizing it would be beneficial (see Chapter 6).

```
# Empty vector to store the average value of the linear predictor
pp <- numeric(n.draws)

for(k in 1:n.draws){ # Second for loop goes over the simulated coefficients

# Empty vector to store the value of the linear predictor
# for each observation in the data set
lp <- numeric(nrow(nominees))

for(i in 1:nrow(nominees)){ # Final for loop goes over each observation
lp[i] <- as.matrix(nominees.x[i, ]) %*% nominees.sim[k, ]
} # End observed value loop

# Compute the mean value of linear predictor
# values across all the observations
pp[k] <- mean(lp)
cat("Just finished k =", k, "of", n.draws,
"(j =", j, "of", length(distance), ")", "\n")
} # End coefficient loop


# Compute the point estimate on the probability scale for a given value of
# distance
pe.ov[j] <- mean(inv.logit(pp))
lo.ov[j] <- quantile(inv.logit(pp), .025) # CIs on the probability scale
hi.ov[j] <- quantile(inv.logit(pp), .975)
gc() # Clear out RAM
} # End distance loop
```

We plot the results in Figure 9.6; the average case point estimate and 95% confidence intervals are in black and the observed value estimate and 95% confidence intervals are in gray. The black line shows that the probability of a "yea" vote is about 99% when there is no distance between the senator and nominee and drops to just below 50% at the maximum of eucldist. However, notice from the rug plot at the bottom of the graph that most of the observations fall toward the left side (i.e., smaller values). Between the minimum value of eucldist and its 95th percentile, the probability of a "yea" vote only drops to about 92% according to the average case method.

The observed value method (gray line) shows a somewhat different story. It has the same downward trend, but is much steeper. Between the minimum and maximum of eucldist, the estimate moves from 99% to about 22%. At the 95th percentile of eucldist, the estimate is approximately 79%. In short, the observed value method suggests that the impact of eucldist on confirmation votes is stronger than is the average case method using the means and modes of the control variables. Most important, the observed value method produces estimates that average over all of the heterogeneity in the data rather than for one specific and arbitrary case.

9.2.5 The Benefits of QI Simulation

Many statistical models produce coefficient estimates that are unintuitive, and even those that are do not fully capture the results researchers care about. Reporting only those coefficients and their standard errors might let researchers evaluate the statistical significance of some parameter estimates, but it does not facilitate evaluating substantive importance. Such a limited reporting of results sells the analysis short by not connecting the statistical evidence to substantive theory. Simulating QI helps convey more meaning from the results to the reader.

Additionally, the method makes quantifying uncertainty easier compared with computing standard errors and confidence intervals analytically. Using the variance–covariance matrix of the coefficient estimates along with the uncertainty embodied in the stochastic portion of the model allows researchers to compare expected and predicted values and to evaluate the findings of a model based on a full accounting of uncertainty.

Figure 9.6 Expected Probability of a Vote to Confirm a Supreme Court Nominee by `eucldist`, Computed With the Average Case and Observed Value Methods (With 95% Confidence Intervals)

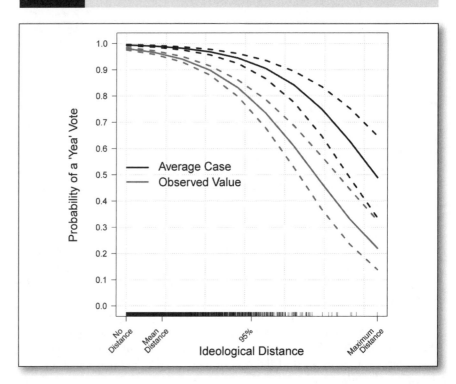

Finally, conducting a simulation based on the variance–covariance matrix of the model estimates means that anything that can be computed with the estimated coefficients can also be computed with the simulated coefficients. No matter how complex the QI one wants to report, it can be computed and evaluated relatively easily with simulation.

9.3 CROSS-VALIDATION

Our second topic for this chapter is a model evaluation method called cross-validation (CV). Though CV takes on many forms, the general goal is to assess the fit of a statistical model based on how well it performs in making predictions of "new" observations. Because researchers rarely have multiple data sets to employ, CV involves partitioning the one data set a researcher has such that the model is fit on one portion of the sample (often called the "training" or "estimation" data) and evaluated on another portion (the "testing" or "evaluation" data). Assuming that the two types of data come from the same population, CV will provide a more realistic measure of model fit compared with estimating and evaluating the model on the same data.

As a result, CV helps guard against overfitting the model to the particular sample of data at hand. As our previous discussions of the systematic and stochastic components of a model have illustrated, any sample of data is made up of "signal" (systematic), which reflects the true relationship between variables in the DGP that is present in all samples, and its own unique oddities, which we often label "noise" (stochastic). This noise influences the estimates of a model's parameters to some degree—in any given sample, the empirical relationship between X and Y might be a bit stronger or weaker than it is in the true DGP. In fact, this sort of noise is the source of estimation uncertainty.

However, this noise can also "masquerade" as signal. Consider the following example. In the R code below, we create a data set of 1,000 observations and 20 variables using the rmvnorm() command. We draw 20 variables from a multivariate normal, each with a mean of zero. Additionally, all of these variables are generated such that their expected covariances, which we set in the matrix object rand.vcv, are zero. Thus, in the true DGP there is *no relationship between any of these variables*. We arbitrarily choose the first variable to be the dependent variable and the remaining 19 to be independent variables. We then estimate an OLS regression model.

```
# Regression with Random Variables
library(mvtnorm)
set.seed(843749)

rand.vcv <- matrix(0, nrow = 20, ncol = 20)
diag(rand.vcv) <- 1
```

```
rand.data <- as.data.frame(rmvnorm(1000, mean = rep(0, times = 20),
  sigma = rand.vcv))
colnames(rand.data) <- c("y", "x1", "x2", "x3", "x4", "x5", "x6", "x7",
  "x8", "x9", "x10", "x11", "x12", "x13", "x14", "x15", "x16", "x17",
   "x18", "x19")

rand.model <- lm(y ~ x1 + x2 + x3 + x4 + x5 + x6 + x7 + x8 + x9 + x10 +
  x11 + x12 + x13 + x14 + x15 + x16 + x17 + x18 + x19, data = rand.data)
```

The model output is given below. Of the 20 estimated parameters (intercept and 19 slope coefficients), exactly one of them, $x3$, is statistically significant at the 0.05 level. This is despite the fact that we know in the true DGP there is no covariance between y and $x3$. However, this is not a surprising result. By the very definition of a p value, we know that under the null hypothesis such an estimate should appear about 5% of the time.[13] In this case, one out of 20, or 5%, of our estimates generated a large enough t statistic and small enough p value to be considered "significant."

```
summary(rand.model)

Call:
lm(formula = y ~ x1 + x2 + x3 + x4 + x5 + x6 + x7 + x8 + x9 +
    x10 + x11 + x12 + x13 + x14 + x15 + x16 + x17 + x18 + x19,
    data = rand.data)

Residuals:
    Min       1Q    Median      3Q      Max
-3.06592  -0.69443  0.01892  0.65948  2.72683

Coefficients:
             Estimate  Std. Error  t value  Pr(>|t|)
(Intercept)   0.025093   0.033052    0.759    0.4479
x1           -0.004887   0.032006   -0.153    0.8787
x2            0.019572   0.032647    0.600    0.5490
x3            0.065960   0.032221    2.047    0.0409 *
x4            0.016389   0.032241    0.508    0.6113
x5           -0.018243   0.033537   -0.544    0.5866
x6           -0.015481   0.032983   -0.469    0.6389
x7           -0.004819   0.034414   -0.140    0.8887
x8            0.024821   0.033149    0.749    0.4542
x9           -0.021343   0.032585   -0.655    0.5126
x10           0.028944   0.032373    0.894    0.3715
x11          -0.002242   0.033880   -0.066    0.9473
x12           0.024388   0.032577    0.749    0.4543
x13          -0.029578   0.033077   -0.894    0.3714
```

---

[13]Or 1%, or 10%, or any other critical value you choose.

```
x14              0.001502    0.031966    0.047   0.9625
x15              0.017520    0.031754    0.552   0.5812
x16              0.010401    0.033124    0.314   0.7536
x17              0.030702    0.033236    0.924   0.3558
x18             -0.023462    0.033376   -0.703   0.4823
x19              0.025898    0.031808    0.814   0.4157
---
Signif. codes:  0 `***' 0.001 `**' 0.01 `*' 0.05 `.' 0.1 ` ' 1

Residual standard error: 1.032 on 980 degrees of freedom
Multiple R-squared: 0.01163,   Adjusted R-squared: -0.007534
F-statistic: 0.6068 on 19 and 980 DF, p-value: 0.9035
```

What we see in this example is a case in which the stochastic component of the model (noise) happened by chance to produce a statistically significant estimate. There is nothing systematic that connects y and x3. Rather, the result is just an odd quirk of this particular sample of data. You could repeat the process with a different seed and a new estimate might be significant, even though the DGP itself remained the exact same. Thus, it is easy to be tricked into thinking that a significant estimate automatically implies that something systematic is going on. CV is one way of guarding against that problem.

9.3.1 How CV Can Help

The problem in evaluating a model on the same data used to estimate the parameters is that some of the noise in the data gets mistakenly "picked up" as signal, leading to overly optimistic measures of model fit.[14] CV addresses this problem by keeping the evaluation data independent of the estimation data.

An example of CV in action is the "Netflix Prize" competition. The online movie rental company Netflix utilizes a five-star rating system for users to evaluate movies that they have seen. Netflix then uses this information to make predictions about how users will rate new movies. The company places a high priority on making good predictions; if it can connect users to movies that they like, those users will likely continue to subscribe to the service. In 2009, the company held a competition, offering a $1 million prize for beating its current prediction system.

To begin the competition, Netflix provided 100 million ratings from 480,000 users of 18,000 movies. Each competitor (or team of competitors) created a prediction model using those data. However, the performance of the final submissions were *not* evaluated on how well the models fit these 100 million ratings. Rather, they were evaluated on how well they predicted 2.8 million ratings that were *not included* in the original data given to teams.[15] The purpose of setting aside these 2.8

---

[14]In fact, the difference between an in-sample and a CV fit measure is often termed optimism (Efron & Tibshirani, 1993).

[15]This is often referred to as out-of-sample prediction or out-of-sample forecasting and is quite common in time series models.

million ratings was to prevent "gaming" the system, or what we would call overfitting the model. Competitors could find the odd, random quirks of that particular sample and design the model specifically to account for those odd quirks. The result would be a model that would look good on that one sample, but would not be generalizable to future users and movies. By separating training and testing data, Netflix made sure that the winning entry would be useful to them in the future.[16]

CV with statistical models in social science follows a similar procedure. However, most social scientists do not have 2.8 million observations to set aside for later use. Below, we show some examples of CV in practice, with a particular focus on working with small samples. We do this for two reasons: (1) to reassure those who work with small samples that CV is still feasible and (2) because the bias associated with using in-sample model evaluation is largest when the sample size is small.

9.3.2 An Example

Harden (2012b) uses data coded from American state legislators' websites to assess the determinants of their "representational priorities," or the types of activities state legislators focus on in providing representation to their constituents. The data set "websites.csv" contains data from a sample of 100 of these websites. We estimate a logit model predicting whether a legislator mentions constituent service (e.g., an offer to help constituents who have problems with government agencies) on the front page of his or her website. There are several independent variables, including state-, district-, and individual-level characteristics (for more details, see Harden, 2012b).

```
websites <- read.csv("websites.csv")

front.service <- glm(frontservice ~ s.proscaled + s.incscaled +
s.distpctblack + competitive + ambition + female + black + republican,
family = binomial (link = logit), data = websites)

summary(front.service)
Call:
glm(formula = frontservice ~ s.proscaled + s.incscaled + s.distpctblack +
    competitive + ambition + female + black + republican,
    family = binomial(link = logit), data = websites)

 Deviance Residuals:
     Min       1Q    Median       3Q       Max
-1.96768  -1.05459  -0.00022  1.18539  1.49580
```

---

[16]Ironically, the winning entry was never actually put into place due to computational constraints. See http://techblog.netflix.com/2012/04/netflix-recommendations-beyond-5-stars.html.

```
Coefficients:
                 Estimate  Std. Error  z value  Pr(>|z|)
(Intercept)    -4.766e-01   1.056e+00   -0.451   0.65182
s.proscaled     6.861e-01   2.334e-01    2.940   0.00328 **
s.incscaled     7.590e-02   2.726e-01    0.278   0.78064
s.distpctblack  9.565e-01   5.032e-01    1.901   0.05734 .
competitive    -4.749e-03   1.282e-02   -0.370   0.71109
ambition       -1.708e+01   1.057e+03   -0.016   0.98711
female          2.536e-02   4.838e-01    0.052   0.95820
black          -1.855e+00   1.699e+00   -1.091   0.27508
republican      1.015e-01   5.579e-01    0.182   0.85563
  ---
Signif. codes:  0 *** 0.001 ** 0.01 * 0.05 . 0.1  1


(Dispersion parameter for binomial family taken to be 1)

    Null deviance: 138.59  on 99  degrees of freedom
Residual deviance: 119.69  on 91  degrees of freedom
AIC: 137.69


Number of Fisher Scoring iterations: 15
```

The first step with CV is to select an appropriate measure of model fit. CV is so general that virtually any model fit statistic could be used (e.g., R^2, Adjusted R^2, AIC [Akaike's Information Criterion], BIC [Bayesian Information Criterion]). In this case, we will compute the percentage of observations correctly classified by the logit model—the proportion of cases for which the predicted value of the dependent variable matches the actual value.

K-Fold CV

Next, we choose the type of CV to use. In our first example, we will illustrate a simple version of "K-fold" CV, in which we randomly divide the data into two sets (a 75% subsample and a 25% subsample), estimate the model on one set, and evaluate it on the other. Our training set in this case is 75 observations, and our testing set is the other 25 observations.

```
# Divide the data into training and testing sets
n <- length(front.service$y)
train.size <- .75*n
test.size <- n - train.size

# Randomly draw the training sample observation numbers
train <- sample(1:n, train.size, replace = FALSE)
train.data <- websites[train, ] # The training data
test.data <- websites[-train, ] # The testing data
```

Notice the use of `replace = FALSE` in this case because we do not want observations repeated. Then, using the `data` argument we fit the model only on the training data.

```
# Fit the model only on the training data
front.service.cv <- glm(formula(front.service),
family = binomial (link = logit), data = train.data)
```

After estimating the model on the training data, the next step is to loop through all of the observations in the testing data and compute the expected probability for each. We create an empty vector to store the results, then use a `for` loop to go through each observation in the testing data. In each iteration, we matrix multiply the observation's values of the independent variables by the coefficients from the model estimated on the training data, `front.service.cv`. Once this is done, we use the `inv.logit()` function to compute the CV expected probability.

```
# Empty vector to store the value of the linear predictor
cv.lp <- numeric(test.size)
# Loop through all the observations in the test data
for(i in 1:(test.size)){

# Calculate the value of the linear predictor
# for each observation in the testing data
cv.lp[i] <- as.numeric(c(1, test.data[i, -1])) %*% coef(front.service.cv)
}
predicted.cv1 <- inv.logit(cv.lp) # Use inv.logit to get a probability
```

Finally, we compare three different models for prediction. The first is the null, or intercept-only, model. In this case, we compute the mean of the dependent variable, which is 0.49, and plug it into `rbinom()` to produce 100 predicted 1s and 0s. We then compute the mean of these 1s and 0s to get the percentage correctly predicted if we just guessed "1" for every observation. In this case, we get exactly 49% correctly predicted with that strategy.

```
set.seed(750437)

correct.null <- mean(rbinom(n, 1, mean(front.service$y))) # The null model
correct.null
[1] 0.49
```

Our second prediction model is to compute in-sample predicted values based on the model fit to all the data points. The code below uses an `ifelse()` statement to record which observations' actual values of the dependent variable match with their predicted values. We generate the predicted values by plugging the probabilities computed from the model (extracted with the `fitted()` function) into `rbinom()`. In other words, we get the probability of observing a 1 for each observation from the `fitted()` function, then use `rbinom()` to include a stochastic element in predicting a 1 or 0 (as we did with the intercept-only model). The `ifelse()` statement evaluates to TRUE or FALSE depending on whether the actual and predicted values match up. By taking the mean of that vector of TRUEs or FALSEs (which R recognizes as 1s and 0s), we arrive at the in-sample percent correctly classified of 59%, an improvement of 10 percentage points over the null model.

```
correct.is <- mean(ifelse(front.service$y ==
rbinom(n, 1, fitted(front.service)), 1, 0))
correct.is
[1] 0.59
```

The third method is to compute the prediction based on the CV expected probabilities. We repeat the process from the in-sample method above, but substitute `predicted.cv1`, the expected probabilities from the CV routine, for `fitted (front.service)`. The result is a percent correctly classified of 52%, which is a slight improvement of 3 percentage points over the value for the intercept-only model.

```
correct.cv1 <- mean(ifelse(front.service$y ==
rbinom(n, 1, predicted.cv1), 1, 0))
correct.cv1
[1] 0.52
```

In short, while the in-sample measure suggests that the model gives a moderate improvement in our ability to predict the dependent variable (10 percentage points), computing the fit measure with CV suggests that the improvement over simply guessing 1 every time is much smaller (3 percentage points). However, this computation was based on only one division of the data. A true K-fold CV routine would likely divide the data into more than two groups, repeat the procedure many times, and take the average of the repeated computations to reduce noise (see Burman, 1989; Stone, 1974, 1977).

Leave-One-Out CV

A specific version of K-fold CV that can be particularly useful is called "leave-one-out" CV. As its name implies, the procedure for leave-one-out CV is similar to that of the jackknife from Chapter 8: Each observation is iteratively dropped from the data, the model is fit to the remaining observations, then the fit statistic is computed for the dropped observation using that model. As with our first example, this renders the training and testing data independent of one another. In this approach, however, each observation takes one turn at becoming the testing data.

We can repeat the example from above using leave-one-out CV with a few modifications to the code. First, we create an empty storage vector of length n (the sample size) and start a new `for` loop.

```
# A vector to store the value of the linear predictor
# on each observation when it is excluded
cv.lp <- numeric(n)
for(i in 1:n){ # Loop through all the observations
```

Next, we estimate the model on all of the data points except one. Again, we use the `data` argument to tell R which data points to use. Once the model has been estimated, we compute the expected probability for the left-out observation using the coefficients from that model and the `inv.logit()` function.

```
# Estimate the model without observation i
cv.model <- glm(formula(front.service), family = binomial (link = logit),
data = websites[-i, ])

# Calculate the value of the linear predictor for the left out observation
cv.lp[i] <- as.numeric(c(1, front.service$model[i, -1])) %*% coef(cv.model)
cat("Completed", i, "of", n, "\n")
}
predicted.cv2 <- inv.logit(cv.lp)
```

Then, we repeat the calculation from above by inserting `predicted.cv2` into `rbinom()` to get the predicted values. We compute the proportion that are correct and arrive at a value of 56%. This is larger than the 52% calculated above from just one division of the data.

```
# The % correctly classified using CV computations
correct.cv2 <- mean(ifelse(front.service$y ==
rbinom(n, 1, predicted.cv2), 1, 0))
correct.cv2
[1] 0.56
```

This result suggests that the model does fit the data better than the intercept-only model, with an improvement in correct classifications of 7 percentage points. Figure 9.7 plots the percent correctly classified from the intercept-only model, the in-sample computation, and our two CV computations. Notice that the CV value improves when we switch to leave-one-out CV, but it still does not reach the in-sample value of 59%, which shows an optimistic bias.

As with many of the methods discussed in this book, CV relies on an RNG to produce its results. In the K-fold example, we used the `sample()` function to divide the data into subsamples. In both examples, we used `rbinom()` to generate predicted values. Because of this, it is important to set the seed as we have done throughout the book for the sake of reproducibility. Furthermore, we recommend using leave-one-out CV or averaging over several iterations of a K-fold CV procedure in a real analysis to minimize the chance of the RNG throwing off the results and to maximize the use of the information available in the data set you have.

| Figure 9.7 | Intercept-Only, In-Sample, and Leave-One-Out CV Percent Correctly Classified Values From the Logit Model of Constituent Service Website Content (Harden, 2012b) |

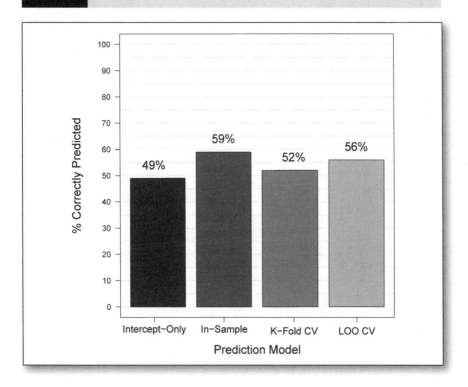

Separation Plots

Another informative way to use CV expected probabilities from a binary model is a separation plot (Greenhill, Ward, & Sacks, 2011). This method plots the observations in ascending order of their CV expected probabilities on the *x*-axis against the values of the probabilities on the *y*-axis (shown by the black line). Dark vertical shading in the background indicates observations with an actual value of 1 on the dependent variable, and light shading indicates observations with an actual value of 0. The arrow at the bottom of the plot denotes where the expected values of 0 ends and expected values of 1 begins. This is created by summing the expected probabilities generated by the model. A perfect-fitting model would produce all dark shading to the right of the expected number arrow and all light shading to the left of that arrow, implying that CV predictions from the model produce perfect separation of the actual 1s and 0s in the dependent variable (see Greenhill et al., 2011, p. 995). More realistically, a model that fits "well" should produce a higher concentration of dark shading toward the right side of the plot and a higher concentration of light shading to the left.

As an example, consider the following code, which is based on the logit model simulation from Chapter 6. Here we simulate a sample of 100 observations, estimate a logit model, and produce a separation plot just like above.

```
# Separation Plot
library(separationplot)

# The example from Chapter 6

# Inverse Logit Function
inv.logit <- function(p){
return(exp(p)/(1 + exp(p)))
}


library(separationplot)
set.seed(32945) # Set the seed for reproducible results

b0 <- 0 # True value for the intercept
b1 <- 2 # True value for the slope
n <- 100 # Sample size
X <- runif(n, -1, 1) # Create a sample of n observations on the
                     # independent variable X

Y <- rbinom(n, 1, inv.logit(b0 + b1*X)) # The true DGP, Bernoulli trials
cv.data <- data.frame(Y, X)
model <- glm(Y ~ X, family = binomial (link = logit)) # Estimate logit model

# LOOCV
# A vector to store the value of the linear predictor
# on each observation when it is excluded
cv.lp2 <- numeric(n)
for(i in 1:n){ # Loop through all the observations

# Estimate the model without observation i
cv.model <- glm(formula(model), family = binomial (link = logit),
data = cv.data[-i, ])

# Calculate the value of the linear predictor for the left out observation
cv.lp2[i] <- as.numeric(c(1, model$model[i, -1])) %*% coef(cv.model)
cat("Completed", i, "of", n, "\n")
}
predicted.cv22 <- inv.logit(cv.lp2)

par(mar = c(5, 5.25, .5, .5))
separationplot(predicted.cv22, model$y, lwd2 = 3, show.expected = TRUE,
 BW = TRUE, newplot = FALSE)
axis(1)
```

```
axis(2, at = seq(0, 1, .1), las = 2)
title(xlab = expression("Observations"), cex.lab = 1.5)
title(ylab = expression("CV Probability"), line = 3.75, cex.lab = 1.5)
text(34, -.1, expression(paste(""%<-%"")~"Expected y = 0"))
text(63.5, -.1, expression("Expected y = 1"~paste(""%->%"")))
box()
```

The separation plot is given in Figure 9.8, Panel (a). Notice that the dark lines tend to fall to the right side, indicating that most of the observations for which the model assigns a high probability of having a 1 on the dependent variable actually have a 1 on the dependent variable. Likewise, most of the left side of the plot has light lines, indicating that most of the observations with low expected probabilities actually have 0s.

In contrast, consider the separation plot for the front.service model from above in Figure 9.8, Panel (b). The code for that graph is as follows.

```
library(separationplot)

par(mar = c(5, 5.25, .5, .5))
separationplot(predicted.cv2, front.service$y, lwd2 = 3, show.expected = TRUE,
  BW = TRUE, newplot = FALSE)
axis(1)
axis(2, at = seq(0, 1, .1), las = 2)
title(xlab = expression("Observations"), cex.lab = 1.5)
title(ylab = expression("CV Probability"), line = 3.75, cex.lab = 1.5)
text(37, -.1, expression(paste(""%<-%"")~"Expected y = 0"))
text(66, -.1, expression("Expected y = 1"~paste(""%->%"")))
box()
```

In Panel (b), the plot shows that the model does not fit the data well. There are many dark lines on the left side of the plot, indicating legislators whose websites mention service but have low expected probabilities of mentioning service on their websites. There are also several light lines near the right side of the plot, which indicate legislators for whom the model produces a high expected probability of mentioning service, but do not have such a mention on their websites. In other words, the simulated data model fits much better than does the website data model.[17] Overall, by computing the expected probabilities via CV and plotting these probabilities and the actual values, a separation plot provides an honest and thorough assessment of model fit with binary dependent variable models (for more details, see Greenhill et al., 2011).

---

[17]This is another reason to incorporate simulation into your research—the data are more well behaved!

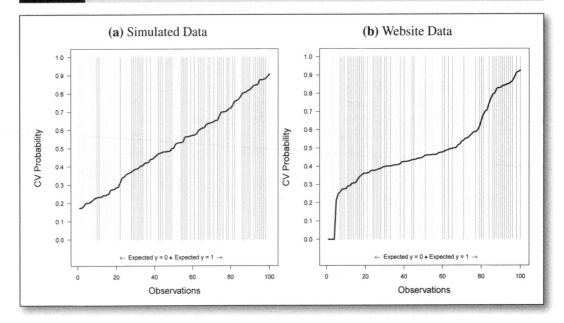

Figure 9.8 Separation Plot From the Simulated Data Logit Model and Constituent Service Website Content Model (Harden, 2012b)

9.3.3 Using R **Functions for CV**

Finally, while CV can be done manually as in the examples above, there are also several R packages and functions you can use to perform CV, including the `validate()` function in the `rms` package and several functions in the `DAAG` package. Here we briefly illustrate the use of `cv.glm()`, which can be found in the `boot` package.

The `cv.glm()` function requires three main arguments to perform leave-one-out CV. The first is the name of the data object, the second is the name of the model object, and the third is the "cost function," which is the formula for the fit statistic of interest. There is also an argument K for K-fold CV. This argument defaults to the sample size, which is equivalent to leave-one-out CV. The default fit statistic is mean squared error. In this case, we want to compute the percent correctly classified. We first write the formula into a function called `pcc()`. This is the exact same formula we used above, with parameters y for the actual values of the dependent variable and `yhat` for the fitted values (expected probabilities).

```
library(boot)

# This cost function computes the % correctly classified
pcc <- function(y, yhat){
return(mean(ifelse(y == rbinom(n, 1, yhat), 1, 0)))
}
```

As a test, we can use the function to do the in-sample computation on the websites data. Remember that there is an element of randomness associated with the `rbinom()` function, so, in this case, we get a value of 56%, which is slightly different from above.

```
# Use the pcc() function for in-sample computation
example.is <- pcc(front.service$y, fitted(front.service))
example.is
[1] 0.56
```

Finally, we can compute the CV percent correctly classified with the following code. The value itself gets printed in the object $delta. Here we see that the function returns a value of about 55%, which is close to the value we computed above.[18] Most important, we see again that the CV value is smaller than the in-sample value.

```
# CV with the cv.glm() function
example.cv <- cv.glm(websites, front.service, pcc)
example.cv$delta[1]
[1] 0.5484
```

Overall, this is only a small sampling of the possible uses for CV. Indeed, many more types of model fit statistics could be used (e.g., mean squared error, median absolute deviation, individual log-likelihood contributions, residuals, etc.). Furthermore, many other types of model choices can be made with CV. Variable selection, model specification, and functional form are all important modeling decisions for which CV can be useful. For more on CV, see Efron (1983), Efron and Tibshirani (1993, 1997), or Harrell (2001).

9.4 CONCLUSIONS

In this chapter, we provided an overview of two of the many other simulation-based methods employed by social scientists. We covered a lot of ground in this chapter. Both of the main topics in this chapter can and should be explored in much greater detail, but we hope the introduction we provided helps readers begin to develop a basic understanding of these tools. We include these methods because they are useful, because they share a common underlying logic and similar properties with simulation and resampling methods, and because quantifying uncertainty about meaningful information (QI simulation) and proper evaluation of statistical models (CV) lie at the heart of the goal of empirical social science.

---

[18]The `cv.glm()` function uses a slightly more complex formula to adjust the final result. Type `?cv.glm` for more information.

QI simulation is useful for translating the specialized, technical results from a statistical model into a meaningful way to communicate results that will resonate with other researchers as well as people without specialized knowledge. The statement "the expected probability of voting increases by 29 percentage points for strong partisans compared to independents" is much more helpful than "the logit coefficient was positive and statistically significant at the 0.05 level." Moreover, QI simulation provides an easy way to report uncertainty around virtually any estimate that can be produced using the model's coefficients. This allows researchers to do more with their analyses, reaping more benefits from the data that they have collected.

We also showed a few applications of CV, which is a general method of evaluating the fit of statistical models. CV forces researchers to avoid "double-dipping" by separating the data used to fit the model and the data used to test the model. Evaluating the model on the estimation data runs the risk of overfitting, or making the model seem to fit well, but only on that particular sample of data. Assessing a model's capacity to make out-of-sample predictions produces a tougher test and ultimately a more rigorous assessment of the connection between theory and empirics.

10

Final Thoughts

As we said at the start of this book, social scientists try to answer really important questions. Much of social science research rests on observational data, where the leverage available to experimentalists in evaluating the impact of a treatment variable on an outcome is lacking. At the same time, many experiments in the social sciences are based on small, nonrepresentative samples and/or impose unrealistic restrictions on how treatment variables are experienced. Simulation and resampling methods do not solve all of these problems, but they do allow researchers to bring together many of the best elements of observational and experimental research. These methods allow researchers to use computers as "experimental laboratories" and to extract more information from the data they have. These tools are powerful, flexible, and available to all social science researchers. In short, these tools give social scientists greater leverage in answering important questions and evaluating the quality of those answers. If you find this paragraph convincing, compelling, or at least somewhat plausible after working through this book, we have achieved our goal.

Monte Carlo simulation and resampling methods have become increasingly useful tools for academic research and training over the past several decades. This is particularly evident in the social sciences, where, for example, these methods have been used to evaluate statistical models (e.g., Cameron & Trivedi, 2005; Feng et al., 1996; Green & Vavreck, 2008), compute quantities of interest from model results (e.g., Gelman & Hill, 2007; King et al., 2000), and assess uncertainty of estimates through bootstrapping (e.g., Chernick & LaBudde, 2011; Good, 2005). Computer simulation and resampling methods are flexible and intuitive, which makes them accessible and useful tools for social scientists.

In this book, we highlighted the advantages of Monte Carlo simulation and resampling methods for social scientists. We focused on the most broad application to social science research: evaluation of statistical models and substantive theory. We demonstrated the benefits of using simulation to turn the computer into a laboratory. This can be useful in at least two distinct ways: (1) for researchers interested in using Monte Carlo simulation to conduct rigorous assessments of statistical tools or to directly test substantive theories and (2) social science students looking for a more intuitive approach to understanding the concepts presented in a traditional textbook.

10.1 A SUMMARY OF THE BOOK

The first three chapters provided an introduction to the book, a basic primer on probability theory, and a short introduction to R, respectively. The probability chapter is comprehensive enough to lay the groundwork for the main chapters, but also contains citations to other books for further reading. The introduction to R chapter also provided sufficient material to understand the rest of the book with suggested citations for further study.

Chapter 4 began the heart of the book with an in-depth treatment on random number generation (RNG) in R. RNG is central to understanding simulation and resampling methods because both rely on iteratively drawing random numbers from either a theoretical probability distribution or a sample of data. We discussed how to draw random numbers using existing functions in R and how to create functions that draw random numbers. We introduced the concepts of systematic and stochastic components in a statistical model through a basic simulation of ordinary least squares (OLS). We also described some basics of programming in R and outlined the standard components of a script file of R code.

Chapter 5 was devoted entirely to simulation, using the linear model as a running example of how to evaluate an estimator. We began by discussing bias and efficiency and different ways of measuring estimator performance with a simulation. This included the evaluation of coefficient estimates and standard errors. We then went through seven different simulations illustrating some of the consequences of violating different OLS assumptions. Our emphasis in these examples was to show how to simulate data with each of these problems and how to efficiently assess the results.

In Chapter 6, we moved to simulations of generalized linear models (GLMs). We began by reframing OLS as a GLM, then went through examples of several common models used by applied social scientists (e.g., binary, ordered, and unordered dependent variables). We also provided extended examples with ordered, unordered, count, and duration models. These were designed to show how simulation can be used as a tool for developing new methods. Finally, we ended Chapter 6 with a discussion of computational issues that arise with simulation. We described how research on computing clusters and parallel processing can be used to complete simulations faster. We also gave a step-by-step example of how to parallelize simulation code across multiple cores on a standard desktop computer.

In Chapter 7, we switched from purely statistical simulations to simulations about substantive theory. We made the point that simulation need not be all about understanding and evaluating the methods we use to test hypotheses. It can also be used to directly understand a substantive process. Using three examples from the social sciences, we demonstrated how simulation of a DGP can be used to directly assess theory, with particular attention directed at whether patterns offered as evidence for a theoretical claim differ in a meaningful way from patterns that might result from randomness.

Chapter 8 focused on three of the most common resampling methods used in social science as a means of estimating uncertainty in statistical models. We began with permutation and randomization tests. We made the point that these methods lend themselves best to experimental data, where creating a null distribution for the treatment effect is useful. Next, we introduced jackknifing and showed in a simulation how it outperforms the conventional OLS standard errors in the presence of heteroskedasticity. Finally, we devoted the most attention to bootstrapping. We began with basic code, then progressed to multiple regression models. We also showed an in-depth example on bootstrapping clusters of observations rather than individual observations.

In Chapter 9, we highlighted "other simulation-based methods." Specifically, we presented detailed discussions on two techniques that share similar properties with simulation and resampling methods. First, we discussed the simulation of quantities of interest (QI) from statistical models. Using simulation from statistical models, analysts can generate quantities such as expected values, expected probabilities, or first differences as well as measures of uncertainty to give readers a clearer sense of the results from a statistical model (see King et al., 2000). The second technique we highlighted was cross-validation (CV). CV is a general method of evaluating the fit of statistical models by separating the data used to fit the model and the data used to test the model. This helps researchers guard against "overfitting."

10.2 GOING FORWARD

A central message we hope this book conveys is that the techniques described here are not just for the methodologists in one's department. Rather, they are tools that can be used by anyone conducting empirical research. We filled the book with examples and sample code so that readers can execute them on their own computers. We encourage you to make changes to our code to expand the examples and learn more. Overall, we emphasize the necessity of learning through hands-on experience. To that end, all of the code and examples in this book can also be found online at `www.sagepub.com/carsey`.

A logical question after reading this book might be "What could I do to apply the information in this book to my own work?" We recommend the following five possibilities to get started.

1. Identify a possible problem or assumption violation in one of your own projects or in a published paper. Write down a simulation that constructs the DGP with that problem and then use the estimator from the paper on the simulated data to see how it performs. If there are other possible estimators, evaluate those as well and compare the different options. Use what you learn from those simulations to replicate the original analysis employing the plausible alternatives your simulation uncovered and defend which one is best based on the results from your simulation.

2. Think of a way to simulate the substantive theoretical mechanism in one of your papers or a published paper. Write down one or more simple formulas that you think

describes the DGP you are interested in. Consider how you would create the DGP, including necessary assumptions or simplifications, in R. Execute the simulation and evaluate the results. Consider alterations to the DGP and evaluate their impact on the resulting patterns you observe after rerunning the simulation. Think about the pros and cons of evaluating theory in that simulation rather than with observed data and consider what data you would need to collect to access the theory empirically.

3. Use a resampling method to evaluate the hypotheses in one of your papers or a published paper. Compare the results with a conventional method. Think about the structure of your data and how the resampling method might be used to adapt to that structure.

4. In your next paper, simulate QI from the model results. Devote more space to the interpretation of QI rather than the sign and significance of the coefficient estimates. Consider how to construct graphs to present those results.

5. Also in your next paper, evaluate the fit of your model(s) using CV. Choose an appropriate model fit statistic and compute it with either a K-fold or leave-one-out CV procedure. Compare the result with the in-sample measure of fit.

10.3 CONCLUSIONS

As we discussed at the beginning of this book, the phrase "in repeated samples" is commonly used in statistics and quantitative research methods courses in the social sciences. It is important because we want to know more than just what patterns exist in our sample of data; we want to draw inferences from our sample of data about the DGP in the population. However, the concept of repeated samples in the abstract can be difficult to understand. Monte Carlo simulation solves this problem. Simulation allows the analyst to easily create many samples of data in a computing environment, then assess patterns that appear in those repeated samples. This book has shown the utility of Monte Carlo simulation in three different areas: (1) as a means of learning and understanding fundamental principles of statistical methods, (2) as a powerful tool for assessing new methods and comparing competing methods, and (3) as a method of evaluating substantive theory about social processes.

We have provided a foundation for those interested in comparing statistical techniques in a controlled environment as a means of advancing knowledge about statistical methods as well as the substantive problems to which statistical methods are applied. We tried to provide a starting point for researchers who know the topic they want to study, but are unsure of how to go about creating the DGP, recording the simulated results, and presenting them effectively. Over the course of the book, we touched on topics such as investigation of the finite sample properties of an estimator under assumption violations, hypothesis testing when a sampling distribution is unknown, comparing the quality of two or more inference methods, and checking the robustness of parametric assumptions in an analysis.

Monte Carlo simulation is advantageous in studying these types of problems for several reasons. First, the method gives the analyst full control over the DGP, which is important because accurate evaluation requires that the data being tested precisely reflect the characteristics of the problem of interest. Second, simulation provides clear, conclusive results. Comparison of estimators with simulated data allows the analyst to set a standard by which the estimators can be judged. In contrast, evaluation with observed data is disadvantaged because the true parameters are unknown. Furthermore, even in cases where there is a mathematical proof that one estimator has a certain problem like bias, simulation can show the extent of the bias under common conditions defined by the analyst. This informs judgments on trading off between bias and efficiency when selecting estimation methods. Finally, simulation results are easy to interpret and present graphically, making the communication of findings approachable to a wider audience. This book makes conducting Monte Carlo studies accessible to researchers even if they do not have extensive experience with computer programming.

Additionally, we believe that simulation methods can be a complement to traditional social science methods training. From our own experience, illustrating statistical concepts through simulation helps students develop a greater intuition about applied statistical analysis while still providing a look at what is going on "under the hood." For example, being able to create a DGP that induces heteroskedasticity lets students really see what the problem looks like and helps them develop a more thorough knowledge of the concept. To paraphrase the comment made by our colleague, Jim Stimson, we do not truly understand a problem in our data until we can create that problem in a simulated data set.[1] Indeed, simulation helps students explore statistical principles under a variety of plausible conditions they might encounter in their own research.

Empirical social scientists can produce their best research when they have a clear sense of both the tools they are using and their assumptions about the DGP in the larger population they are studying. While it may be quicker to view methods as recipes and simply select the one that seems to fit best by pointing and clicking your way through menus in canned software, engaging the data through simulation and adapting the chosen methods appropriately can help in accurately estimating how the data were generated, thereby promoting deeper understanding. The methods described here can all be used to help researchers focus on adapting their methodological plan to the substantive problem, rather than redefining their substantive problem to fit a standard method. This will ultimately yield more understanding and better insights of important social processes.

---

[1] We noted this comment in the acknowledgments section of this book, and we thank Jim again for it here.

REFERENCES

Adler, E. S. (2000). Constituency characteristics and the "guardian" model of appropria-
tions subcommittees, 1959–1998. *American Journal of Political Science, 44*(1),
104–114.

Adler, E. S., & Lapinski, J. S. (1997). Demand-side theory and Congressional committee
composition: A constituency characteristics approach. *American Journal of Political
Science, 41*(3), 895–918.

Agresti, A., & Coull, B. A. (1998). Approximate is better than "exact" for interval estimation of binomial proportions. *The American Statistician, 52*(2), 119–126.

Arai, M. (2011). Cluster-robust standard errors using R. Retrieved from `http://
people.su.se/~ma/clustering.pdf`.

Arceneaux, K., & Nickerson, D. W. (2009). Modeling certainty with clustered data: A
comparison of methods. *Political Analysis, 17*(2), 177–190.

Bailey, D., & Katz, J. N. (2011). Implementing panel-corrected standard errors in R: The
`pcse` package. *Journal of Statistical Software, 42*(1), 1–11.

Bates, D., Maechler, M., & Bolker, B. (2011). `lme4`: Linear mixed-effects models using
s4 classes. R package version 0.999375-42. Retrieved from `http://
CRAN.R-project.org/package=lme4`.

Baumgartner, F. R., Foucault, M., & Francois, A. (2006). Punctuated equilibrium in French
budgeting processes. *Journal of European Public Policy, 13*(7), 1086–1103.

Baumgartner, F. R., & Jones, B. D. (1993). *Agendas and instability in American politics*.
Chicago, IL: University of Chicago Press.

Beck, N., & Katz, J. N. (1995). What to do (and not to do) with time-series cross-section
data. *American Political Science Review, 89*(3), 634–647.

Bednarski, T. (1989). On sensitivity of Cox's estimator. *Statistics and Decisions, 7*(3),
215–228.

Bednarski, T. (1993). Robust estimation in Cox's regression model. *Scandinavian Journal
of Statistics, 20*(3), 213–225.

Bollen, K. A., Ray, S., Zavisca, J., & Harden, J. J. (2012). A comparison of Bayes factor
approximation methods including two new methods. *Sociological Methods & Research,
41*(2), 294–324.

Box-Steffensmeier, J. M., & Jones, B. S. (2004). *Event history modeling: A guide for
social scientists*. New York, NY: Cambridge University Press.

Braun, W. J., & Murdoch, D. J. (2007). *A first course in statistical programming with R*.
New York, NY: Cambridge University Press.

Burman, P. (1989). A comparative study of ordinary cross-validation, v-fold cross-validation
and the repeated learning-testing methods. *Biometrika, 76*(3), 503–514.

Cameron, A. C., & Trivedi, P. K. (1998). *Regression analysis of count data*. New York,
NY: Cambridge University Press.

Cameron, A. C., & Trivedi, P. K. (2005). *Microeconometrics: Methods and applications*. New York, NY: Cambridge University Press.

Canty, A., & Ripley, B. D. (2011). boot: Bootstrap R functions. R package version 1.3-2. Retrieved from http://CRAN.R-project.org/package=boot.

Carsey, T. M., & Desmarais, B. A. (2013, April 11–14). "Punctuated equilibrium and the policymaking process: Empirical evidence and theoretical implications." Paper presented at the Midwest Political Science Association Annual Meeting, Chicago, IL.

Chambers, J. M. (2008). *Software for data analysis: Programming with R*. New York, NY: Springer.

Chang, J. (2011). lda: Collapsed Gibbs sampling methods for topic models. R package version 1.3.1. Retrieved from http://CRAN.R-project.org/package=lda.

Chasalow, S. (2010). combinat: Combinatorics utilities. R package version 0.0-8. Retrieved from http://CRAN.R-project.org/package=combinat.

Chernick, M. R., & LaBudde, R. A. (2011). *An introduction to bootstrap methods with applications to R*. Hoboken, NJ: Wiley.

Cohen, Y., & Cohen, J. Y. (2008). *Statistics and data with R*. West Sussex, UK: Wiley.

Cook, R. D. (1977). Detection of influential observation in linear regression. *Technometrics*, *19*(1), 15–18.

Cox, D. R. (1972). Regression models and life-tables. *Journal of the Royal Statistical Society, Series B (Methodological)*, *34*(2), 187–220.

Cox, D. R. (1975). Partial likelihood. *Biometrika*, *62*(2), 269–276.

DebRoy, S., & Bivand, R. (2011). foreign: Read data stored by Minitab, S, SAS, SPSS, Stata, Systat, and dBase. R package version 0.8-48. Retrieved from http://CRAN.R-project.org/package=foreign.

Dehejia, R. H., & Wahba, S. (1999). Causal effects in nonexperimental studies: Reevaluating the evaluation of training programs. *Journal of the American Statistical Association*, *94*(448), 1053–1062.

Desmarais, B. A., & Harden, J. J. (2012). Comparing partial likelihood and robust estimation methods for the Cox regression model. *Political Analysis*, *20*(1), 113–135.

Durrett, R. (2010). *Probability: Theory and examples* (4th ed.). New York, NY: Cambridge University Press.

Efron, B. (1979). Bootstrap methods: Another look at the jackknife. *Annals of Statistics*, *7*(1), 1–26.

Efron, B. (1983). Estimating the error rate of a prediction rule: Some improvements on cross-validation. *Journal of the American Statistical Association*, *78*(382), 316–331.

Efron, B. (1987). Better bootstrap confidence intervals. *Journal of the American Statistical Association*, *82*(397), 171–185.

Efron, B., & Tibshirani, R. J. (1993). *An introduction to the bootstrap*. Boca Raton, FL: Chapman & Hall/CRC.

Efron, B., & Tibshirani, R. J. (1997). Improvements on cross-validation: The .632+ bootstrap method. *Journal of the American Statistical Association*, *92*(438), 548–560.

Ehrlich, I. (1973). Participation in illegitimate activities: A theoretical and empirical investigation. *Journal of Political Economy*, *81*(3), 521–565.

Eldredge, M., & Gould, S. J. (1972). Punctuated equilibria: An alternative to phyletic gradualism. In T. J. M. Schopf (Ed.), *Models in paleobiology* (pp. 82–115). New York, NY: Doubleday.

Epstein, L., Lindstädt, R., Segal, J. A., & Westerland, C. (2006). The changing dynamics of Senate voting on Supreme Court nominees. *Journal of Politics*, *68*(2), 296–307.

Erikson, R. S., Pinto, P. M., & Rader, K. T. (2010). Randomization tests and multi-level data in state politics. *State Politics & Policy Quarterly*, *10*(2), 180–198.

Evert, S., & Baroni, M. (2008). zipfr: Statistical models for word frequency distributions. R package version 0.6-5. Retrieved from http://zipfR.R-Forge.R-project.org/.

Faraway, J. J. (2006). *Extending the linear model with R: Generalized linear, mixed effects and nonparametric regression models*. Boca Raton, FL: Chapman & Hall/CRC Press.

Feinerer, I., Hornik, K., & Meyer, D. (2008). Text mining infrastructure in R. *Journal of Statistical Software*, *25*(5), 1–54.

Feng, Z., McLerran, D., & Grizzle, J. (1996). A comparison of statistical methods for clustered data analysis with Gaussian error. *Statistics in Medicine*, *15*(16), 1793–1806.

Fisher, R. A. (1935). *The design of experiments*. New York, NY: Hafner.

Fox, J. (2008). *Applied regression analysis and generalized linear models* (2nd ed.). Thousand Oaks, CA: Sage.

Fox, J., & Weisberg, S. (2010). *An R and S-plus companion to applied regression* (2nd ed.). Thousand Oaks, CA: Sage.

Gamerman, D., & Lopes, H. F. (2006). *Markov chain Monte Carlo: Stochastic simulation for Bayesian inference*. Boca Raton, FL: Chapman & Hall/CRC.

Gelman, A., & Hill, J. (2007). *Data analysis using regression and multilevel/hierarchical models*. New York, NY: Cambridge University Press.

Gelman, A., Su, Y.-S., Yajima, M., Hill, J., Pittau, M. G., Kerman, J., & Zheng, T. (2012). arm: Data analysis using regression and multilevel/hierarchical models. R package version 1.5-08. Retrieved from http://CRAN.R-project.org/package=arm.

Gentle, J. E. (2003). *Random number generation and Monte Carlo methods*. New York, NY: Springer.

Gentry, J. (2012). twitteR: R based twitter client. R package version 0.00.19. Retrieved from http://CRAN.R-project.org/package=twitteR.

Genz, A., Bretz, F., Miwa, T., Mi, X., Leisch, F., Scheipl, F., & Hothorn, T. (2011). mvtnorm: Multivariate normal and *t* distributions. R package version 0.9-9991. Retrieved from http://CRAN.R-project.org/package=mvtnorm.

Gill, J. (2007). *Bayesian methods: A social and behavioral sciences approach* (2nd ed.). Boca Raton, FL: Chapman & Hall/CRC.

Good, P. I. (2004). *Permutation, parametric and bootstrap tests of hypotheses* (3rd ed.). New York, NY: Springer.

Good, P. I. (2005). *Resampling methods: A practical guide to data analysis* (3rd ed.). Boston, MA: Birkhäuser.

Green, D. P., & Vavreck, L. (2008). Analysis of cluster-randomized experiments: A comparison of alternative estimation techniques. *Political Analysis*, *16*(2), 138–152.

Greene, W. H. (2011). *Econometric analysis* (7th ed.). Upper Saddle River, NJ: Prentice Hall.

Greenhill, B., Ward, M. D., & Sacks, A. (2011). The separation plot: A new visual method for evaluating the fit of binary models. *American Journal of Political Science*, *55*(4), 991–1002.

Grün, B., & Hornik, K. (2011). topicmodels: An R package for fitting topic models. *Journal of Statistical Software*, *40*(13), 1–30.

Gujarati, D. N., & Porter, D. C. (2008). *Basic econometrics* (5th ed.). New York, NY: McGraw-Hill.

Hanmer, M. J., & Kalkan, K. O. (2013). Behind the curve: Clarifying the best approach to calculating predicted probabilities and marginal effects from limited dependent variable models. *American Journal of Political Science*, *57*(1), 263–277.

Harden, J. J. (2011). A bootstrap method for conducting statistical inference with clustered data. *State Politics & Policy Quarterly*, *11*(2), 223–246.

Harden, J. J. (2012a). Improving statistical inference with clustered data. *Statistics, Politics, and Policy*, *3*(1), 1–27.

Harden, J. J. (2012b). *Multidimensional democracy: The supply and demand of political representation*. Unpublished doctoral dissertation, University of North Carolina at Chapel Hill.

Harden, J. J., & Desmarais, B. A. (2011). Linear models with outliers: Choosing between conditional-mean and conditional-median methods. *State Politics & Policy Quarterly*, *11*(4), 371–389.

Harrell, F. E. (2001). *Regression modeling strategies: With applications to linear models, logistic regression, and survival analysis*. New York, NY: Springer.

Harrell, F. E. (2012). rms: Regression modeling strategies. R package version 3.4-0. Retrieved from http://CRAN.R-project.org/package=rms.

Horton, N. J., & Kleinman, K. (2011). *Using R for data management, statistical analysis, and graphics*. Boca Raton, FL: Chapman & Hall/CRC.

Imai, K., King, G., & Lau, O. (2012). Zelig: Everyone's statistical software. R package version 3.5.4. Retrieved from http://CRAN.R-project.org/package=Zelig.

Jackman, S. (2011). pscl: Classes and methods for R developed in the Political Science Computational Laboratory, Stanford University. R package version 1.04.1. Retrieved from http://pscl.stanford.edu/.

Jones, O., Maillardet, R., & Robinson, A. (2009). *Scientific programming and simulation using R*. Boca Raton, FL: Chapman & Hall/CRC.

Jurka, T. P., Collingwood, L., Boydstun, A. E., Grossman, E., & van Atteveldt, W. (2011). RTextTools: Automatic text classification via supervised learning. R package version 1.3.2. Retrieved from http://CRAN.R-project.org/package=RTextTools.

Keele, L., & Kelly, N. J. (2006). Dynamic models for dynamic theories: The ins and outs of lagged dependent variables. *Political Analysis*, *14*(2), 186–205.

Keele, L., McConnaughy, C., & White, I. (2012). Strengthening the experimenter's toolbox: Statistical estimation of internal validity. *American Journal of Political Science*, *56*(2), 484–499.

Kennedy, P. E. (1995). Randomization tests in econometrics. *Journal of Business & Economic Statistics*, *13*(1), 85–94.

Kennedy, P. E., & Cade, B. S. (1996). Randomization tests for multiple regression. *Communication in Statistics B: Simulation and Computation*, *25*(4), 923–936.

King, G. (1998). *Unifying political methodology: The likelihood theory of statistical inference*. Ann Arbor, MI: University of Michigan Press.

King, G., Tomz, M., & Wittenberg, J. (2000). Making the most of statistical analyses: Improving interpretation and presentation. *American Journal of Political Science*, *44*(2), 341–355.

Koenker, R. (2011). quantreg: Quantile regression. R package version 4.76. Retrieved from http://CRAN.R-project.org/package=quantreg.

Koenker, R., & Bassett, G. (1978). Regression quantiles. *Econometrica*, *46*(1), 33–50.

Komsta, L., & Novomestky, F. (2012). moments: Moments, cumulants, skewness, kurtosis and related tests. R package version 0.13. Retrieved from http://CRAN.R-project.org/package=moments.

Kristensen, I. P., & Wawro, G. (2003, July). "Lagging the dog? The robustness of panel corrected standard errors in the presence of serial correlation and observation specific effects." Presented at the 20th Annual Meeting of the Society for Political Methodology, Minneapolis, MN.

Kropko, J. (2008, April). "Choosing between multinomial logit and multinomial probit models for analysis of unordered choice data." Presented at the 66th Annual National Conference of the Midwest Political Science Association, Chicago, IL.

Künsch, H. R. (1989). The jackknife and the bootstrap for general stationary observations. *Annals of Statistics*, *17*(3), 1217–1241.

LaLonde, R. J. (1986). Evaluating the econometric evaluations of training programs with experimental data. *American Economic Review*, *76*(4), 604–620.

Lave, C., & March, J. (1993). *An introduction to models in the social sciences*. Lanham, MD: University Press of America. (Original work published 1975 by Harper & Row)

Lee, L. (1995). Asymptotic bias in simulated maximum likelihood estimation of discrete choice models. *Econometric Theory*, *11*(3), 437–483.

Li, W. (1992). Random texts exhibit Zipf's-law-like word frequency distribution. *IEEE Transactions on Information Theory*, *38*(6), 1842–1845.

Long, J. S. (1997). *Regression models for categorical and limited dependent variables*. Thousand Oaks, CA: Sage.

Long, J. S., & Ervin, L. H. (2000). Using heteroscedasticity consistent standard errors in the linear regression model. *The American Statistician*, *54*(3), 217–224.

Loprinzi, C. L., Laurie, J. A., Wieand, H. S., Krook, J. E., Novotny, P. J., Kugler, J. W., … Moertel, C. G. (1994). Prospective evaluation of prognostic variables from patient-completed questionnaires. *Journal of Clinical Oncology*, *12*(4), 601–607.

Maindonald, J., & Braun, W. J. (2012). DAAG: Data analysis and graphics data and functions. R package version 1.12. Retrieved from http://CRAN.R-project.org/package=DAAG.

Manly, B. F. J. (2006). *Randomization, bootstrap and Monte Carlo methods in biology* (3rd ed.). Boca Raton, FL: Chapman & Hall/CRC.

Matloff, N. (2011). *The art of R programming: A tour of statistical software design*. San Francisco, CA: No Starch Press.

Mayr, E. (1954). Change of genetic environment and evolution. In J. Huxley, A. C. Hardy, & E. B. Ford (Eds.), *Evolution as a process* (pp. 157–180). London, England: Allen & Unwin.

Miller, G. A. (1965). Introduction. In G. K. Zipf & G. A. Miller (Eds.), *The psycho-biology of language: An introduction to dynamic philology*. Cambridge: MIT Press.

Mineo, A. M., & Ruggieri, M. (2005). A software tool for the exponential power distribution: The normalp package. *Journal of Statistical Software*, *12*(4), 1–24.

Mitchell, M. (2009). *Complexity: A guided tour*. New York, NY: Oxford University Press.

Mooney, C. Z. (1997). *Monte Carlo simulation*. Thousand Oaks, CA: Sage.

Mooney, C. Z., & Duval, R. D. (1993). *Bootstrapping: A nonparametric approach to statistical inference*. Thousand Oaks, CA: Sage.

Murrell, P. (2005). R graphics (2nd ed.). Boca Raton, FL: Chapman & Hall/CRC.

Oken, M., Creech, R., Tormey, D., Horton, J., Davis, T., McFadden, E., & Carbone, P. (1982). Toxicity and response criteria of the Eastern Cooperative Oncology Group. *American Journal of Clinical Oncology*, *5*(6), 649–655.

Pitman, E. J. G. (1937). Significance tests which may be applied to samples from any population. *Journal of the Royal Statistical Society Supplement*, *4*(1), 119–130.

Press, W. H., Teukolsky, S. A., Vetterling, W. T., & Flannery, B. P. (2007). *Numerical recipes: The art of scientific computing* (3rd ed.). New York, NY: Cambridge University Press.

Prindle, D. F. (2012). Importing concepts from biology into political science: The case of punctuated equilibrium. *Policy Studies Journal*, *40*(1), 21–43.

Rao, M. M., & Swift, R. J. (2005). *Probability theory with applications*. New York, NY: Springer.

R Development Core Team. (2012). *R: A language and environment for statistical comput-ing*. Vienna, Austria: R Foundation for Statistical Computing. Retrieved from `http://www.r-project.org`. (ISBN 3-900051-07-0)

Revolution Analytics. (2011a). `doSNOW`: Foreach parallel adaptor for the `snow` package. R package version 1.0.5. Retrieved from `http://CRAN.R-project.org/package=doSNOW`.

Revolution Analytics. (2011b). `foreach`: Foreach looping construct for R. R package version 1.3.2. Retrieved from `http://CRAN.R-project.org/package=foreach`.

Ridgeway, G., McCaffrey, D., Morral, A., Griffin, B. A., & Burgette, L. (2012). `twang`: Toolkit for weighting and analysis of nonequivalent groups. R package version 1.2-7. Retrieved from `http://CRAN.R-project.org/package=twang`.

Rizzo, M. L. (2008). *Statistical computing with R*. Boca Raton, FL: Chapman & Hall/CRC Press.

Rosenbaum, P. R. (2002). *Observational studies* (2nd ed.). New York, NY: Springer.

Skinner, B. F. (1948). "Superstition" in the pigeon. *Journal of Experimental Psychology*, *38*(1), 168–172.

Spector, P. (2008). *Data manipulation with R*. New York, NY: Springer.

Steenbergen, M. R., & Jones, B. S. (2002). Modeling multilevel data structures. *American Journal of Political Science*, *46*(1), 218–237.

Stone, M. (1974). Cross-validatory choice and assessment of statistical predictions. *Journal of the Royal Statistical Society, Series B (Methodological)*, *36*(2), 111–147.

Stone, M. (1977). An asymptotic equivalence of choice of model by cross-validation and Akaike's criterion. *Journal of the Royal Statistical Society, Series B (Methodological)*, *39*(1), 44–47.

Stroock, D. W. (2011). *Probability theory: An analytic view* (2nd ed.). New York, NY: Cambridge University Press.

Therneau, T. (2012). `survival`: A package for survival analysis in S. R package version 2.36-12. Retrieved from `http://CRAN.R-project.org/package=survival`.

Tibshirani, R., & Leisch, F. (2012). `bootstrap`: An introduction to the bootstrap. R package version 2012.04-0. Retrieved from `http://CRAN.R-project.org/package=bootstrap`.

Tierney, L., Rossini, A. J., Li, N., & Sevcikova, H. (2011). `snow`: Simple network of workstations. R package version 0.3-6. Retrieved from `http://CRAN.R-project.org/package=snow`.

Tukey, J. W. (1958). Bias and confidence in not-quite large samples. *Annals of Mathematical Statistics*, *29*(1), 614.

Varadhan, S. R. S. (2001). *Probability theory*. New York, NY: Courant Institute of Mathematical Sciences.

Venables, W. N., & Ripley, B. D. (2002). *Modern applied statistics with S*. New York, NY: Springer.

Wackerly, D. D., Mendenhall III, W., & Scheaffer, R. L. (2002). *Mathematical statistics with applications* (6th ed.). Pacific Grove, CA: Duxbury.

White, H. (1980). A heteroskedasticity-consistent covariance matrix estimator and a direct test for heteroskedasticity. *Econometrica*, *48*(4), 817–838.

Williams, R. L. (2000). A note on robust variance estimation for cluster-correlated data. *Biometrics*, *56*(2), 645–646.

Wilson, S. E., & Butler, D. M. (2007). A lot more to do: The sensitivity of time-series cross-section analyses to simple alternative specifications. *Political Analysis*, *15*(2), 101–123.

Wooldridge, J. M. (2002). *Econometric analysis of cross section and panel data.* Cambridge, MA: MIT Press.

Wu, C. (1986). Jackknife, bootstrap and other resampling methods in regression analysis. *Annals of Statistics, 14*(4), 1261–1295.

Yee, T. W. (2010). The VGAM package for categorical data analysis. *Journal of Statistical Software, 32*(10), 1–34.

Zeileis, A. (2006). Object-oriented computation of sandwich estimators. *Journal of Statistical Software, 16*(9), 1–16.

Zeileis, A., Kleiber, C., & Jackman, S. (2008). Regression models for count data in R. *Journal of Statistical Software, 27*(8), 1–25.

Zipf, G. K. (1932). *Selected studies of the principle of relative frequency in language.* Cambridge, MA: Harvard University Press.

INDEX

ⓈSAGE research**methods**

The essential online tool for researchers from the world's leading methods publisher

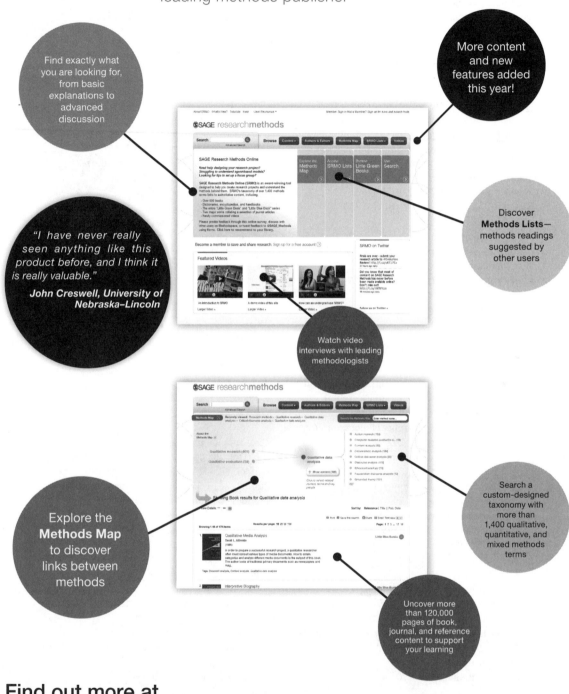

Find exactly what you are looking for, from basic explanations to advanced discussion

More content and new features added this year!

"I have never really seen anything like this product before, and I think it is really valuable."

John Creswell, University of Nebraska–Lincoln

Discover **Methods Lists**— methods readings suggested by other users

Watch video interviews with leading methodologists

Explore the **Methods Map** to discover links between methods

Search a custom-designed taxonomy with more than 1,400 qualitative, quantitative, and mixed methods terms

Uncover more than 120,000 pages of book, journal, and reference content to support your learning

Find out more at
www.sageresearchmethods.com